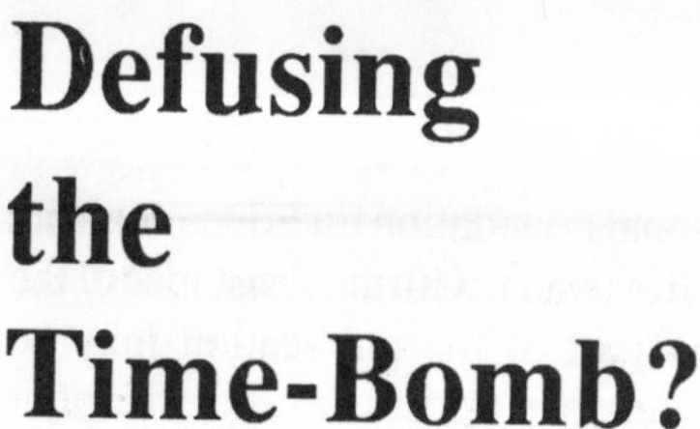

Defusing the Time-Bomb?

Report on a Seminar on Education and Training for Employment and Employment Creation in the SADCC Countries, held in Zimbabwe between April 20 and 28, 1989

INTERNATIONAL FOUNDATION FOR EDUCATION WITH PRODUCTION

GABORONE **JUNE 1990**

The Seminar was jointly organised by the Zimbabwe Ministries of Education, the Dag Hammarskjold Foundation and the International Foundation for Education with Production.

This Report is published by the International Foundation for Education with Production, P O Box 20906, Gaborone, Botswana, with the assistance of the Dag Hammarskjold Foundation.

First published: June 1990
ISBN 99912-0-022-3

Typesetting by Gaogakwe Tlhaloganyang, IFEP Graphics Department
Printed and bound by Printing and Publishing Co., Gaborone, Botswana

CONTENTS

PART 1

THE SEMINAR AT VICTORIA FALLS

Introduction......3

Section 1

Opening Address by His Excellency, Cde Robert Gabriel Mugabe, President of the Republic of Zimbabwe......9

Message of Goodwill from the Prime Minister of Norway, Mrs Gro Harlem Brundtland......15

Statement by the Executive Director of the Dag Hammarskjold Foundation on the Foundation's Role in Identifying Issues in the Fields of Education for Liberation, Education for Development and Education for Job-Creation, through Seminars sponsored between 1974 and 1989:
Dr Sven Hamrell......17

Presentation by Professor Nicholas Kuhanga, Chairman, Foundation for Education with Production......25

Section 2: The Anatomy of Unemployment

Thoughts on the Political Economy of Development, and the Role of Education, in relation to Unemployment: The Hon. Cde Fay Chung, Zimbabwe's Minister of Primary and Secondary Education......27

Section 3: Education for What?

Country Reports: Critical Reviews of Employment-Creation Strategies, with Special Reference to Policies, Programmes and Innovations in Education.

The experience of Botswana including a Report on the Brigade Movement....33
The experience of Lesotho....37
The experience of Malawi including a Report on the Young Pioneers....45
The experience of Mozambique....57
The experience of Swaziland....63
The experience of Tanzania....69
The experience of Zambia, including a Report on the Education Reform and SHAPE....75
The experience of Zimbabwe, including a Report on ZIMFEP and Education with Production....83

Education-for-Employment and Self-Employment Interventions in Developing Countries: Past Experience and Present Prognosis: Dr. Kenneth King, University of Edinburgh....89

Section 4: Where to Go from Here

Critical Innovations in Education for Employment - The Education of the Future: Patrick van Rensburg, Director of the Foundation for Education with Production (FEP)....107

Report on Discussion of the Recommendations of the Harare mini-Seminar....119

Report on a Panel Discussion of Issues arising out of the World Bank's Role in Vocational Training, viewed from the perspective of Job-Creation....121

The Cuban Experience in Linking Education and Training to Development and Job-Creation: Dr Ernesto Fernandez Rivero....127

The Chinese Experience in Linking Education and Training to Job-Creation within the Policy of "Walking on Two Legs": Yang Dong Liang....135

Section 5: Coordination of Multi-Sectoral Planning, and Financial Implications

Report on a Panel Discussion on Comprehensive Multi-Sectoral Planning for Job-Creation at National, District and Local levels and the Role of Education within Broader Strategies....143

Report on a Dialogue between Employers and Employees about the Role of the 'Formal Sector' in Expanding Job-Creation....147

Section 6: Regional Cooperation

Possibilities of Improving and Extending Regional Cooperation in the Fields of Education and Training and Manpower Development with particular emphasis on Employment-Creation, within SADCC. Report on Introductory Remarks by E.S. Nebwe, Special Advisor to the Executive Secretary of SADCC, and on the discussion that followed....151

Section 7: Resolutions of the Seminar in Plenary Session....161

Section 8: Co-Directors' Overview and Report on Participants' Evaluations....175

Closing Address: The Hon. Cde Dr Bernard Chidzero, Zimbabwe's Senior Minister of Finance and Development Planning....181

PART 2

CURRICULUM DEVELOPMENT MINI-SEMINAR, HARARE

Introduction.......189

Opening Address by Dr C. Chikombah, Dean of the Faculty of Education of the University of Zimbabwe.........191

Section 1: Country Reports on Curriculum Policies and Principles

Botswana.......197
Lesotho.......205
Malawi.......211
Mozambique.......217
Namibia.......221
Swaziland.......227
Tanzania.......233
Zambia.......239
Zimbabwe.......243

Section 2: Resource Papers

The Botswana Brigades: Experiences in Education for Employment, 1965 to 1989: Dr Q.N. Parsons.......247

Education for Self-Reliance: The Tanzanian Experience: Professor N.A. Kuhanga.......261

The FEP Curriculum: An Anatomy of Education with Production: Patrick van Rensburg.........277

The Core Curriculum for Education with Production: Simon Matsvai, the Director of the Zimbabwe Foundation for Education with Production (ZIMFEP).........287

Section 3: Recommendations of the mini-Seminar........293

Section 4: Co-Directors' Overview and Evaluation.......299

ANNEXURES

The Seminar Description.........305

List of Participants.........313

PART 1

THE SEMINAR AT VICTORIA FALLS
24TH TO 28TH APRIL, 1989

INTRODUCTION
THE TIME BOMB

"Unemployment - or more accurately, low productivity non-wage employment - is emerging as one of the major problems confronting the SADCC Member States and a major challenge to the region as a whole". These are the words of a Macro-Economic Survey commissioned by the SADCC Secretariat.

"Unemployment of young people leaving school is especially high and is a source of great concern to every Government in the region, considered by many to be a 'time-bomb'", read the seminar description relating to this Seminar which was sent out to participants in advance. According to the SADCC Survey quoted, only two of the Member Countries have more than 20% of their labour force in the 'formal' wage sector of their economies. In all the other countries, the percentages are well below 20% and vary from country to country.

The 'formal' or 'modern' sector, reflected in advanced industrial and commercial enterprises and finance houses in modern buildings in inner cities, and served by well-built high schools and universities, all set within reach by private cars along paved roads of affluent residential areas, is sometimes viewed as an 'enclave', or a complex of 'enclaves', if we include agricultural estates and commercial farms as well as large scale mines, in relation to urban slums and the traditional countryside.

The comparison may seem too stark because we must take account of gradations of wealth and poverty in both towns and countryside, of adequate housing in many townships around cities, of smaller enterprises in less affluent surroundings, and of many quite lucrative backyard businesses, as well as successful, well-housed small farmers and businessmen in rural areas.

But for all that, the underlying reality is that the 'modern' sector is an extension of the industrialised world rather than a natural historical outgrowth of indigenous societies. Whatever may have happened subsequently, it is a colonial legacy, and in the post-colonial era the juxtaposition of 'enclaves' of wealth and urban and rural poverty, accentuated by increasing unemployment - notwithstanding other contributing causes - continues to reflect the exploitative dependency relationships inherent in the prevailing international economic order.

Economic growth is determined fundamentally by patterns of international trade and in the interests of external ownership of large enterprises existing primarily to promote such trade, which derive much of their profits from exports of valuable local resources and the use of advanced, labour saving technologies. Countries in the SADCC region "sell cheap and buy dear", in the words of Mwalimu J.K. Nyerere and most of them face desperate shortages of foreign exchange earnings, dependent as they are on imported plant, material inputs critical to advanced production, and a variety of manufactured goods.

Rising unemployment on a massive scale is accentuated by population explosions and has arisen acutely among young people who leave school because school systems grow more quickly under population pressure than the 'modern' wage-paying sector of the economy. The problem is also seen by many as being the result of inappropriate, predominantly academic, conventional schooling which is geared towards producing employees for the limited number of jobs in the formal sector and ill-prepares them for the challenges of joblessness.

The seminar description had noted the belief of the organisers that solutions to the problems of prevalent, widespread unemployment throughout the region lie in the interaction and relationship of appropriate socio-economic policies and programmes on the one hand, and appropriate educational policies and programmes on the other.

The organisers noted, moreover, that some countries in the region had embarked on radically different socio-economic policies in earlier attempts to provide education and employment for all, and meet mass basic needs. These were not notably successful for a variety of reasons related to international factors as well as internal factors, which it was intended to examine at the Seminar, but which examination may not have been entirely successfully accomplished.

It was the hope of the organisers that the Seminar would try to formulate the outlines of appropriate multi-sectoral and co-ordinated policies and strategies geared to job-creation and also try to identify crucial innovations in educational policies and strategies that would link in better with such new and wider socio-economic approaches and play their own part in more effective job-creation. To this end, participating countries were invited to send delegations which included economists and planners as well as educators, and which included representatives of employers' as well as employees' organisations and of voluntary associations active in the field of education for development and job-creation. The selection of speakers also bore this aim in mind. Speakers were invited from outside the region as well so that participants could learn from international experiences in accelerated job-creation served by revitalised educational practice.

Recognising that the formal sector of the economy was able to absorb only a proportion of the labour force and of educated youth, the organisers made the point in the seminar description that education and training for the formal sector should be seen as but one of the roles of the various components and modes of the educational system, and not the only one as many economists and planners as well as educators tend to treat it.

The organisers suggested that within the framework of comprehensive multi-sectoral action, schooling and training can play an important role in shaping the attitudes of young people and in better preparing them to meet the challenges of development and job-creation. The seminar description assumed that changes in the organisation and management, and the activities and curriculum of schools, better linkages between schools and their communities, between theory and practice and education with production, might inculcate and generate skills, knowledge, experience and confidence in young people to enable many of them to create their own gainful production opportunities, individually and collectively and with adults in their communities.

A major focus of the Seminar was on the potential for, and constraints on, expanded regional co-operation in the field of education generally and in respect of education for employment generation in particular. With this in mind, Ministers of Education were invited to lead their country delegations, and the deliberations of the Seminar benefited greatly by the presence of seven of the SADCC Education Ministers at the head of high level delegations.

Not all the speakers that the organisers had invited were able to attend. But the deliberations were greatly enriched by panels drawn from the participants, which introduced the plenary discussion of several of the topics in the stead of absent speakers, and reflected the high quality of delegations from which the organisers were able to find well-qualified replacements. The Seminar also benefited from the input of a mini-Seminar on the Curriculum for Employment that was organised a few days earlier for that purpose, whose participants took part in the main Seminar and were able to contribute their collective expertise to the deliberations.

This Report comprises two Parts, the first covering the proceedings at the Main Seminar at Victoria Falls, attended by some 80 participants representing all the nine SADCC Countries as well as the ANC of South Africa and Swapo of Namibia, and the second covering the proceedings of the mini-Seminar in Harare at which only Angola was not represented.

The participants at both the Main Seminar and the mini-Seminar on the Curriculum broke up into several working groups which drafted recommendations for discussion and adoption by the final plenary session. These are presented in Section 7 of Part 1 and towards the end of Part 2, with only such minimal changes of wording as was required by collation, consolidation, clarification, and the resolution of minor contradictions.

The Seminar was jointly organised by the Ministries of Higher Education and of Primary and Secondary Education of Zimbabwe, the International Foundation for Education with Production, FEP, assisted by its Zimbabwe associate, ZIMFEP, and the Dag Hammarskjold Foundation of Sweden which also bore the main costs of the Seminar. Zimbabwe's two Ministers concerned with Education set up a Planning and Organising Committee, chaired by the Principal Economist in the Ministry of Finance and Development Planning (who is also the Chairperson of ZIMFEP), and otherwise comprising officials of the Ministries of Higher Education and of Primary and Secondary Education and of Labour and Manpower Development, and the Director of FEP International, which Committee liaised with the Dag Hammarskjold Foundation largely through FEP International's Director.

This Committee has also been charged with the editing of this Report, with The Director of FEP International given the role of Executive Editor.

The various bodies responsible for planning and organising the Seminar brought their collective and varied experiences and expertise to the task. A special word here on the role of the Dag Hammarskjold Foundation is in order, because the Foundation is not primarily engaged in education in the usual sense.

Since 1974, the Dag Hammarskjold Foundation has been a major party to a number of seminars which have helped define the nature of the mutually interacting relationship between education and society, and the nature and process of education for liberation, and of education for development and employment. The address by the Foundation's Director, Dr Sven Hamrell, is one of the documents in Section 1 of Part 1 of this Report.

The importance attached to the Seminar by the Zimbabwe Government is evidenced by the presence on the first day at Victoria Falls of His Excellency the President, Cde R.G. Mugabe, to open the deliberations, and the attendance of The Honourable Minister of Finance and Development Planning, Cde Bernard Chidzero, on the last day to close the Seminar. Both addresses are reproduced fully in the pages that follow. The Prime Minister of Norway, Mrs Gro Harlem Brundtland, who had come to Zimbabwe to receive the 1989 Third World Prize from President Mugabe, accompanied him to the Seminar and briefly addressed the participants after President Mugabe had delivered his opening address, adding gracefully to the Scandinavian dimension to the Seminar already provided by the Dag Hammarskjold Foundation.

This Introduction is not the place in which to review the Seminar or the mini-Seminar on Curriculum, or to evaluate the success and likely future impact in the region and elsewhere of either. That is a task undertaken by the Co-Directors at the end of Part 1 and Part 2. It is sufficient to say here that the proceedings and deliberations merit the publication of this Report as a book, the more so because the successful implementation of the recommendations and resolutions are acknowledged to depend on the support of educators at all levels,and especially of teachers, and on a wide measure of public support, and especially of parents and local communities. This, in turn, depends on distributing the Report to as wide a readership as possible.

The Editors

SECTION 1

ADDRESS BY HIS EXCELLENCY THE PRESIDENT OF ZIMBABWE, CDE R.G. MUGABE, AT THE OPENING OF THE SEMINAR.

Comrade Chairman,
Honourable Ministers,
Your Excellencies,
Members of the Diplomatic Corps,
Ladies and Gentlemen,
Comrades and Friends.

It gives me great pleasure to perform two important tasks this afternoon. Firstly, I would like to welcome you all but, more especially, those of you who have travelled far to be with us at this Seminar. A special welcome is due to the Honourable Ministers of Education from our sister SADCC countries and their officials, to our visitors from China, Cuba, India, Mauritius, Great Britain, ANC and SWAPO, to the World Bank, and last but not least to the Dag Hammerskjold Foundation which is sponsoring this Seminar. I would like to wish you all a productive and happy stay in Zimbabwe.

Secondly, I accepted with enthusiasm an invitation to open this Seminar because the subject matter is dear to my heart. I believe that a commitment to education is a commitment to development and that manpower training is essential for the many development tasks that require a trained and enlightened cadre. The prosperity of the SADCC region will depend, among other interrelated forces, on the effective and efficient utilisation of human resources. In addition, all of us in this region face the exciting challenge of employment creation over the next few decades. The solution of unemployment is necessarily related to the education and training programme.

Since Independence in 1980, my Government has made significant strides in the sphere of education and training. Enrolment in primary schools increased from 820 000 in 1979 to 2 220 900 in 1988, and from 66 000 to 653 000 at secondary level in the same period, while enrolment at teacher education colleges rose from 3 082 to 15 750. Considerable progress has also been made in non-formal education, with the adult literate population rising to 70 per cent.

In the area of vocational and technical education, significant progress has similarly been made. Enrolment at technical colleges rose from 3 600 in 1980 to 25 104 in 1988. Enrolment at agricultural colleges rose from 171 in 1979 to 1 050 in 1988. There are about 90 non-government technical/ vocational colleges of various sizes offering a wide range of skills. A National Vocational Training Centre has also been opened. It will be the focal point for the training of skilled manpower through the development of training modules and curricula.

At University level, significant progress has been registered. Enrolment rose from 2 240 in 1980 to 7 700 in 1988. Between 1980 and 1985 alone, $57 million were spent on capital projects, the bulk of which was provided by Government. Despite these achievements, the pressure of specialised manpower requirements and the demand for a university education have prompted plans to set up another university, with a science and technology bias. This university should be operational within the next few years.

Having outlined our achievements in quantitative terms, I would hasten to say, as you all know, that a linear expansion of existing systems of education is not enough. Quality and relevance are essential, and we do not perceive the quest for quality in education as necessarily at variance with the democratisation process. There should be a balance. In Zimbabwe, our success in the area of quality and relevance has not been of a comparable magnitude to our quantitative expansion. We have had very successful experiments, which I am sure you will hear about, but these have not been sufficient to solve our problems. We still have to inter-relate our education and training more closely to the world of work. This is particularly challenging when we consider that the developed industrial sector in SADCC countries is at present only capable of absorbing a small proportion of our school leavers. Thus, the majority will have to seek gainful work in the traditional and non-formal sectors of employment.

The traditional sector, namely, small-scale or peasant agriculture, presents an immense challenge. There is little doubt that the extension of modern technologies and management systems to this sector, coupled with improved inputs in terms of draught power, implements, seeds and fertilizers, will enhance the productivity and wealth of the peasants, thereby providing greater economic power to these peasant farmers. This will in turn provide a boost to the manufacturing sector, taking up the presently under-utilized capacity in our factories.

Whilst small-scale agriculture provides a great potential for employment creation and the increase of wealth, I would like to remind this august gathering that greater productivity and wealth must be seen within the context of societal progress and transformation. Moreover, our countries need to move from the constraints of the traditional feudal and colonialist infrastructures we have inherited to more cooperative and nationalist social structures, in keeping with our aspirations to provide a more equitable distribution of resources.

Comrade Chairman, the developments I have outlined in the case of Zimbabwe may resemble those experienced in other countries except on points of detail. But there are difficulties and constraints which are even more identical. There are problems of foreign currency, shortage of qualified personnel to man our institutions, and insufficient tools and equipment in our schools, tertiary colleges and institutions of higher learning. In the case of higher education there is also the issue of establishing a sound relationship between the education and training system and industry. But perhaps it is the financing of education and training at all levels that poses a greater challenge. In Zimbabwe, expenditure on education has been growing at a rate faster than that of any other sector, including defence. All these issues are compounded by a rapid population growth, especially the school age population and, subsequently, of young school leavers.

For example, since independence, a million students have left school in Zimbabwe, most of them with 'O' levels. The job market has not been able to expand commensurately. It is optimistically estimated that only one quarter of the school leavers have been absorbed into employment in the developed industrial sector. My Government has been paying very serious attention to this issue through its Cabinet Task Force on Employment Creation. This Task Force has already completed a great deal of work in setting out possible solutions to this grave problem. In the near future, my Government will be taking decisive steps to initiate a number of programmes to enhance employment creation by the public sector, local authorities, parastatals, private enterprise and cooperatives.

I invite this Seminar to assist SADCC Governments in resolving these problems. These are areas for which machinery for greater coordination should be explored in the SADCC region to complement and strengthen arrangements already in place. This brings me to the theme of your Seminar. I would like to congratulate the organisers for an interesting programme and look forward to its findings.

The theme for this Seminar represents a great challenge for the participants gathered here as it does for the countries they represent. The relationship between education and training on the one hand and employment and development on the other is a complex one. There is no simple equation whereby the elimination of illiteracy, universal primary education, expanded secondary education opportunities, increased tertiary and university level training could automatically lead to economic growth and development. Experience of various strategies attempted in the past in our region and others shows limited achievements in providing solutions to the dynamic and complex problems that confront our Governments, in particular in the area of education and employment.

Comrades and Friends, what we need are policies and programmes that take cognisance of the need to tailor our investment in education and training in line with investment needs on the farm and in the factory. Our strategies should ensure that the productive sectors, namely, agriculture, mining, industry and commerce continue to grow as we build a development-oriented manpower base. These strategies must reconcile, through a dynamic and progressive approach, the apparently competing claims on the resources available. In the SADCC region, the formulae we design should stand the test of problems imposed on us by the political circumstances of this sub-region and the drought conditions that we have to contend with from time to time.

Comrade Chairman, one of the essential elements for development in any country is the availability of highly skilled manpower to man the private, public and parastatal sectors of the economy. But of course, this is not the only essential variable. In the past, the democratisation of education has tended to be associated with unemployment, because education had little relevance or relationship to the country's development programmes. Our education and training plans should be aggressive, designed to produce people who are innovative and willing to exploit the available resources to generate more jobs and create more wealth. In particular, there is need to emphasise science and technology. Perhaps the challenge before us now is to concentrate policy attention not only on the education system but also on the employment system, though this would appear to be more complex.

Moving on to another front, I would like to make reference to the paradox that has been persistent in all SADCC countries since independence, a paradox that is discussed at several human resource development seminars and which appears in our development plans.

It is the phenomenon of persistent manpower shortages in certain fields, often termed critical areas, in the face of hundreds of youths qualified to undergo training in those fields. How much time do we need to resolve this paradox, or will we forever resort to cursing the unjust colonial practices of the pre-independence era? In some cases the numbers justify training abroad but in other cases the answer lies in regional cooperation among SADCC countries. This gathering, the first among Ministers of Education of this region, is a positive sign.

A related question one may ask regarding skills shortages and manpower plans is the availability of baseline information as a timely basis for planning purposes. Just how recent are our latest figures? Does the scope of our manpower plans and training programmes extend to all sectors of the economy? These are vital questions to answer if we are to make informed judgements, policies and plans. Perhaps these questions require a multi-disciplinary approach, an integrated approach at all levels of planning.

I note that the spectre of unemployment is one of the themes of your Seminar. I will not be drawn into the various definitions given the phenomenon, but I would wish to urge this Seminar to remember that human resources are the greatest asset this region has. I challenge the participants gathered here to design and recommend programmes that will provide opportunities for our youth to take part in national development. The youth must be trained while at school and after, if they are to realise their full potential. The provision of basic education to all children is a fundamental right, but this education should not only comprise carefully planned alternative forms of training but be linked to employment at all terminal points in the system. It is poor planning to leave some of the youth to fend for themselves while taking interest in those who will have qualified for the next rung of the ladder at any terminal point.

I have noted from your seminar programme that national experiences will be shared in the areas of curricular diversification, education and production, the vocationalisation of secondary education, and the unemployment problem. These are major societal issues and in your search for answers to them I would urge you to go beyond isolated interventions in the skills training and work experiences. Perhaps the persistent and growing unemployment might be rooted in the very structures of our economies. Hence I would urge you to continue to intensify your research efforts and to extend the existing research and experimentation frontiers in search of solutions to the problems of this region.

Comrade Chairman, the task before this Seminar is also important from a political point of view, particularly in Southern Africa. Events are moving quickly in this part of the world, and, as you are aware, the world is currently focussing its attention on this region. The year 1989 may herald the independence of Namibia. As we strengthen our economies through careful, purposeful planning and plan implementation, we must, at the same time, be better prepared to withstand the tribulations the liberation process demands of us. SADCC needs unity and stronger regional cooperation to withstand and win the struggle against ignorance, disease and poverty. Above all, we need to unite against apartheid and to remain vigilant and conscious of the destabilising designs of South Africa.

I now have the pleasure to declare this Seminar open.

MESSAGE OF GOODWILL FROM THE PRIME MINISTER OF NORWAY, GRO HARLEM BRUNDTLAND

It is indeed a privilege to attend this seminar in Victoria Falls on "Education and Training in the SADCC Countries". Only a few hours ago I was at another seminar in Harare arranged by the Third World Foundation on the related theme of "Enviroment and Development". As you know, there is a close connection between enviroment and education, as the pamphlet from the Dag Hammarskjold Foundation reminded me when I looked through the list of seminars that have been held over the years.

These issues are not only related to each other in terms of subject matter, but also because they are common to many different parts of the world and sectors of society. On this occasion we are focusing on the regional aspects of these issues as they apply to Southern Africa. As a supporter of the Dag Hammarskjold Foundation, Norway has worked together with the other Nordic countries to promote regional development cooperation with the Third World. All the Nordic countries have benefitted from this process. We have exchanged and compared experiences in many vital sectors of development such as education, which you are dealing with here, child care, the enviroment and other issues.

There is a special understanding between the Nordic and the SADCC countries, which has evolved during the long years of their struggle for liberation and independence. This understanding between two widely separated parts of the world has deepened during the years of development cooperation.

The world is growing smaller by the month. More than ever, people in different parts of the world need to reach out to each other across national boundaries and across sectoral divisions.

And obviously the education of children and young people is essential for our common future. To quote President Mugabe, it is, in whatever way you look at it, "the only possible option". Looking at the linkages between development and enviroment, it is obvious that without education, we will never be able to address these issues in time.

In the 1990s we need more than ever to realize that economic growth is essential in order to deal with enviromental issues as well as with poverty and other social evils. This lesson was not obvious five or ten years ago. On the contrary, the enviroment was a controversial issue. In many parts of the world it was looked upon as a kind of luxury problem which concerned only the rich. Today we know that the depletion of the world's basic resources and the retention of non-sustainable development patterns will undermine economic development and the social and economic prosperity of nations wherever they are. This is why we need to couple economy and ecology. This is why there will be no real development if we do not realize that all of us are responsible for the development of human resources and human dignity in all parts of the world. And this development can be achieved only through education. The right to knowledge is fundamental to democracy, it is fundamental to justice, and it is fundamental to the future of us all.

In closing, I would like to congratulate you on this seminar and to wish you every success with your future endeavours in the field of education.

Thank you for your attention.

STATEMENT BY THE EXECUTIVE DIRECTOR OF THE DAG HAMMARSKJOLD FOUNDATION, DR SVEN HAMRELL, ON THE FOUNDATION'S ROLE IN THE FIELDS OF EDUCATION FOR DEVELOPMENT AND LIBERATION, THROUGH SEMINARS SPONSORED BETWEEN 1974 AND 1989

Hon. Ministers, Ladies and Gentlemen

The Dag Hammarskjold Foundation was established in 1962 - on the basis of a spontaneous collection of money among the Swedish people - to honour the memory of the late Secretary-General of the United Nations, who met his death at Ndola, not so far from here, in September 1961. The purpose of the Foundation is to organise and sponsor seminars and conferences on the political, economic, social, legal and cultural problems facing the Third World and to do so in consonance with the aspirations of the peoples of the Third World. It should also be emphasised that it is an international Foundation, which, although it operates from its offices in Dag Hammarskjold's home town Uppsala in Sweden, has an international Board of Trustees, among whose members are the Zimbabwean Senior Minister for Finance, Economic Planning and Development, Dr Bernard Chidzero, and the Tanzanian Ambassador to the United Nations in Geneva, Dr Amir Jamal.

Over the last almost three decades, the Foundation has organised or been privileged to co-sponsor a large number of seminars and conferences in Africa, Asia and Latin America. They have focused more and more on the sectoral aspects of the alternative development strategies proposed in the 1975 Dag Hammarskjold Report to the Seventh Special Session of United Nations General Assembly. Extensively elaborated in the Foundation's seminars on rural development, health, education, science and technology (especially plant genetic resources and biotechnology), international monetary policy, information and communication, and participation, the results have been regularly published in the Foundation's journal *Development Dialogue*.

As an important appropriate part of its activities, the Foundation has over the past 15 years been closely involved in a series of primarily African seminar initiatives to define the nature and processes of education for liberation and endogenous development as opposed to conventional externally induced development, i.e. what we have termed 'Another Development' to distinguish it from the conventional development models that are still being indiscriminately applied by quite a number of international donor agencies.

In the course of these primarily African education seminars, there has emerged from seminar to seminar a constantly broadening vision of what education can be when conceived as a whole social process in a society that produces and develops with the public interest at heart rather than in the interest of a small elite.

The education seminars and panels of experts which the Foundation has co-sponsored or organised itself in the Southern African region and at the Dag Hammarskjold Centre in Uppsala, Sweden, have brought together committed individuals, representatives of organisations, governments and liberation movements, and thus ensured a wide range of perspectives from which to view education and its relationship to society and its role in promoting regional cooperation in the interest of liberation and as an integral component of the anti-apartheid struggle.

The 1974 Dar es Salaam IDS/DHF Seminar, which began the series of seminars in the Southern African region, was opened by President Nyerere, who entitled his address *Education and Liberation*. The seminar was held in Tanzania because Tanzania had behind it seven years of experience of its policy of Education for Self-Reliance, a policy which, in President Nyerere's words, "recognised the need for an education, which is relevant to our conditions and our aspirations". In proposing to "integrate education and life, and education and production", the policy was far-sighted and captured the essence of a radical transformation of education. "Our peoples", President Nyerere said, "do have a conception of what education is; and although it might be wrong and contrary to their real needs, this conception cannot be wished away". He therefore urged the seminar to "think about how we can move away from what is, to what should be".

The 1975 Dag Hammarskjold Report on Development and International Cooperation, which is better known under its title *What Now: Another*

Development, included a section on education prepared by a panel of Third World experts under the chairmanship of the co-director of this seminar, Patrick van Rensburg. The panel, drawing on the inspiration of the Dar es Salaam seminar, developed a dynamic new conception of education, beautifully and succinctly phrased.

"Education in a new conception would become the permanent duty and responsibility of the whole society and towards everyone in it, and the continuous function of the total social environment. Education would be a vast cooperative effort of everyone in society, and it would not be divorced from work and production. Then everyone would be a learner, a worker and a teacher".

The 1978 Maputo seminar on 'Educational Alternatives for Southern Africa', organised by the Mozambican Ministry of Education in cooperation with the Dag Hammarskjold Foundation, was of special significance because it highlighted the fact that education was not only part of but central to the liberation struggle. In the words of the then Minister for Education and Culture, H.E. Mrs Graca Machel, who opened the seminar: "In the process of armed struggle for national liberation, we learned that education is one of the principal aspects of our revolution - a decisive factor, because to the degree that it triumphs or fails, the new man and the new society will or will not emerge...Because of this, education is seen as a fundamental battlefield, where we are carrying on a permanent fight for the transformation of mentalities, a fight against the actions of the enemy ... It was in the course of the struggle that the education of the future was forged in the liberated zones of Mozambique and in neighbouring Tanzania".

The discussion of this aspect of the Mozambican experience suggested the need for a seminar on 'Education and Culture in Southern Africa' focusing primarily on the role of education and culture in the liberation struggle. Liberation movements had participated both in the Dar es Salaam and Maputo seminars - as they are in this seminar - and a seminar on this subject was held in Lusaka in October 1980, organised in cooperation with ANC (SA), the Patriotic Front of Zimbabwe (ZANU-ZAPU), SWAPO and the Government of Zambia, providing the movements an opportunity to exchange ideas, insights and experiences among themselves and with movements like Frelimo.

In the meantime, a seminar on 'Alternatives and Innovations in Education' had been organised in 1979 at the Dag Hammarskjold Centre in Uppsala as a follow-up to the panel of educationalists who had helped to prepare the 1975 Dag Hammarskjold Report *What Now: Another Development.*

This seminar, to which African educators made an important contribution, elaborated the notion of education as part of and central to the process of social transformation, not only in terms of schooling but in terms of the wider educative functions of other social agencies, activities and processes. It emphasised in its conclusions that "society is an arena of conflict and educational institutions are a part of as well as a result of conflict ... For education is not only the product of the schools or formal teaching, but rooted in the economy and society as a whole - the family, the work place, the community, and in political and social movements.

"An urgent and vital question in the struggle for structural transformation is therefore how to reform schools, which now preoccupy themselves in social and production systems that divide mental and manual labour and fragment both. The assimilation of knowledge, especially science, and the ability to conceptualize, are in general best served by the active linking of theory and practice, with the allocation of time to both used as a means of systematically guiding the learners. These processes are best learned, too, when rooted as much as possible in the social and cultural environment, itself changing as the result of conflict".

The liberation movements of Southern Africa established schools in the frontline states both for freedom fighters and for the thousands of people escaping from persecution and oppression at home. As a member since 1964 of the Swedish Government Committee on Humanitarian Aid, which has contributed considerable sums to the funding of these schools and still continues to do so, it has been especially gratifying for me to note that they can also serve as models for the future education systems of liberated societies by promoting an education system accessible to all, catering for all kinds of talents and abilities. And this was, of course, a natural consequence of the fact that under these conditions, people had to work and live together in collective and communal arrangements, gaining an understanding of the processes of production and of organisation and management.

As in the case of the previous seminars, the 1980 Lusaka seminar paid a great deal of attention to the practical implementation of ideas and policies linking theory and practice, focussing on the supply and training of teachers, the curriculum and syllabus and the provision and content of teaching materials and, finally - running as a red thread through all these efforts - the organisation and relevance of production in education, in short all the issues that are now placed on the agenda for this seminar and placed - for the first time - in a comprehensive regional context.

One of the organisational outcomes of this long series of seminars was the establishment in 1980, actually at a meeting in Harare, of the Foundation for Education with Production International (FEP) with Patrick van Rensburg as Director and, within a year, with Professor Nicholas Kuhanga, the Tanzanian former Minister of Education and then Vice-Chancellor of the University of Dar es Salaam, as Chairperson.

Professor Kuhanga has, in his speech to this Seminar, told the story of FEP and its activities, but I must be allowed to say that the Dag Hammarskjold Foundation was very happy to join forces with FEP in assisting in a modest way the Zimbabwe Ministry of Education and Culture in the organisation of its 1981 Seminar on 'Education in Zimbabwe - Past, Present and Future'. This was a huge effort, intended to re-link educational thinking in the newly independent Zimbabwe with the current educational trends in independent Africa as they had emerged over the preceding decade and a half. And it was significant that the new Prime Minister of Zimbabwe, now H.E. President Robert Mugabe, in his opening speech should emphasise that the future educational system of Zimbabwe should break away from the colonial heritage and aim at inculcating "an attitude and a sense of commitment to the development of our people as a collectivity rather than the development of the self as an individual. Our schools must not merely teach such commitment, they must themselves practise it as well. Pupils must learn to work together productively for the good of their schools and their community". Zimbabwe has since then pursued this policy and through organisations like the Zimbabwe Foundation for Education with Production (ZIMFEP), which is co-sponsoring this seminar, gained the respect of many African countries and the respect and well-deserved material support of countries like my own, Sweden.

This has been a rather lengthy and hopefully not too tedious attempt to give a short historical background to what has brought us together here today and to explain the long involvement of the Foundation in a process, which it has been privileged to be able to assist but whose strength is truly endogenous.

Further examples of this and of the strength of the movement towards the formulation of alternative development strategies in Southern Africa are two seminars which the Dag Hammarskjold Foundation and its sister organisation, the Foundation for Education with Production, were in a position to co-sponsor in the mountain kingdom of Lesotho with the full support of H.M. King Moshoeshoe II. The first one, held at the Royal Palace in Maseru in November 1985, dealt with the overall development problematique in the region and counted participants from most of the SADCC countries, who met to discuss what should be done in an integrated manner to fulfil the basic human needs of food, health, habitat and education in the SADCC countries. It also discussed the instrumentalities required for this by way of infrastructural and communications development and the safeguarding of the human rights of the individuals and the rights of the SADCC states to pursue their development objectives without interference from the apartheid Government in South Africa. The second seminar, held in Maseru in December 1987, which also enjoyed the whole-hearted support of H.M. King Moshoeshoe II and the Matsieng Development Trust, applied the experience gained at the regional SADCC seminar to the national situation in Lesotho.

Both these seminars are fully accounted for in two publications, appropriately entitled *Another Development for SADCC* and *Another Development for Lesotho*, and copies of these two reports, published by FEP with the support of the Dag Hammarskjold Foundation, will be made available to the participants this seminar.

Needless to say, it is my hope that this Seminar will also result in a similar publication, formulating an Agenda for Action highlighting the need for Another Development in Education in the region and outlining a strategy designed first and foremost to contribute to a truly African solution of the enormous employment and training problems in the region thereby disarming a 'time bomb', which is ticking away at an alarming speed and whose inner mechanics have been so well analysed by Minister Fay Chung.

It is therefore gratifying to note the very positive response to the invitation extended by the Ministers Fay Chung and Dzingai Mutumbuka of Zimbabwe to this seminar and the presence of so many important ministers and leading officials from the region and from key non-governmental organisations and so many highly qualified speakers and resource persons. So let me in concluding express the special gratitude of the Dag Hammarskjold

Foundation to the Ministries of Education in Zimbabwe and the Organising Committee of the Seminar, which has spared no effort to bring us together, and, of course, also to the seminar directors, Ms Heather Benoy and Mr Patrick van Rensburg.

Foundation and the Ministry of Education in Zimbabwe and the Organising Committee of the Seminar, which has saved no effort to bring us together, and of course, also to the seminar directors, Mr Heather Brown and Mr Patrick van Rensburg.

PRESENTATION BY PROFESSOR NICHOLAS KUHANGA, CHAIRMAN OF THE FOUNDATION FOR EDUCATION WITH PRODUCTION (FEP)

The Foundation for Education with Production is proud to be associated with the Zimbabwe Ministries of Higher Education and of Primary and Secondary Education and the Dag Hammarkjold Foundation in the organisation of this Seminar on Education and Training for Employment in SADCC Countries.

The Foundation believes that the combination of education with production has tremendous potential in terms of the economic, social and pedagogical benefits it can offer. Possible economic benefits include the generation of income or the development of physical infrastructure through the use of student work, especially when they are engaged in a measure of skill training. Educational institutions can help set up farms, workshops and factories which can promote development and create employment. The educational benefits of combining work and study, relate to both the cognitive and affective domains. Students can practise technical skills in the course of production, and they can more effectively learn and apply organisational and management skills in a real way, within production enterprises linked to their educational institutions. Practical experience in production and socially useful work offers the basis for developing personal skills and character traits in ways that cannot be achieved in classroom settings alone. All production, moreover, has roots in science and mathematics, and even in other disciplines like economics, and production provides a practical basis for easier learning of many scientific principles. Engagement of educational institutions in production is the key to their self-reliance, and offers the means by which they can take part in national, district and local social and economic development within the framework of appropriate development plans. This creates the possibility of more closely linking educational institutions to their communities.

FEP, as we call the Foundation, believes that the combination of learning and working productively will be most effective in achieving its economic, social and pedagogical potential if backed up by curriculum reform, closer linkages between theory and practice, democratic and participatory management of educational institutions, and the mutual involvement of education institutions and their surrounding communities in each others' affairs and activities. In these circumstances the relations between teachers and learners will be beneficially transformed.

The Foundation accepts that education with production may be manifested in a variety of forms and models, including production units and enterprises in schools at all levels, out-of-school organisations like national service and brigades, producer co-operatives, or the education of working people. Learning is, we feel, both a total social process and a lifelong process.

FEP, which was formed in October 1980 in Zimbabwe with Cde Fay Chung as first Chairperson, is a regional organisation associated with counterpart national organisations like Botswana FEP, Lesotho FEP, the Zambian Society for Education with Production, ZIMFEP and more recently Kenya FEP. These national organisations are fully autonomous, they make their own policies and are responsible for their own policy implementation. FEP's activities have included direct participation in projects in conjunction with national FEPs, although our tendency is to disengage from purely national projects, leaving these to national FEPs or associated organisations and confining ourselves to advisory roles. FEP also works directly with Governments in activities like evaluations and the organisation of seminars. FEP's Board is elected by national FEPs, and interested Ministries of Education may also appoint Board members. The headquarters are in Gaborone, Botswana, and we may be looking into the possibility of establishing offices in some of the countries where we have counterpart organisations to bring the advisory services closer to the member countries.

Currently our activities include association with project planning and development, the publication of a journal twice a year, curriculum development, the writing of a handbook on production that educational institutions can undertake, the organisation of seminars, textbook writing and production, the promotion of research and promotion of producers' cooperatives as a means of employment creation.

FEP strongly supports regional cooperation in the educational sector and we look forward to the adoption by this Seminar of recommendations in this connection, and in general to the success of the Seminar.

SECTION 2

THOUGHTS ON THE POLITICAL ECONOMY OF DEVELOPMENT, AND THE ROLE OF EDUCATION, IN RELATION TO UNEMPLOYMENT

The Hon Cde Fay Chung, Zimbabwe's Minister of Primary and Secondary Education

The Reality of Neo-Colonialism

The countries of our region inherited the power to make laws and administer, but we did not inherit power over our economies. Within the countries of SADCC, we thus have political power without economic power. The economic rules of the game are determined by the international division of labour. In terms of these rules, manufactures are produced in the industrialised countries whilst raw materials are supplied by the poorer countries. The prices of raw materials have fallen whilst generally the cost of manufactures have risen. Moreover, industrialised countries are increasingly engaged in the production of synthetic replacements which compete with raw material supplies and threaten the economies of poorer countries. Generally speaking, ownership of the capital invested in extractive industry lies abroad in the industrialised world, which draws interest, profits and patent rights. Over a recent twelve-month period, financial inflows to Third World countries, including aid and investments were estimated at US$ 8 billion against outflows of US$ 25 billion.

The development of industry in countries like ours is subject to competitiion with the industry of economically more advanced coutnries. The industries of many Third World countries are technologically 20 to 30 years behind those of industrialised countries. This is certainly the case in Zimbabwe.

Our societies are characterised by the existence of formal, wage employment sectors and traditional, predominantly agricultural sectors. In Zimbabwe only one out of nine people is engaged in wage employment in the formal sector. The more traditional sector is characterised by social formations different from the formal sector and dominated by a large peasantry. Largely a hangover from pre-colonial society, this traditional sector has been re-made in subordination to the formal sector and kept in an underdeveloped state so that it could for instance be a source of cheap labour.

The Class Situation in Our Countries

Who was capable of taking power from the colonial rulers during the struggles for independence? The peasantry could not read and whilst they knew how they suffered under colonial domination, they were not aware of its fullest implications, of the scope of the struggle against it and of the demands of post-colonial development. At the same time, there was no fully developed working class. There was also no national bourgeoisie. There were intellectuals, linked to a petty bourgeoisie made up of various strands of limited local privilege. This petty bourgeoisie was the most advanced social force of the dying colonial era, and it effectively inherited political power from the departing colonial rulers. This brought in its train a return to some of the historical contradictions of the pre-colonial period, however. The choice before the new rulers was either to align themselves with capitalism or with the workers and peasants. For a revolution to take place, there may have to be a mass revolutionary party, but the class formation is very important to its continued success. Transnational capital is very powerful, but local capital if there is any is weak. It is realistic to ask the petty bourgeoisie to commit class suicide?

The Technological Chasm

The technological chasm between the industrialised and the third world is expressed in technological domination by the advanced countries and a technological backlog in the poorer world. Hence the dependence on expatriates from the economically richer countries. Our educational and training systems are inappropriate to our needs. We have taken them over with very little adaptation from the colonial rulers. They are overly academic and geared to the conditions of the former colonial power. At independence, Zimbabwe inherited a schools system that was not only racially divided but hopelessly inadequate for the numbers of Zimbabweans seeking entry.

Philosophical Conceptualisation of Our Situation

Let us look at the sociological underpinnings of our societies and analyse these in terms of prevailing philosophical and ideological assumptions. There is a powerful 'clientelism', a word to describe the traditional system of patronage, inherited from the pre-colonial past, which characterises the relationship between leaders and their followers. Then we have capitalism, but without indigenous capitalists and with no real market economy. This is a real contradiction in terms. It is a situation in which outside capital can do what it likes. We also have socialism, but without a large, skilled and educated working class to build and control a large, diversified and complex economy and manage the socialist revolution. The contradiction is only exacerbated by the reality of a peasantry constituting 80% of the population - a peasantry that has no knowledge of nor interest in Marx nor fully understands the complexity of capitalism and its workings. Our socialisms are rhetorical rather than real in these circumstances. We do have free education and free health in many of our countries but they constitute 'welfarism' rather than socialism.

Instability and High Defence Costs

The countries of SADCC are interdependent so instability in one affects the others. We are all affected when our lifelines are cut and by the destabilising activities of South Africa and its agents, the MNR and UNITA. These are like Nazi groups. They simply wipe out people. As a result of the terror that these groups have unleashed, and of South African cross-border attacks, we all have heavy defence burdens to carry which pre-empt funds that could otherwise be available for education and development.

Population Increase

In 1984, Sweden, which is the same size as Zimbabwe, had the same population. Now, 5 years later, Zimbabwe has 2.3 million more people than Sweden. There is a popular delusion that the country can carry 20 million, but with such a high rate of population expansion, economic growth has to be at the same rate - which is exceptionally high - just to keep pace. One of the reasons for the population explosion is that the peasants need more labour and they acquire it either by marrying it or giving birth to it. The average woman bears 7 children in her lifetime, although research suggests she would rather only have four. It may be that contraceptive technology may not be readily available everywhere (only 30% of women practice some form of contraception) but it also appears that there are social reasons for the high birth rate and that women defer to men in decisions to have children. Children are also seen as social security for old age.

Involving Education Ministers in Job-Creation

Former Minister of Higher Education Cde Dr Dzingai Mutumbuka had wanted this Seminar so that SADCC Education Ministers could involve themselves in the problems of unemployment of educated youth, and exchange views on what to do about the problem both in the educational systems but also in terms of broader socio-economic strategy. The question is what can we do? Perhaps we can start by looking at alternative solutions at the broader socio-economic level that are on offer. There are the Lagos Plan of Action on the one hand and the World Bank and IMF model, on the other. The Lagos Plan advocates self-sufficiency in basic foods and the satisfaction of basic needs as well as in high and middle level manpower. It also advocates regional co-operation. The World Bank and IMF model advocates specialisation within the international division of labour. It advocates devaluation and the opening up of economies to competitive access, for foreign made goods.

The problem with the World Bank and IMF solution is that the technologically superior goods manufactured outside our region displace the technologically inferior goods we produce with our often outdated machinery, and that we do not have equal free access to the markets of industrialised countries. Another criticism from the IMF and World Bank is that there is too much fiscal regulation, state ownership, control of prices and wage determination. They demand privatisation of state-owned enterprises and liberalisation of economies.

Proponents of state involvement hold that local industry would be destroyed without state protection and inputs. For example, the Rhodesian Front regime under UDI had started industries which were too risky or large for private venture capital, and which once they had succeeded were privatised. Governments in Taiwan, South Korea and Singapore - show-cases of capitalism - intervened to assist and protect local capitalists and even provided the initial research for key industries. It is not that state intervention is wrong per se but that our Governments may have been intervening in the wrong way, generating and protecting inefficiency to a degree.

Whilst we would all want to see rapid industrialisation, if the finances are available, we must have regard for the relationship between investment and the rate of job-creation. It is possible to invest $200 million to create 50 jobs. There may of course be downstream effects which need also to be taken into account. But in this respect, too, the state must have a watching brief. Since independence in Zimbabwe, as a result of the rapid expansion of the school system, some 1 million students have left school with 'O' levels but only one quarter of them have been able to find paid employment in the formal sector.

What is the absorptive capacity of the traditional and informal sectors. Can we learn from the post-revolutionary experience of China? Can the peasant sector absorb more workers? In Zimbabwe, as peasants become more productive, there is a tendency towards more polygamy and the education of young girls is limited. There are also the negative effects of clientelism described earlier. But it is possible, with the right incentives and with appropriate education, for the peasants to move beyond present technological levels and to expand and diversify their production and so increase the absorptive capacity of the sector.

Our task in the next five days is to find the ways out of these problems.

SECTION 3

COUNTRY PAPER: BOTSWANA

Introduction

Since Independence one of the major development strategies of the Botswana government has been to work for rapid economic growth. In order to attain this objective, emphasis has been placed on employment creation and rural development. It is rural development which has proved difficult to achieve. One of the main problems is that Botswana has both a shortage of educated and skilled personnel and a surplus of unskilled personnel. The labour force is growing but the capacity of the economy to absorb labour has been constrained.

Population and the Labour Force

According to the 1981 Population and Housing Census, 941,00 people were resident in Botswana with 477,000 of the population being of working age. It was estimated that the population would grow to 1,345,000 in 1991 with 676,000 people of working age. By the year 2001, there would be approximately 980,000 people available for work.

The 1984-5 Labour Force Survey carried out by the Central Statistics Office showed that 274,000 people were in employment at the time of the survey; 159,000 (57.9%) of these people were in the agricultural sector. The survey estimated that 93,100 unemployed people were available for work; two-thirds of this number were women living in the rural areas. In both the rural and urban sectors it was found that women had a higher unemployment rate than their male counterparts.

It was reported that, in general, those who were employed had low levels of education; 44% had no schooling, 43.4% primary schooling only and 12.5% secondary schooling.

Education and Training

Over the period 1966-86, formal employment in Botswana has grown at an average compounded growth rate of 8.8%. Equally important is the expansion of primary and secondary enrolments. New vocational training centres and teacher training colleges have also been established.

At primary level, enrolments have grown from 78,442 in 1971 to over 230,000 in 1986 and are projected to reach just under 400,000 in the year 2001. Enrolments at secondary level have increased from 5778 in 1971 to over 33,000 in 1986 and enrolment is projected to rise to over 100,000 by 2001. This is largely because of the introduction of community junior secondary schools. University enrolments have also increased with an average growth rate of 15% per annum.

In addition to these achievements in the formal schooling system, expansions have been made at local training institutions such as Botswana Institute of Administration and Commerce(BIAC), National Health Institute(NHI), Botswana Agricultural College(BAC), Botswana Polytechnic and the Auto Trades Training School(ATTS). All these have seen major upgradings, not only in terms of physical facilities, but also in terms of the number of course offerings and levels of these courses.

Technical education aims to produce manpower with craft and technical qualifications. The main institutions providing such training are the Vocational Training Centres (VTCs), Auto Trades Training School, Botswana Polytechnic and the Brigades. The Vocational Training Centres will each year enrol about 300 full time students and 1,400 part time students.

The ATTS trains artisans in auto trades and auto mechanics. It currently achieves its planned annual output of 40 trained artisans. It is planned to increase the output of auto mechanics by fully utilizing the existing facilities through reorganization.

The Polytechnic changed its status from a Vocational Training Centre to a polytechnic in 1979 and subsequently expanded at all levels. It is planned to affiliate the polytechnic to the University and to institute degree courses in engineering and technical education. The training of technical education teachers is a priority.

Existing subject areas are to be expanded at the Polytechnic and the number of full time students is to be increased to 1,250. New areas of study will also be introduced.

The Botswana Brigades

The Brigade concept, which is unique to Botswana, was put into practice in 1965 by Patrick van Rensburg. It combines academic and practical training. The movement aims to provide a vocational training for primary school leavers outside the formal education system which also meets the needs of the individual local community. It combines training and productive work so that what is produced helps cover the cost of the training.

The government has given financial subsidies to the Brigades and the Ministry of Education has accepted full responsibility for all Brigades with reference to training and rural industrialization. Ministry support is given to the Brigades through the Brigades Development Centre (BRIDEC). There are fifteen Brigades; most of them are administered by local authorities.

In 1987 enrolment for the Brigades was reported at around 1,000 and three-quarters of them were in building and carpentry. The annual output of the Brigades is estimated to rise to 300-400 by the 1990s and there is a concerted effort to make the concept of Brigades compatible with the new apprenticeship provisions. Brigades training covers a wide range of subjects and this allows trainees to graduate with a strong combination of theoretical and vocational skills.

Employment Creation Measures

A number of programmes have been initiated to combat unemployment. The problems of unemployment and underemployment are further compounded by lack of development in the rural sector. The number of unemployed in the urban areas is increased by migrants from the rural sector.

Therefore, government development strategies are aimed at encouraging businesses to relocate in major villages and thus create employment in rural households. Schemes also exist to encourage and assist farmers to be more productive.

Other packages include the Financial Assistance Policy (FAP) and Business Advisory Services which assist entrepreneurs to set up businesses in urban and rural areas. Other programmes aimed at employment creation and income generation have involved Drought Relief Schemes and labour intensive public works programmes.

However, more remains to be done and government is aware of the need to broaden and diversify the economic base in order to encourage employment creation, especially as it appears unlikely that there will be another discovery of viable mining deposits.

COUNTRY PAPER: LESOTHO

General Economic Background

The principal characteristic of Lesotho's economy is its great dependence on South Africa. Lesotho's vulnerability in this respect is further exacerbated by South Africa's protection policies and its incentives for economic development which ensure that new investments are attracted into its economy and thus lead to the polarization of Lesotho and the other Southern African countries.

Another major feature of the economy is the considerable difference between GNP and GDP. GNP far exceeds GDP because of the net factor income from abroad, mainly remittances from migrant workers in South Africa. Almost 25% of Lesotho's total labour force is employed in South Africa and about 95% of Lesotho's merchandise imports and tourist traffic come from this country.

Lesotho's geopolitical and historical background make it vulnerable to factors beyond its immediate control. Lesotho's currency is tied to the South African rand international exchange rate and it is a member of the Rand Monetary Area (RMA). This limits Lesotho's scope for implementing monetary policies to support employment promotion and severely limits its control of foreign exchange.

Lesotho is a member of the South African Customs Union (SACU) but this union mainly benefits South Africa since it is the major producer of goods within the union. More than 60% of Lesotho Government revenue comes from SACU receipts but this is not advantageous because member states are obliged to give priority to South African goods. Lesotho, therefore, like the other states in the union, is severely constrained in terms of fiscal and trade policies to promote industrial development and expand its production base to benefit employment creation.

Demographic Indicators

According to the 1986 Population Census, the total population of Lesotho is estimated at 1.58 million and grows at an annual rate of 2.6. The potentially active labour force is approximately 865,374 or 54.8% of the total population. For a small country like Lesotho this represents a sizeable reservoir of human resources which could be utilized for the development of the country. However, at the moment there are very few employment opportunities in Lesotho. In 1985/6 more than 40% of the active population were recorded as unemployed or never employed. However, one should note that those in full-time education and those who are underemployed are included in the term 'unemployed'.

The Employment Situation

If one excludes the migrant labour in South Africa, then the government of Lesotho is the largest employer of the labour force. However, growth of employment in the wage sector has declined in recent years. What is more, since 1979, the annual number of Basotho recruits to the South African mines has been falling at a rate of about 2%. Indications are that this process of decreasing labour intake may be accelerated which could lead to gradual, or even immediate, repatriation of migrant workers.

This declining demand for Basotho migrant workers is accompanied by an increasing number of new entrants into the domestic labour force. Past trends indicate that even if the modern sector manages to achieve a relatively high economic growth rate, it is not likely to absorb more than 10% of the additional labour force.

Some Causes of Unemployment

The main reason for the high level of unemployment is that the structure of the economy has remained fundamentally unchanged. Despite Lesotho's fairly rapid economic growth, employment opportunities in productive sectors have not increased significantly. This economic growth did not lead to capital accumulation nor future productive investment. Instead, it seems to have provided an opportunity for an unprecedented increase in consumption of non-capital goods and services originating almost exclusively from South Africa.

The failure to broaden the production base has led to a steady decline in crop production since the late 1970s, the stopping of mining activities, the freezing of posts in the public sector and underutilisation of industrial capacity due to shortages of skilled manpower and entrepreneurial ability.

It has also become clear that the country's educational system, which is mainly formal, prepares school leavers primarily for employment in the modern sector and civil service, both of which have demonstrated limited capacity to absorb increasing numbers of labour force entrants.

Manpower Shortages

Employment in the modern sector is characterised by acute shortages in managerial, professional, technical, craft and other production level skills in all spheres of economic activity. Skilled manpower is concentrated in the modern sector, which employs only about 6% of Lesotho's labour force. The 1980 Survey revealed that only 39% of the estimated 41,000 people in this sector were skilled. At the end of 1984 there was an average vacancy rate of about 31% in the established posts in the civil service which required skilled personnel. It is clear that Lesotho has a relatively small number of skilled personnel in the midst of an abundance of unskilled labour. At the end of 1984, there were about 700 expatriates occupying established posts in the civil service and more than 3000 vacancies.

Despite the institution of training programmes Lesotho continues to lose some of its skilled manpower to the neighbouring Bantustans in South Africa as these offer lucrative benefits which Lesotho is unable to match.

Education and Training Sector

Education and training for employment in Lesotho is not the responsibility of one ministry but a joint venture by government ministries, private organisations and individuals. Lesotho has the problem of the incompatibility of job requirements and education. No comprehensive manpower plan has been produced and the studies carried out have tended to address only individual issues. However, vacant positions and posts occupied by expatriates indicate where there are skills shortages.

Our main concern is to provide basic education to the vast majority of primary school students who will not go on to secondary level, since they cannot afford to do so, and who will end up working in agriculture and the informal sector. The policy of the government is to provide education for self-reliance. Our objectives at primary level are to introduce the concept of education with production and to improve basic literacy and numeracy skills. The emphasis is on teaching practically, and making learning more relevant to real life so that learning becomes enjoyable and useful.

In both primary and secondary education the curriculum has been reviewed in order to make it more relevant. In primary education the practical studies curriculum has been revised and is being pilot tested in 22 schools. Our contention is that children must learn to use their hands at an early stage so that they learn by doing. As a result of this revision we have produced a number of teaching materials.

The strengthening of Lesotho's technical and managerial cadres is recognized as a government priority during the current Fourth Five Year Development Plan period. Thus efforts are being made to improve the teaching and learning of mathematics and science at all levels. Special programmes such as in-service courses for unqualified mathematics and science teachers (AMSTIP) and a science pre-entry course (LESPEC) are already making an important contribution.

The policy of government in secondary education is that every school should teach at least two practical subjects with a view to introducing vocational skills to students. The introduction of the Secondary Technical Teachers Programme enabled the spread of a curriculum diversification programme. In addition, a few schools were assisted with workshops. Many schools are willing to offer vocational subjects but are hampered by a shortage of qualified teachers. However, our teacher training programme cannot be expanded because the government is not in a position to employ more teachers because of stringent financial constraints. Intensive in-service programmes for teachers are required but funding is inadequate.

In Lesotho the importance of maximizing the utilization of land for agriculture cannot be over-emphasized because we have inadequate land. In an attempt to achieve self-sufficiency in food production all secondary schools are being encouraged to start income generating projects in addition to teaching agriculture as a subject. Students are expected to run manageable production units so that they can practise what they learn inside the classroom. Food aid assistance from WFP is being phased out in primary schools and this should foster self-reliance.

The shortage of manpower with managerial skills is being addressed by the Lesotho Centre for Accounting Studies (CAS), the Institute of Extra Mural Studies (IEMS), Lesotho Cooperative College and Lesotho Distance Teaching Centre (LDTC). CAS trains about 100 full time and 60 part time trainees in accountancy; the other three organizations run short term courses in business and management, bookkeeping and management of cooperatives or group activities.

The Technical and Vocational Training Board was established in 1984 and the Department of Technical and Vocational Education (TVE) within the Ministry of Education in 1987. The Board is the overseer of all technical and vocational education in order to ensure that training in this sector is closely linked to manpower requirements.

While the prospects for modern wage employment in Lesotho are modest, some improvement can be expected in the coming years as a result of the Lesotho Highlands Water Project. Many jobs in the Highlands Development Authority (LHDA) itself, and in all the implementation stages of the project, require skills not currently available. Training for the project is a joint responsibility between the existing training institutions, LHDA and contractors. Training is expected to be of both short and long term duration. Training of general and semi-skilled labour will be based on instructional modules. In addition, contractors will provide on-the-job training.

Training for engineers and other high skilled professionals will be conducted partly in Lesotho and partly abroad. A new Department of Water Technology is being established at the Lerotholi Polytechnic in preparation for the operations stage of the Lesotho Highlands Water Project. The Department will produce about fifteen technicians annually, starting in 1993.

Non-Formal Education

The non-formal education programmes are used to address the training needs of the informal sector, which is large and growing. Several ministries and organizations are involved. In the area of agricultural education, there is the Thaba-Khupa Farm Institute whose main objective is to train out of school youth through learning by doing.

The Institute was set up to train young people to start their own farms so that they become self-employed. Training is divided into two sections. In the first year students study the basic techniques of vegetable growing, poultry and dairy farming, fish pond farming, sewing, knitting, cookery, leather-work and artisanal skills, spending half a day on theory and the other half in practicals. Second year students study these subjects in depth, but with more emphasis on simple costing and management.

As part of the programme the trainees are given the opportunity to manage a small enterprise within two of the four main subjects taught. This method of teaching enables the students to experience some of the difficulties in managing an enterprise whilst still at the Institute where advice and guidance are readily available. After completing the course and returning home, the students continue to receive advice and help from the Institute through extension follow-up and from staff in the Department of Agriculture.

In the area of vocational training we have institutions like Lesotho Opportunities Industrialization Centre (LOIC) and Thaba Tseka Training Centre (TSTC). Their objective is to combat youth unemployment by providing vocational skills during a shorter time than formal vocational schools. They prepare participants for self employment through simultaneous business and skills training. In addition, LOIC upgrades the business skills and knowledge of entrepreneurs.

Priority is given to the most deprived people from the educational and social standpoint. All training is tuition-free and based on the philosophy of helping the deprived to help themselves. The programme has an inherent system of on-going fund raising in order to pay at least part of its training cost. The LOIC has recently embarked upon training its vocational trainees in business skills as a result of the awareness that there is a trend for job opportunities to decrease. It is, therefore, necessary to prepare the skill-training participants in techniques that will enable them to be self-employed when the need arises.

At the end of the training programme both LOIC and TSTC encourage trainees to make use of the Assistance Fund. Students are free to borrow as partners or groups of cooperatives in order to start any business. The Fund provides initial capital outlay and has easier terms than those for ordinary bank loans. However, people are reluctant to take up this assistance as they are scared to take risks.

There is also the Lesotho Distance Teaching Centre (LDTC) as an institution which helps us achieve and spread basic education to both out of school youth and adults. LDTC is engaged in designing and developing instructional materials and training income generating groups which have shown interest in benefiting from the Assistance Fund. The groups receive step by step guidance and training in the planning and running of a successful business or activity.

The LDTC staff carry out monitoring visits once a month to assess the progress of each group and to reinforce good practices and help eliminate bad ones. It is through these visits that the additional training needs of each group and problems of loan repayment are identified so that precautions to correct the problems are taken in time.

In short, LDTC is involved in educational activities that involve raising awareness of social, economic and health problems and communication skills designed for the improvement of rural employment opportunities.

While skills and financial resources are essential for any income generating activity, we are convinced that concerted efforts should be made towards motivating our people to become entrepreneurs. Our youth appear to be reluctant to take risks by making use of the money available to them and would rather be in salaried jobs. There is, therefore, a need for flexibility and continuous reviews of the programmes.

COUNTRY PAPER: MALAWI

From the time of Independence the government of Malawi has placed a significantly greater emphasis on the development and support of productive sectors than on social services. Accordingly, government expenditures over the last two decades have been concentrated in such areas as agriculture, transport and communications. The expansion of education has been balanced with the availability of resources and the competing needs of other social services as well as the productive sectors. Additionally, the growth of post-primary education and training opportunities were controlled and geared to meeting the skilled manpower requirements of the economy. Given the limited availability of resources the development of education is likely to continue to be tempered by resource constraints.

Structure of the System

Formal education and training in Malawi is, for the most part, centrally controlled by government. The Ministry of Education and Culture (MOEC) has responsibility for general education and some post-secondary education institutions, regulating or controlling both private and state institutions. However, the University of Malawi is essentially autonomous. The MOEC also shares responsibility for coordinating and supervising technical and vocational training with the Ministry of Labour. In addition, some technical ministries or departments such as Agriculture, Health, Posts and Telecommunications, Works and Youth conduct training directly related to their organizations. Some major entreprises in the private sector also conduct or sponsor in-service training programmes.

The structure of the education system is as follows: eight years of primary education is followed by four years of secondary education. Secondary education is conducted in two stages. The first part prepares students for the Junior Certificate of Education which is taken after two years. Successful students at JCE may proceed to the Malawi Certificate of Education which is the normal entry qualification for the University. Students who do not gain entry for the MCE course may proceed to other forms of post-secondary education or training courses.

The distribution of enrolments by level in the educational system resembles an inverted T. In 1985-6, 97% of the students were in primary school, 2.6% in secondary education, 0.4% at the University and in primary teacher training and 0.1% in technical and vocational education and training.

Primary Education

The administration of primary schools is shared among the MOEC, missions, local education authorities and the community in which a school is located. There are three types of schools: central government schools, government assisted schools and unassisted schools. In 1985/6, there were 2,520 primary schools, of which 1,914 were government assisted. At present, about 48% of children of primary school age attend primary school. Over 25% of primary school pupils in 1985/6 were over-age and about 4% were under-age, resulting in a gross enrolment rate of 67%.

Primary education is characterised by high drop-out and repetition rates and low completion rates for any given cohort as it progresses from Standard 1 to 8. The completion rate is estimated at 3.5%. The average number of years taken to complete the eight year cycle is about fifteen. The average pupil/teacher ratio in 1985/6 was 1:61 and classes of over 100 are common. Pass rates at Primary School Leaving Certificate have averaged about 70% in recent years but secondary school places are available for only about 11% of those who pass.

Secondary Education

There are only 79 secondary schools in Malawi at present. Sixty institutions, including 27 boarding schools, are government assisted. Although secondary school enrolments have increased four-fold since Independence, they are still low and amounted to less than 5% of the secondary school age (14-17 years) population in 1985/6. Pass rates for JCE and MSCE in 1986 were about 76% and 65% respectively.

Post Secondary Education

Post secondary education in Malawi falls almost outside the jurisdiction of the MOEC. Although the University of Malawi is nominally part of the

MOEC, for all practical purposes, it is an autonomous body. The Ministry of Labour has joint responsibility with the MOEC for technical training and apprenticeship programmes. The system of technical education is particularly complex. There is a considerable proliferation of training activities within various ministries and the major parastatal organizations. In addition, there are a number of privately owned and operated vocational training schools.

Population, Labour Force and Employment

Malawi is one of the most densely populated African countries. Acute land pressure problems are currently being experienced as a result of rapid population growth. It is forecast that pressure on the land will intensify further. The implications of such a scenario for employment are considerable and require new initiatives and urgent action to stimulate and develop productive employment opportunities. The potential for the development of wage employment must, of course, be assessed within the context of the resources of the economy.

Of an estimated economically active population of 2,951,500 in the 15-64 age group in 1987 about 75% were engaged in subsistence agriculture. It is estimated that the economically active population will exceed 5.5 million by 1997 and will include over 3 million people engaged in subsistence agriculture. Between 1987 and 1997 it is estimated that 900,000 new labour force entrants will have to earn their living from subsistence agriculture or other forms of non-wage employment.

Urban informal sector employment probably numbered fewer than 30,000 in 1987. It is projected that only an additional 10,000 people will be able to find permanent employment in this sector by 1997.

The situation with regard to migrant labour has changed since 1974. While many Malawians continue to live and work abroad, export of labour no longer appears to be a viable option for the employment problems of Malawi.

Subsistence Agriculture Employment

In the agricultural smallholder sector there was a two pronged approach: firstly, there was a gradual improvement in extension and farmer training throughout the country, supported by a number of low-cost special activities in such areas as dairy improvement and secondly, much more expensive and management intensive comprehensive rural development projects were set up in selected areas. Within a decade, this latter approach was found to be prohibitively expensive and by 1978 it had been replaced by the National Rural Development Programme (NRDP) which aimed at broader geographical coverage but focussed more directly on support services.

Estate Agriculture

The government improved the investment climate by limiting wage increases, making leasehold land available on very favourable terms and allowing considerable freedom in marketing. Low wages relative to capital costs resulted in a labour intensive and hence employment generating growth pattern. Looking to the future, one needs to consider whether the present structure of the economy provides a strong basis for continued growth. Agriculture's dominance of the private sector is declining and so the growth of employment since 1977 has also declined.

Vocationally Oriented Curricula

Faced with problems of youth unemployment, Malawi has re-examined syllabuses to try to incorporate vocational content. Agriculture has been made a compulsory subject in the last three years of primary and throughout both junior and senior secondary school, except where teaching facilities are lacking. In secondary schools time is allocated to technical drawing and woodwork/metalwork and home economics. With regard to these, the most that secondary schools should attempt to do is to impart appreciation of skilled manual work and to stimulate sufficient interest in these trade skills for a minority to consider pursuing them.

Vocational Training

In addition to the vocational content of its secondary school curriculum, Malawi has established technical schools or trade schools which concentrate entirely on technical subjects.

There are five basic trades schools in Malawi which have trained mostly bricklayers and carpenters. Courses offered include three year full-time courses, courses for apprentices and upgrading courses. Those trained pass almost entirely into the urban formal sector.

There are three other trades schools which attempt to cater partly or wholly for the rural areas: Nasawa Technical College, the Malawian Entrepreneurs Development Institute (MEDI) at Mponela and the Salima Trades School. Nasawa is linked to youth employment, being associated with the Malawi Young Pioneers. Graduates go, for the most part, either into large urban establishments or into the Ministry of Works.

The courses offered at MEDI relate to the mechanical and electrical with some entrepreneurship development incorporating accounts. A high proportion of graduates seems to be engaged in subsistence farming and not, therefore, practising their newly acquired trade. The proportion is much greater in the case of primary leavers, reflecting their reduced opportunities for formal sector employment. Falling back into farming might be a sign either of lack of demand for the skills in question due to local market saturation which would be of major significance in the light of plans to expand production of skilled trainees, or of special difficulties faced by graduates in establishing themselves as self-employed entrepreneurs.

Salima Rural Trades School is the institution which has so far made the greatest effort to direct its graduates, predominantly carpenters, bricklayers and metalworkers, towards the rural areas. Unlike MEDI, its intake consists entirely of Malawi Young Pioneer graduates who have had basic agricultural training in addition to a craft. The course is a two year course. Part of the second year is spent in a rural location under supervision and efforts are made through an extension service to establish leavers in rural self-employment and subsequently to monitor their progress. Moreover, the School avoids putting its trainees through the standard trade test which might facilitate their absorption into urban formal sector employment, but instead awards, at the equivalent level, a Rural Craftsman Certificate. The School offers the best opportunity within the formal training system for primary leavers to acquire technical skills.

However, Salima and MEDI, on the experience of the past few years, are supplying no more than about 30-40 trainees to the rural areas. If another eight such trade schools were to be established, they would still provide for no more than 1% of the school leavers. This implies that the case for vocational training cannot be based on the employment objective but on other benefits, specifically the supply of more and cheaper goods and services which artisans can make available to rural consumers. The main factor restricting the demand for these skills is the general level of purchasing power, a particular constraint in the case of Malawi.

This does not mean that there is no need to raise the present scale of vocational training which is clearly extremely small. It is likely that the drift of trained artisans to the urban areas reflects higher remuneration obtainable by artisans in the formal sector and is not entirely undesirable. In part, of course, it may represent the substitution of more trainees or more educated workers for less trained and less well educated rather than a net increase in jobs. How far this supply can be increased without saturating the market is not certain. As far as the rural areas are concerned, the present output is low so that the size and number of institutions involved could be safely increased, so long as proper measures for settling graduates in the rural areas are taken.

Conclusion

Malawi has in the past adopted a number of strategies to help ease the problems of unemployment, such as the National Rural Development Programme. Migrant labour is no longer a safety valve and paid employment will almost be static in the near future unless new, viable initiatives are taken in employment creation. The subsistence sector equally calls for other new initiatives to promote productive employment. All in all, education and training is seen as only a factor in the complex problem of employment creation.

The Malawi Young Pioneers

Aims and Objectives

The main youth development programme in Malawi is the Malawi Young Pioneers (YP). The aims and objectives of the programme are as follows:

(a) direct employment creation;
(b) training;
(c) attitude- forming, including the inculcating of discipline and patriotism

The Leadership Course

The Malawi Young Pioneers movement is centred upon a 10 month leadership/agriculture training course aimed at self-employment in agriculture, but also offering priority access to technical trades training at Nasewa Central Training School, Salima Rural Trade School or to agricultural settlement schemes. The MYP also supports the development of youth clubs.

The MYP was established by Act of Parliament in 1965, following a visit paid to Ghana in 1963 to study a similar Youth Pioneers movement there. The leadership course is offered at 24 training bases distributed throughout the country with an average annual intake of 50 -100 boys and girls, per base. In addition to classes, the youth work in groups, on demonstration farms, producing most of the basic food requirements for the bases. Apart from agriculture classes, there are classes in political education (mostly relating to the history of Malawi), home economics, crafts and physical education. From the general objectives listed above, in addition to the training function there is a strong attitude forming objective, the course being intended to inculcate patriotism, personal discipline and certain other values such as respect for parents as well as imparting an appreciation of agriculture as a means of livelihood. Those who return to the villages (the majority) are expected to spearhead or pioneer agricultural change there.

The original target group was that of primary school leavers and out-of-school youth. Probably about half are now primary school leavers. As in the case of technical schools, the scarcity of standard academic school opportunities has made the MYP a well sought - after venue, despite its rigorous approach. This has occurred fairly rapidly, since only as recently as the late 1970's MSCE candidates were not forthcoming.

In assessing the value of the programme, we can consider the nature of the training programme itself and the post training results through the settlement schemes or the village.

The training programme itself has a number of positive aspects. The excess demand for places is an indication of perceived benefits among school leavers. It is agriculture-oriented, directed towards the sector where possibilities of labour absorption are greatest (though problems of labour absorption due to land shortage are already affecting graduates from the programme in the Southern Region). Tractors and tractor driving are not elements of the training or associated subsequent settlement and establishment programmes as found in some other countries. MYP courses focus on simple economic improvements in agricultural practices capable of implementation at the village level.

The programme is the only one which is available to cater for the broad target group of primary school leavers and out-of-school youth and for which recruitment is not simply based on academic qualifications. It is also open to both sexes.

The programme also reaches a significant number of the target group unlike most youth programmes in Africa. Over the 12 years 1969/70 to 1981/82 over 34,000 passed through the leadership course, an average annual rate of some 2,600. This is a useful contribution equivalent to some 8 - 9% of standard 8 leavers in any year, about 60 per cent of the figure for form 1 enrolment and about 5 - 6 times the size of annual technical schools enrolment.

The programme still does not cover anything like the majority of standard 8 leavers, absorbing about only 1 1/2% of the annual output of school youth. This emphasises the need for maintaining an agricultural content in the school syllabuses but the limited access to school education and the limits on how far teaching in the schools can go in imparting practical skills suggest that the MYP programme could profitably be substantially expanded.

Such a decision would need to be based on anticipated returns to training for the village economy rather than for settlement schemes since, as will be seen, the latter absorb only a very small proportion of trainees. It would need to be justified against the alternative of spending more on an already deprived primary school sector and that of providing agricultural training to older, established smallholders through farmers' training centres. The case would be based on the advantage of learning improved agricultural methods at a young age.

Although there is much evidence on the performance of farmer trainees, the general view of those directly concerned with MYP programmes, particularly Training Base Discipline Officers who are charged with acting as extension agents in this regard, is favourable. These have found MYP graduates to be generally more active and responsive. While this is difficult to measure and we may note that there is no clearly recognised vehicle through which MYP graduates might make an impact at the village level, it is probably true to say there have been some beneficial effects. Some positive indicators are that new MYP recruits have sometimes been influenced to apply by the example of returning graduates, and the fact that MYP graduates appear to be welcomed as members of agricultural credit clubs, being known as good farmers.

Settlement Schemes

There are now over 30 settlement schemes including 14 active rice irrigation schemes and a proportion of these regularly accept MYP graduates as settlers in addition to local farmers and some from other parts of Malawi. Between 1964 and 1976 government settled some 1400 graduates of MYP bases.

The number of settlers now on the schemes is much lower than this due to a high rate of departures, particularly among MYP settlers. It is difficult to state exactly how many settlers there are on the schemes; it is even more difficult to attempt a cost benefit exercise. The institution of an effective monitoring and evaluation system incorporating economic aspects should be considered a priority.

MYP settlers are given a plot, food provisions up to the time of their first sale and, on a loan basis, inputs. They are not provided with housing; this they must construct themselves. A Discipline Officer is attached to the scheme, charged with extension responsibilities.

A feature of settlement schemes as a whole in Malawi is their small size. Thus among the 14 rice irrigation schemes at the end of 1984 the mean hectarage was 241 and the number of farmers 403. In general the membership of both MYP and non-MYP members at the settlement schemes has remained constant.

It would be useful to compare the performance of MYP and non-MYP settlers on the various schemes, but the relevant information is generally not available. A recent report on irrigation schemes states that:

"Despite their initial training and the special assistance provided to them in the form of housing materials, tools etc. the MYPs are generally thought to be at a disadvantage because they lack experience. They are normally single and therefore do not have family labour."

Reference is made to the high rate of desertion among MYP settlers and consequently higher rate of default on loans. This was true particularly during the earlier years and does not appear to have been due to strong economic reasons. In some cases it was because MYPs saw the schemes as a means of earning money for a few years, as they may have viewed employment on the large estates or in town, before returning to their home areas. In the early periods, also, a higher proportion of settlers were from MYP bases. With the increasing intensity of land use there has been more interest in the schemes among local farmers and the number of those participants has risen steadily. The mix of young settlers and experienced farmers has been viewed as having a beneficial effect. Other countries which have settled youth in separate schemes might well take note of this experience. In recent years repayment rates appear to have been excellent in line with the exceptional record of Malawian Farmers Credit Clubs. The latter appear to have been a key supportive element.

The agricultural economic performance of the schemes appear to have been comparatively good, though needing more systematic evaluation than has been accorded so far. Apart from the successful credit element a number of positive features include the avoidance of uneconomic tractorisation and decentralised operations without an excessive number of supervisory staff.

Rural Youth Clubs

The programme of Rural Youth Clubs was instituted in 1968 to spread the ideology of the Malawi Young Pioneers movement of which one of the main objectives is to carry to the villages of Malawi the spirit of National Service and progress among the rural youth in rural communities. This implies that the clubs are viewed at least as a potential vehicle for achieving the training programmes' impact on the village. Among the specific objectives are the teaching of methods of agriculture, engagement of the youth in community activities and the encouragement of literacy education. Literacy classes are carried out in most clubs.

A key element is a demonstration plot, which all clubs have. This may be associated with a credit club. In 1986, 9 of the clubs have had loans. It is the intention of the Department of Youth to expand the programme in each district of the community, with each of the 24 districts having a District Youth Officer. As an indication of the agricultural production emphasis envisaged, it may be worthwhile to have a diplomate in agriculture from the University of Malawi (the officer should also have some knowledge of community development).

COUNTRY PAPER: MOZAMBIQUE

Introduction

Mozambique faces an enormous shortage of skilled personnel in the different sectors. The education system has been revised but the New System of Education (NSE) has not yet been fully implemented. The information provided in the paper is, therefore, based on the revised colonial curricula. It is important to note that the impact of NSE on training has not yet been felt.

The war in the country has also compromised the early efforts in education. Many training institutions have been destroyed or paralysed. Resources earmarked for education have been transferred elsewhere to attend the needs imposed by war. In the process, many future technicians have been physically, psychologically, morally and intellectually affected, thus reducing their ability to perform the work successfully.

The Labour Market in Mozambique

The National Commission for Planning (NCP) and the Ministry of Labour (Mitra) are the two government bodies in charge of the periodical gathering of data on the labour situation. Difficulties in obtaining information from provinces and districts and the fact that the Ministry of Labour is still in the process of setting up its Department of Statistics makes existing data unreliable.

The census of 1980 is the only source of reliable data on the country's economically active population. According to this census, 82.5% of the economically active population works in agriculture, 6.2% in industry, 2.1% in commerce and 0.6% in education and culture. The shortage of skilled workers is countrywide. A study carried out by SIDA in 1987 showed that the demand for middle-level skilled workers was ten times more than available graduates.

The Need for a Specialised Workforce

A study carried out as part of the National Technical Cooperation Programme (NATCAP) shows workforce needs per sector and education levels in relation to the number of graduates. In 1986 the demand for specialised technicians reached a total of 780 against 373 available graduates. The main deficit is for technicians with middle-level training as the total number of graduates represents only 41.6% of needs.

It should be noted that although this study is a worthwhile indicator, it is only partial and refers to only three economic sectors, industry, agriculture and commerce. Even in these sectors the data does not represent the real demands as the methods used to obtain information were inadequate.

The Agricultural Sector

A study was carried out on this sector by MONAP in 1986. The study aimed to determine the distribution of human resources in agriculture, animal husbandry, forestry and managerial services related to the sector. Results showed that, discounting the private and family sectors, the following are needed; 2328 basic level technicians, 1325 middle level technicians and 226 higher level technicians. However, in the same year, the total number of graduates from technical-professional institutions for both basic and middle levels was a mere 1,286.

The Industrial Sector

Here demands are quantitative as well as qualitative. Studies show that 20% of the workforce have no training whatsoever, whilst 70% have only primary education, 9% have secondary education and a mere 1% have middle or higher level training. The training of clerical staff is known to be inadequate.

The Education Sector

The current problems in the education sector are largely the consequences of the relatively recent colonial legacy which aimed at reproducing colonial values. During the colonial period, the majority of the teaching corps were

Portuguese nationals who left the country at Independence. The subsequent extension of access to education to all social groups meant not only the replacement of those teachers who had left but also a massive increase in the number of teachers. Thus it was necessary to take on people without adequate training. This is especially evident in the primary sector. In addition to the need for more teachers, there is a need for managerial and administrative staff in the education sector.

The System of Workforce Deployment

The shortage of specialized technicians led to a centralized system of workforce deployment. The official body in charge of deployment is the National Commission for Planning which carries out placements after approval of a ministerial consultative council.

The distribution system begins in the ministries and directorates whose departments undertake surveys of needs at different levels. This information is conveyed to the NCP which then furnishes each ministry with technicians. After approval by the consultative council, the University and the Ministry of Labour place the graduates.

The System of National Education

The System of National Education (SNE) was instituted in 1983 and is still being phased in. The SNE results from a radical alteration to the education system inherited from the colonial period. It consists of five distinct subsystems: General Education (SSEG), Teacher Training (SSFP), Professional Technical Training (SSETEP), Adult Education (SSEA) and Higher Education (SSHE).

The principal changes include an extra year of primary education (extended from four to five years of schooling) and thus the extension of secondary and pre-university schooling to twelve classes. Another important alteration has been the transfer of professional-technical training to the Ministry of Education from the Ministry of Labour. Lastly, adult education became part of formal education, thereby extending opportunities to a wider group of citizens who are illiterate or have little schooling.

The sub-section of Teacher Training is the source of qualified teachers for educational institutions whilst that of Professional-Technical Education tries to respond to the various needs of the economic sectors.

The SNE includes the principle of obligatory schooling for seven classes. Thus, application on a national basis demands a vast expansion in terms of educational facilities and the number of fully trained teachers. Mozambique now finds itself in a transitional stage between the old system and the new. Standard 8 classes will be introduced in 1990.

The Main Difficulties in the Educational Sector

Changes implemented since Independence have permitted notable progress: the illiteracy rate has been reduced from 93% to 70%; primary school enrolments have tripled; in secondary education, there were five times as many enrolments in 1980 as in 1960.

However, the war of aggression sponsored by the system of apartheid through armed bandits has harmed thousands of school children and created difficulties in the training of a skilled workforce for the country. By 1987, terrorist aggression had caused the closure of the following: 2,629 primary schools (affecting 500,000 students); 22 secondary schools (affecting 8,000 students); three teacher training centres; two technical institutions; 36 boarding institutions (affecting more than 5,000 students). The economic situation of the country hampers the development of strategies to counter these problems.

In numerical terms, enrolments have dropped since 1984 and about 50% of the school population is currently outside the school network. In qualitative terms, at all levels of education there have been notable indications of low retention, high failure rates and drop-outs.

As regards the question of the relevance of the educational system to employment needs, it is unfortunate that, so far, no studies have been undertaken by any of the sub-systems of the SNE. The failure to identify the needs of the various sectors in terms of specialization and workforce demands makes it difficult for professional-technical education to respond to needs. The fact that Ministries and companies have to undertake additional professional training programmes for their own staff is indicative of the shortcomings of formal education. SETEP has made an enormous effort to regulate the activity of such programmes for professional training; SETEP controls more than 85 training centres which are administratively independent of the Ministry of Education.

Educational Priorities

There are three levels of educational priority:
1) educational coverage;
2) effectiveness of the system;
3) relevance of training in relation to labour needs and opportunities.

In relation to coverage, the Ministry of Education aims at universal primary education by the year 2000. The projection is the enrolment of 85% of children at seven years of age. The expansion of secondary and higher education, including vocational education, is another objective, which, if successful, would have a significant impact on the productive sector.

From the point of view of effectiveness, we aim to improve the quality of teaching so as to raise pass rates and to reduce the number of repeaters and the drop-out rate.

With regard to relevance, the priority is to fit training to the labour market. It will, therefore, be necessary to carry out studies to identify needs. Taking into consideration the effects of war and the Programme for Economic Recovery, we plan to prepare students for work, particularly those who could not continue their studies, so that they will be self-employed in small and self-reliant activities and will, eventually, promote employment opportunities for others.

COUNTRY PAPER: SWAZILAND

The Nature and Causes of Unemployment

While the number of Swazis needing productive employment has been increasing rapidly each year, the number of regular jobs in the formal sector has grown only slowly in recent years. As a result, the formal sector has only been able to absorb about one third of each year's school leavers.

The recent recession resulted in the closure of some large manufacturing companies and retrenchments in the construction sector. Another factor has been the relatively capital intensive nature of the major agro-industrial companies and the recent introduction of labour saving technologies. The problem has been further exacerbated by large reductions in the number of Swazi migrant workers.

The available evidence suggests that on balance, ever increasing numbers of future labour force entrants (and, possibly, current holders of regular jobs) will have to be dependent upon self-support in the traditional agricultural sector or in the urban informal sector.

The Measures Taken to Curb Unemployment

The results of the recent National Manpower Study indicate that there will be an oversupply of educated and trained people for the available employment opportunities in the wage sector during the period 1986 to 1993. Overall, the results show that the total output of the education and training system will exceed formal employment opportunities by a ratio of over 4:1 during this period. Consequently, unemployment can be expected to increase.

In an effort to enhance the employability of the youth and in the light of the growing unemployment problem, the government has embarked upon a policy of introducing practical arts and pre-vocational education and training in schools. The following are some of the steps being taken:

1) pre-vocational training and practical arts curricula in schools are being established.

2) the demand and supply of the output of formal technical and vocational training programmes are closely linked and monitored and resources are being concentrated upon improving quality and on producing those trainees who have the most critically needed skills.

3) an expanded programme of informal training courses is being developed for urban informal sector operators and rural workers. This programme is largely provided by NGOs with overall monitoring and co-ordination by the Ministry of Education.

4) localisation is being promoted and an optimal balance between skilled citizens and expatriates is exercised. It is planned that those jobs at all skill levels that can readily be localised should be localised within the 1986-1993 period.

Population Figures

The 1986 Census indicates that the total population is 681,059 and that the rate of growth of the population is about 3.2% per annum which is high by international standards. A large proportion of Swazis are very young, with about 48% being under the age of fifteen. The population of working age is around 332,597 or about 49% of the total population. About 53% of this population is economically active. The labour force is growing even more rapidly than the population as a whole, largely as a result of the relatively youthful age structure of the population.

Training Programmes in Manpower Shortages Areas

A number of institutions in the country offer training in a number of critical areas. They are:

University of Swaziland	-degrees in science, humanities, education, social sciences and agriculture
SIMPA	-management and public administration
IDM	-management
CODEC	-handicrafts

Institute of Health Science	-nursing, health inspection
Nazarene Nursing College	-nursing
Emlalatini Development Centre	-woodwork
Swaziland College of Technology	-technicians courses, craft courses, -business studies, hotel and catering.

A number of other institutions, both government and non-government, offer training in various vocational skills.

Despite this effort, all areas of skilled employment in Swaziland suffer shortages and all the professions are heavily reliant on expatriates. The fact that the country still fails to realise self-sufficiency in food production is enough evidence that agriculture is neither taught nor practised at the desirable levels.

Many employers in industry do not have much confidence in graduates of local institutions, preferring either to employ expatriates or to provide in-service training for their employees. What is more, in a number of specialised areas such as medicine and engineering, training is still not available locally and students have to study outside the country.

Development Plans

In 1978 the government determined "to continue the diversification of the curriculum to achieve a closer relationship with labour market opportunities, necessitating the provision of practical subject classrooms in junior secondary schools and the orientation of the curriculum at all levels towards practical and technical pursuits."

Special Programme

Swaziland has made attempts to address the training needs of school leavers and other young adults. In 1975 the government established seven Rural Education Centres (REC) on a pilot basis. The centres were attached to existing rural secondary schools. The main objective was to provide rural youth with skills that would enable them to make a living within their home areas. The skills taught were those identified by the communities themselves. Today, RECs have spread to several areas. They do not require formal entry requirements. A small revolving fund has been established to give loans to graduates to establish themselves in small businesses.

Successes and Failures

Initially, the RECs had only a limited success. Only women showed any enthusiasm for training. There was also confusion with regard to the sharing of facilities between adult classes and regular school pupils. Often there were problems between school administrators and REC programme co-ordinators. A further problem was that, once trained, REC graduates needed resources to set up on their own.

After the initial set-back, the programme began to pick up in the 1980s. Administrative problems were ironed out and the programme saw over 400 people undergoing training annually. The most popular courses are sewing, knitting, woodwork, masonry, nutrition and cookery, handicrafts and literacy. The RECs have also initiated community projects in piggery and poultry rearing, vegetable gardens, protection of water springs and the building of latrines.

The Curriculum and Manpower Needs

The overall goal of government in the education sector is to provide education for the needs and abilities of all. The achievement of this goal calls for major improvements in the education delivery system which includes development of the curriculum to include practical subjects, both at primary and secondary level; the use of guidance and testing; the substitution of examinations with continuous assessment; the introduction of pre-vocational streams at higher levels; the improvement of teacher training and a general improvement in the system's internal and external efficiency.

Primary School Curriculum

Primary education is for children aged 6-12 years. This level introduces children to practical subjects such as home economics, agriculture and arts and crafts which will be taught alongside more traditional subjects such as mathematics, English and SiSwati.

Secondary School Curriculum

This level is for children aged 12-18 years. Secondary education aims to build on both the academic and vocational skills learnt at primary school. In order to ensure that literacy, numeracy and practical skills are attained by all school leavers, children are given a nine year basic education programme. This will be followed by two years in which pupils choose between academic and pre-vocational subjects. The eighth and ninth years of a student's schooling will be used to determine the career direction a pupil should pursue, with close reference to the manpower survey of 1986 which indicated skill shortages in both the formal and non-formal sectors of the economy.

Post-Secondary Education

To meet the needs of the country's economy, various government ministries, parastatals and private sector institutions have expressed the need for more specialised graduates in particular disciplines at the University of Swaziland (UNISWA), Swaziland College of Technology (SCOT) and Gwamile Vocational and Commercial Training Institute (VOCTIM). At UNISWA certain departments will begin to offer postgraduate programmes during the current plan period. Initially, these programmes will be tailored to meet the specific requirements of employers. With this in mind, UNISWA has established joint faculty/industry committees.

In order to meet the changing needs of the labour market, SCOT activities are being developed to offer degree level courses in technical subjects. During the plan period, government is committed to providing equipment for the commercial, construction and engineering departments.

In order to cater for the 4,000 school leavers who will not have any chance of getting wage employment or being self-employed, VOCTIM has been established. This institution aims to prepare the nation's school leavers for the world of work and self-employment.

Three levels of teacher training are offered, Primary Teacher Diploma, Secondary Teacher Diploma and Graduate Teacher Diploma. The main aims of teacher training over the plan period are to reduce the number of unqualified teachers and to continue with the introduction of a diversified school curriculum into the teacher training programme.

Students' Attitudes

Pupils leave primary school at the age of 13. At that time, they are still too young to go into employment. The primary curriculum aims to develop proper attitudes towards practical work among pupils. The primary curriculum does not make separate provision for boys and girls.

At secondary level, the practical subjects offered are agriculture, woodwork, metalwork, technical drawing and home economics. From its inception, agriculture has been done by both boys and girls and has been taught by both male and female teachers. Although a slight change is now taking place, boys have tended to take technical subjects while girls opt for home economics. There is still not a single male teacher for home economics or a female one for technical subjects.

It is at tertiary level that learners are taught skills that will earn them a living. It is worth noting that it was only in the 1970s that the Swaziland College of Technology opened its doors to female students and it was in the same period that males began to take up nursing as a career. On the whole, opportunities for education and training are offered throughout the system without any discrimination on the grounds of sex.

Guidance and Counselling

The Educational Testing Guidance and Psychological Services (ETGPS) section of the Ministry of Education is used to diagnose students' learning disabilities and to detect their aptitudes and talents. The Guidance Section of ETGPS also advises pupils on available career opportunities and career choices. In every school there is a guidance teacher who works with students and reports on their progress to ETGPS.

COUNTRY PAPER: TANZANIA

Introduction

This paper tries to explore how education systems in Africa, particularly in the SADCC region, can be improved for suitability and relevance to learners with a view to making the school leaver easily employable. In order to achieve this goal, it is important to ask the following questions:

What efforts have so far been made to make primary, secondary and post-secondary school graduates employable? To what extent have they been successful and what lessons can we learn from such attempts?

How should the education system be reorganised and reoriented so that it facilitates the acquisition of knowledge and competencies which can maximise the employability of school graduates?

Before the above questions can be answered in an empirical situation, it is necessary to list certain general observations relating to education, training and employability:

Although additional years of schooling generally give an individual a better chance of finding a job, education is capable of rendering an individual unemployable by raising aspirations which cannot be satisfied.

Evidence suggests that vocationally oriented education, even if it facilitates the acquisition of skills and competencies on the part of the graduates, does not necessarily result in increased employment. Therefore, provision of vocationally oriented curricula is not a panacea for unemployment. It has to be accompanied by structural changes and reforms in labour market practices, i.e. modification in the pattern of wage rates and the introduction of specific employment generating practices.

Education motivates people to leave their communities and move into the formal sector where the same amount of work may be performed by fewer workers. This reduces work per head and, therefore, leads to underemployment.

As education attainment at a given level increases, so does the availability rate of employment decline. The unemployment solution, therefore, to a great extent, rests on factors which are not necessarily educational.

To verify the observations already stated this paper examines the efforts made by Tanzania to grapple with youth unemployment.

Tanzanian Initiatives and the Development of Education for Employment and Self-Employment

1) *Primary Education*

The first seven year cycle constitutes the primary component of education. Primary education is intended to be sufficiently self-contained to serve as a complete education for a substantial proportion of the age cohort. The percentage of primary school leavers who move to secondary education is at present only 7% and is planned to reach 15% by the year 2000.

As a result of the rapid expansion of primary education, the labour market conditions faced by those leaving school now are very different from the conditions faced earlier before the introduction of universal primary education, when primary school leavers were in short supply. For those entering the labour market a generation ago, a primary school certificate was a passport to a white collar job. Today a primary school leaver is fortunate to get a manual blue collar job in the wage sector. For this reason, primary education is diversified and terminal to enable those who complete it to stay in the rural areas and work in the agricultural sector where the majority of their parents earn their livelihood. Therefore, in primary schools, practical skills in arts and crafts, domestic science and agriculture have been increasingly emphasised. Through these activities, children develop insights, interests, creativity and technical skills essential for rural development and for further training.

A two year post-primary course has been introduced to cater for those primary school leavers who do not secure a place in secondary education or other training institutions. These institutions are called Post-Primary Technical Centres (PPTC). The course content in these centres is comprised of technical skills, agriculture, animal husbandry, home economics and accountancy. These centres are meant to produce crafts people who take up self-employment or organise themselves into cooperatives and work commercially after their courses. Problems of implementation do exist and government efforts are directed towards solving them through the provision of qualified teachers and strengthening village projects to enable them to absorb the youth.

Related to rural development, Tanzania, since the mid 1970s, has developed Folk Development Colleges (FDC). These colleges impart to adults knowledge and skills in fields such as agriculture, handicraft, domestic science, health and water supply. These courses are designed to enhance productivity, communal activity and self-employment by raising the level of the knowledge and skills of adults who can then use these skills in their villages. We now have 52 FDCs in the country. There are indications that they are useful and important innovations in as far as there is evidence that village productivity, health and nutrition are reaching acceptable standards. We also hope that these innovations will help to retain primary school leavers in the rural areas.

2) ***Secondary Education Diversification Programme***

Secondary school education consists of a four year cycle (Form I to IV) followed by a two year cycle (Form V and VI). The two year cycle mainly prepares students for university education and is strongly academic.

In the mid 1960s Tanzania started to experience an increasing number of Form IV secondary school leavers who were neither selected for further education nor assigned employment in the formal sector. The situation began to worsen in 1972 when 41% of Form IV leavers could not be assigned any employment or courses of training in the formal sector. Currently this percentage ranges between 50 and 55%. The increasing numbers of the unselected school leavers were seen as stemming from the mismatch between the knowledge and skills that schools imparted and the knowledge and skills that the employment sector demanded. It was alleged that the education system was too theoretical and that very often its content was irrelevant. To meet this challenge, Mwalimu Julius Nyerere argued for a radical view of education that would enable its recipients to earn a living either in the formal or the informal sector.

Thus, from 1967, the educational philosophy in Tanzania was to promote among pupils the culture of self-reliance, both in the economic and intellectual sense. Therefore, efforts have been made to introduce and sensitize secondary school students through a broader curriculum which includes pre-vocational and academic training. The diversified curriculum for secondary education provides students with skills in either agriculture, technical subjects, commerce or home economics. The programme is intended to prepare students for further studies and to equip them with employable skills. Basically, no secondary school can be opened without a specialist bias. Schools can offer more than one specialist bias but students are allowed to take only one in addition to the core curriculum of academic subjects which is compulsory for all.

The bias subjects have both theoretical and practical periods

3) ***Post-Secondary Education***

The most prominent policy in post-secondary education since Independence has been that of expanding tertiary education with the ultimate aim of achieving self-sufficiency in middle and high manpower levels by the year 2000. The thrust has been changing in favour of technical and science education. At university level, the percentage of students studying veterinary science, agricultural science, engineering, medicine, forestry, geology, pharmacy, dentistry and agricultural engineering has increased from 72% in 1981 to more than 82% in 1987.

Tanzania's Experience with the Diversified Curriculum

The primary and secondary diversified programmes have not produced results. Most primary school leavers, aspiring for better paid employment, struggle for places in higher education. If primary school leavers are unable to secure secondary places, they either go back to the villages or seek private avenues to higher education. Those who complete their education privately then swarm to the towns in search, often in vain, of paid employment. Society is now faced with the problem of a frustrated generation of youth. One of the problems is that many villages and urban centres have not provided young people, who have had skills training, with requisite tools and capital with which to start self-reliant self-employment projects.

The secondary school diversified programmes lack the basic educational materials: expert teachers, working tools and raw materials required for practical skills training. This programme has proved to be very expensive.

It was expected that school graduates would emerge with skills and aptitudes relevant for a particular function in society. However, neither the formal nor the informal sector have shown any readiness to receive and incorporate these young people into the economy and have not shown recognition of their skills.

Many African countries, despite their attempts to make their curricula work-oriented by merging theory and practice, are still seriously faced with the school leaver unemployment problem. The problems associated with the teaching of work-oriented curricula in formal educational institutions are diverse and may be summarised as follows:

It is not easy to get qualified teachers for work education. Pre-vocational education graduates suffer from inadequacy of skills and unemployability of the little that they have acquired through crude methods.

In the absence of scientific research data, schools cannot accurately predict those trades which are in great demand in the diverse labour market. Even where prediction can be made, schools cannot adjust their teaching when changes in the labour market occur faster than curricular changes.

There is very little linkage between the programmes of vocationalised schools and the industries which would have been expected to set and ensure standards of skills performance of trainees and to use the latter in actual industrial or field productivity.

Graduates find it difficult to undertake alternative careers when they find that the trades for which they have been prepared in school are no longer in demand. They find themselves ill or inadequately prepared for the heterogeneous activities that characterise the economy. The growth of new technologies and machineries must, therefore, be adhered to in revising curricula after fixed periods in order to match knowledge and skills with new technological developments.

Some parents regard vocational education, especially when introduced at the early stages, as likely to limit their children's future opportunities.

Many employers limit their criteria for employment selection to excellence in academic subjects. They disregard excellence in subjects related to vocational trades by claiming that these subjects do not show a student's academic strength.

Conclusion and Recommendations

In addition to efforts to diversify curricula, manpower planning institutions, in co-operation with local authorities, should devise new strategies to mobilise school graduates who are not absorbed in the formal sector and initiate them into societal functions. Planning at local and central levels should consider how school graduates who are not absorbed in the formal sector can be assisted to undertake self-employment activities or employment in the informal sector.

We suggest that constant research should be made into the nature of the priorities of the various sectors within the economy. On the basis of research findings, education and training should be made to respond to economic needs.

Government should improve their informal sectors so that they become conducive to self-employment. This suggests the restructuring of the informal sector by making available key social services, such as improving rural communication and transport, diversifying production, stabilising market demand and facilitating credit.

Efforts should be made to encourage SADCC countries to arrange conference for educationists, trainers, economists, welfare workers and others to exchange ideas, to deliberate on these issues and to draw up effective and workable strategies to link education, training and employment.

COUNTRY PAPER: ZAMBIA

Background

In traditional African society education was mainly technically and vocationally oriented even though general knowledge for widening children's horizons was also taught. Children had to learn to look after themselves in adult life. In such a society there was no problem of unemployment since most of the activities people did constituted work leading to self-sufficiency within the family. However, with the coming of Western education and Western ways of life, this way of living changed. Wage employment gradually replaced traditional activities and specialisation crept in, particularly in scientific and technological fields.

The Employment Situation in Zambia since 1964

When Zambia attained its political independence in 1964, it had less than one thousand School Certificate holders and a hundred university graduates. Thus it was found fit to place high priority on the expanding provision of education to its citizens and especially of training for the public sector and industry. Indeed from 1964 to date, education in Zambia has been expanded at all levels - primary, secondary and tertiary institutions. There are more than 3,400 primary schools, 200 basic schools and 250 secondary schools and two universities, and 14 technical education and vocational training institutions.

Because of this expansion the labour market is quite flooded with job seekers, particularly in the non-technical fields. With a depressed economy, large-scale unemployment for school leavers and sometimes even for graduates from tertiary institutions has become a common feature.

Nature and Causes of Unemployment

Zambia suffers from both underemployment and unemployment of labour. The Fourth National Development Plan shows that of the 2,365.253 employed persons 10.3% or 243,626 are grossly underemployed (underutilised).

Amongst the unemployed persons (353,357) 34.8% and 65.3% are men and women respectively. The unemployment rate, therefore, is 17.8% for women and 8.6% for men. For urban areas it is 19.2% and 10.6% in rural areas.

In addition to this, there are those people who, having formal education, obtain jobs that are less effective than they might be. And, there is also widespread underemployment in the rural areas because agricultural work is seasonal and the rural economy has not been diversified to offer some other work to the rural communities.

The major causes of unemployment in Zambia could be related to:

1) Low absorption capacity of the modern formal industrial sector which could provide employment to the unskilled additional labour force. As industry grows in complexity as well as in size, manpower is no longer defined in terms of able-bodied people but in terms of more and more highly developed skills and the capacity for rapid adaptation to changing circumstances. It is necessary to secure people with the requisite competence and flexibility to cope with more complex demands. In other words, the old 'investment-employment' ratio has been broken; the pattern is that the more you invest the fewer people you employ.

2) The increased expectation generated by widespread education combined with the high level of diversification in the modern sector has created a demand for wage employment especially in urban areas.

The education system tends to raise the aspirations of students to levels which cannot be satisfied in rural sectors of the economy. For a long time students have looked at education primarily as a means of getting jobs. They have been interested in the 'investment' benefits of education. They obtain education to prevent unemployment.

3) The reluctance of most school-leavers to entertain the notion of taking employment outside the urban white-collar occupations has compounded the problem of unemployment. Manual labour has always been looked down upon. These views about education and about the types of work appropriate for persons with some measure of schooling are in line with prevailing attitudes towards manual work which are bolstered by the existing social stratification where most people think manual work is meant

for those who haven't been to school and those who live in rural areas.

The consequence has been that the rural areas have been deprived of people who could supply the intellectual stimulation needed for development.

4) The concentration of economic development in the urban areas has forced most people, including those who have not been to school, to look for employment in these areas, no matter how meagre a livelihood it may offer.

5) The curriculum has been narrow, geared towards selecting and training pupils for opportunities that are diminishing. The curriculum lacked elements for fostering innovation and increasing productivity.

6) Lack of adequate careers guidance in educational institutions which could have played a prominent role in illuminating the effects of unemployment and also in introducing pupils to opportunities and values that could be found in areas of self-employment, voluntary work, leisure and community service work. Such efforts would assist pupils in learning how to make up the deficits of not having a job.

7) Training programme at tertiary level have remained static. No research programmes have been designed to identify new types of trades and occupations that sustain self-reliance, e.g. soap making. There has also been an absence of Adult Vocational Training schemes.

8) The absence of labour intensive production methods which are capital saving and can create a large number of employment opportunities.

Measures taken to curb unemployment

The Zambian Government has taken serious measures to curb unemployment. These are:

1) ***The Zambia National Service***

The Zambia National Service was established in 1966 with a view to giving school-leavers adequate skills for self-employment, particularly in agriculture.

2) ***The Department of Technical Education and Vocational Training***

This was established in 1968 as a training agency for lower and middle level trained manpower. Its main responsibilities are:

a) training of teachers in technical and commercial subjects for all its institutions;

b) training of craftsmen, technicians/technologists for the public sector and industry;

c) trades testing and certification of trades tested workers. These are unskilled workers who pick up the skill in a trade through practice.

3) ***Educational Reforms***

In 1977 the Government of Zambia adopted a set of Educational Reform recommendations in order to provide education in accordance with the needs and aspirations of the Zambian people. One of the major concerns of the reform was to orientate academic education more towards the world of work and provide an education with a bias to production in which academic education and practical skills training were to be integrated so that the school-leavers can be self-reliant.

4) ***The Department of Youth Development***

This department was established under the Third National Development Plan of 1979-1983. The main objectives are:

a) to reduce youth unemployment through direct participation by youth in production schemes, especially agro-based industries, rural settlements and small-scale industries.

b) to conduct and promote research in youth development

c) to undertake systematic planning and implementation of youth development programmes

d) to develop a cadre of professional youth workers in the country

e) to co-ordinate youth development programmes through local communities, local authorities, village, district and provincial development committees and non-governmental organisations.

The major constraints in the fulfilment of some of the above objectives are:

a) under-capitalisation of youth development projects.

b) lack of an optimum staff establishment to carry out these projects.

5) *Small Scale Industries*

The government has encouraged small scale industries as a way to curb the rising unemployment problem in the nation. And to see that such industries are promoted in the whole country. The government has set up several organisations such as the Small Industries Development Organisation (SIDO) and the Village Industry Service (VIS) and Small-scale Enterprise Promotion (SEP) to spearhead their promotion.

6) *Foreign Investments*

The Zambian government has encouraged a lot of foreign investment as a means of developing the rural economies in which personnel with different skills can be employed.

7) *Other Organisations*

Other organisations like churches, non-government organisations and district councils have embarked on a series of training programmes for school-leavers.

In addition to all these, several tertiary institutions in the fields of health, agriculture, teacher education, as well as the two universities continue to expand their enrolment.

The fourth National Development Plan (1989-1993) advocates the following:

a) achievement of an overall economic growth rate of 3.0% and an increase in formal sector employment from 357,000 in 1987 to 400,000 by 1993;

b) identification and promotion of informal sector productive activities with potential for growth and employment generation.

c) assignment of high priority to the development of agriculture.

d) proper placement and utilisation of manpower by matching individual skills with employment opportunities;

e) establishment of an employment and manpower information system so as to form and maintain a sound base for effective manpower planning.

Guidance and Counselling

A unit for Guidance and Counselling was established in Zambia in 1970 in the Psychological Service Department of the Ministry of Education. Its function was to initiate and monitor the development of Guidance and Counselling services in all educational institutions particularly in secondary schools.

In 1978 a two year Diploma course in Guidance and Counselling was started at one of our teachers' colleges with an initial intake of 20 teachers most of whom had been career teachers in secondary schools.

Self-Help Action Plan for Education (SHAPE)

Production work and resource work have been on-going activities in Zambia schools for a long time. Most schools and colleges established production units following the Presidential Decree in 1975.

By 1980 school based in-service training activities had been started in schools in many parts of the country. INSET co-ordinators were identified who, together with the inspectors of schools, established teacher centres and appointed resource teachers in different subjects who organised and ran seminars and workshops where teachers exchanged ideas and materials. In this way teachers have been learning from one another. The professional meetings, seminars and workshops, which have been organised, are part of the implementation of the Educational Reforms Recommendations of

1977, which the government adopted.

Initially these activities were not easily managed in all areas of the country owing to inadequate financial resources. Furthermore, the process lacked co-ordination at national level as there was no organisational structure to link the various activities.

SHAPE was launched by the two Ministries of Education in January 1987. The programme's main purpose is to enhance the capacity of schools and colleges for self-help in professional and material terms. The programme is mainly sponsored by SIDA and NORAD. Other donor agencies which have contributed are the British Council and the Finnish International Development Agency (FINNIDA) through its Practical Subjects Project (PSP).

The administration and management of the programme are decentralised and participatory. As much as possible activities are planned and managed by the teachers themselves with the assistance of inspectors and administrators. However, teachers, inspectors and administrators are further assisted by SHAPE co-ordinating committees at each level of the education system; zone, district, regional and national level.

The SHAPE programme has now reached a point where the professional and organisational structure is fully implemented at all levels. The programme continues to gain momentum and teachers have become aware of their professional obligations. There is, above all, a change of attitude among teachers and pupils towards production work in schools as well as in teacher training colleges.

The majority of people who co-ordinate the activities of SHAPE also attend to their routine workload of either teaching or inspecting.

The workload of SHAPE co-ordinators poses a critical challenge for the effective implementation of SHAPE.

Conclusion

With new technology and economic developments a constant review of our patterns and policies is necessary as no country can remain immune to the implications or side effects of unemployment as the levels of unemployment remain high or increase. Even though unemployment is one of the inescapable difficulties in the way of achieving modernisation, the problems could be kept to a minimum by:

1) ensuring that the curriculum offered in schools does prepare pupils for the actual realities of life;

2) developing rural areas through the diversification of employment activities in those areas. These would decrease cases of unemployment and underemployment;

3) creating more vocational training programmes to give skills geared towards self-reliance;

4) creating an Employment Service that would have information on all available jobs;

5) effective placement of all skilled manpower

COUNTRY PAPER: ZIMBABWE

Introduction

In pre-independence Zimbabwe, like all former colonies, we had education for power for the minority ruling class and education for subjugation for the majority. During the armed struggle, we asked the question 'education for what' and came up with several answers: education for power for the majority; education for self-reliance for the individual and for the nation; education for the development of Zimbabwe.

Constrained by the war situation we could only explore the prospects of education for self-reliance through our schools in the refugee camps. The schools were established and administered in such a manner that the schools themselves, their students and products had to fit into their society as assets and not liabilities. That is how we came up with the concept of Education with Production.

After Independence in 1980, the government re-stated our socialist philosophy. Steps were taken to expand both formal and informal education, including adult education, while a war was declared on illiteracy.

Developments in Education

Primary school enrolments rose almost 300% from 820,000 pupils in 1979 to over 2.2 million in 1988 with over 95% of school age children in school because of the introduction of universal education, while secondary school enrolments also rose nearly tenfold from 66,000 to 653,000 during the same period. Several technical high schools were also opened. The transition rate from primary to secondary schools has been raised from 25% to 85% with non-formal education taking care of the remainder.

At the tertiary level, enrolments at technical colleges rose sixfold from 3,600 in 1980 to 25,000 and from 170 to 1,050 at agricultural colleges during the same period. More technical and teacher colleges are being established.

At University level, several initiatives have been taken to address the high level manpower needs of Zimbabwe. The infrastructure has been expanded and more developmental disciplines have been introduced, while the general thrust of the University's programmes has been towards employment and development. University enrolment has risen by nearly 400% from just over 2,000 in 1980 to nearly 8,000 in 1988.

Extensive work has been undertaken by the Faculty of Education. All our teacher education colleges now have associate status with the Faculty of Education so that the University of Zimbabwe now issues the certificates and diplomas in conjunction with the Ministry of Higher Education.

The faculty has also introduced the Bachelor of Education degree for technical subject teachers, who may also engage in self-employment if they wish. It has further introduced new masters' degrees; it has established the Human Resources Research Centre as a facility for studies into the manpower needs for Zimbabwe's development. In keeping with this outreach thrust, the Faculty of Education piloted the Zimbabwe Science Programme for secondary school science teaching without physical laboratories and was very much involved in the establishment of the Zimbabwe Integrated Teacher Education Certificate for primary school teachers. It has recently established a programme called TIRA (Teaching in Rural Areas) in which faculty students have to teach in rural areas during the University vacation periods.

To ensure that research undertaken through the Faculty of Education services the community and the region, the University joined the Educational Research Network of Eastern and Southern Africa and has since established a local subsidiary known as the Zimbabwe Educational Research Association which brings together the University and the Ministries of Education for research purposes.

In the engineering and agricultural disciplines, the University has also taken several initiatives to relate theory to practice. A new degree programme, the Bachelor of Technology degree is now in place at Harare Polytechnic and Bulawayo Technical College under the umbrella of the University. In addition to these efforts, we have taken full advantage of external scholarships. The government also has a programme of teacher training in Cuba in an effort to address teacher shortages for science and mathematics.

Zimbabwe Foundation for Education with Production (ZIMFEP), a non-governmental organization established in 1981, had resettled 12,000 people by 1988 in various capacities including further education, job placement, self-employment and collective co-operatives. ZIMFEP has established a number of schools throughout the country. The annual enrolment in these schools is just over 9,000. Because of the success rate in job placement and job creation, the schools are unable to absorb all the candidates applying for enrolment.

Recently a Presidential Commission of Inquiry presented its report recommending the establishment of a second university which will have a developmental bias.

Industrial Training

The government retained the apprenticeship scheme which was the country's main local supplier of artisans and technicians for the majority of industries.

Every year, since 1980, there have been over 5,000 apprentices in training, with an average of 1,000 apprentices graduating each year. To curtail loss of these skilled workers, the government introduced bonding for all apprentices. As a result of this measure, some 9,000 apprentices are currently serving their bonding period. To complement this effort, the government introduced trade testing of skilled workers and this has resulted in the certification of over 30,000 skilled workers at various levels since 1982.

The Education Curriculum in Primary, Secondary and Tertiary Institutions

The government has recognized the need to vocationalize secondary education and to re-structure the education system. The establishment of the Ministry of Higher Education emphasized the government's intention to address the issue of post secondary education and training as a follow-up to the democratization of both primary and secondary education.

The primary education curriculum has been re-oriented to make it more sensitive to the local environment and child centred so that the child can actually participate in the learning situation. The system also draws the parents into the learning of their children.

At the secondary school level, the curriculum which used to be heavily influenced by the overseas Cambridge environment has now been re-oriented to serve the local environment. The '0' level certificate is now jointly issued by the Cambridge Local Syndicate and our Ministry of Primary and Secondary Education. Nearly twenty technical high schools have been authorised to provide technical subjects examinable after four years at the Zimbabwe National Craft Certificate level under the Zimbabwe Further Education Examinations Board.

To ensure that every child at secondary level takes at least two technical subjects, a tool-kit programme has been introduced aimed at supplying basic tool kits for building, carpentry, metalwork, technical drawing, home economics and agriculture. The teaching of science has been greatly improved in rural schools by the expansion of the Zimi-Sci kits, the programme which was piloted by the Faculty of Education and handed over to the Ministry.

Programmes of Education with Production have been extended under the guidance of ZIMFEP. Arrangements have now been made for students in certain secondary schools to be attached to local employers for at least three days a term.

ZIMFEP also maintains very close links with the Ministries of Education so as to feed the general education system and to benefit from the continuous research undertaken by those Ministries. Of late ZIMFEP technical graduates are also being trade tested by the Ministry of Higher Education for skilled worker status recognized in our labour laws and industrial agreements.

ZIMFEP, unlike most education institutions, has followed up its graduates with career guidance and counselling and has also advised employers on methods by which they can fully utilize and benefit from the potential of ZIMFEP graduates.

Problem Areas

A number of problems have been encountered:

1) The shortage of foreign currency has made it difficult to import expensive equipment.

2) Staff shortages have generally led to the underutilization of some of the available facilities.

3) The major constraints in arranging job placements for students have been shortage of funds to support the students and the absence of insurance cover for the students or the employers' equipment and machinery in the event of an accident.

4) Some companies have helped individuals to buy themselves out of their bonding.

5) Despite efforts to place all schools on an equal footing, some rural schools still do not have essential services.

6) Re-orientation is needed for staff to ensure they remain committed to the new educational ideals.

7) Shortage of foreign currency has affected production activities, making it difficult to undertake on-the-job training.

8) How production units should be staffed remains problematic. Teachers do not have enough time to do justice to either academic or production work. However, if production unit managers are hired, it is feared that students will not be fully involved in the units.

9) ZIMFEP has also observed that its graduates without close follow-up for guidance and counselling or assistance with initial start-up capital have found it difficult to establish themselves. It also feels very strongly that there is a need for a deliberate national effort at industrialization and fundamental reforms of the land tenure system if its graduates are to be

expected to play a productive role in future.

10) Individuals have the right to choose where they work, whether in the formal or informal sector or in urban or rural areas.

EDUCATION-FOR-EMPLOYMENT AND SELF-EMPLOYMENT INTERVENTIONS IN DEVELOPING COUNTRIES: PAST EXPERIENCE AND PRESENT PROGNOSIS

Kenneth King

Introduction

Countries in the East, Central and Southern African regions have made many innovations in their education and training systems since independence, ten to twenty five years ago. Many of these initiatives have been homegrown, a few were externally inspired and funded. The result of these efforts by governments, parents, NGOs, and external agencies is that the education and training systems are no longer recognisably the same as in the late colonial period. There have been dramatic changes in the provision, sponsorship, and curriculum of schools. In the training area also there has been considerable development. Along the way, many different institutions have been established, and though the pattern has not been identical in any of the countries in the region, there clearly have been some parallels.

Most countries are likely to learn more from the analysis and evaluation of their own developments and experiments than from neighbouring states. We shall therefore in this discussion avoid detailed descriptions of country specific initiatives, but focus rather upon types of programme that several countries may be able to identify with in their own recent history or in their present policy options. In order to sharpen the outline of the particular issues under discussion, we shall present them in the form of propositions. Not because we feel that there is yet the research evidence to support such generalisations, but because the propositions may capture more effectively some aspect of the past and present debate on a particular policy issue. We start with the present and then look further back at previous interventions.

A. The changing terms of the education-for-employment debate

A1. Traditional definitions of programme success are being challenged.

A2. Institutional orientation to the modern sector is being weakened by programme expansion.

A3. Popular investments in schooling-for-employment continue long after the odds have lengthened against finding a job.

The late 1980s offer a peculiar challenge to education and training systems predicated historically on serving the small modern sector of the economy. At one point in the history of the region it was possible to think of the lower secondary leaver as a manpower category, in the same way as in the late colonial period the Standard VII or VIII leaver could be so considered. The logic and success of school expansion at every level since independence has dramatically lengthened the odds against the bulk of primary or junior secondary school leavers finding paid employment. Indeed, in the countries that have most rapidly expanded secondary education, the size of a single cohort of secondary school leavers is as numerous as the entire body of workers in the manufacturing sector of the formal economy.

There have been, in the first one or two decades of independence, a number of training institutions that have been judged successful in placing their graduates in the modern sector. This success may be protected by very close relations with a particular industry, or through insistence on industrial sponsorship or whatever. But in the present crisis of student numbers, there will often be very strong political and popular pressures to duplicate such institutions, to weaken the special relations with particular employers, and to allow the attendance of self-sponsored students.

To some extent this pressure for access and replication has raised questions about some of the earlier definitions of success. In some cases, the 'success' of a small national youth service scheme was because of its close employment relations with the uniformed services. In other cases, a national polytechnic was judged successful when almost all its students were sponsored by industry and were attending in the inservice training mode. There have been other training institutions, all of whose graduates have traditionally been accepted by a particular ministry, and have had almost a guarantee of employment once they were admitted to training.

In all these cases, there is now strong political and student pressure to broaden access. But in broadening it, the special relationship with employers is weakened, and even broken.

> *A4. Institutions are being asked to add the objective of Training-for-Self-Employment, and thus change their definition of success.*

> *A5. The democratisation of training opportunities is thus follow ing the democratisation of education*

> *A6. The requirements of modern sector industry are no longer seen to be an adequate yardstick for determining training needs.*

For a long time the post-school training institutions have been protected from the pressures for democratisation that have swept through schools, and as a result the training sector has remained very small and much more closely tied to the tiny modern sector than have schools. There is no doubt that the demand for democratisation largely derives from the perception of institutional success in terms of modern sector jobs. But the building of several more similar institutions cannot be entirely justified as merely increasing the opportunity to compete for entry to modern sector jobs. This may continue to be the rationale for parents and students. But the much higher cost of training institutions (as compared with schools) means that external donors, if required, will need to be presented with a different logic for system expansion.

Increasingly the political logic for training system expansion is becoming training-for-enterprise or training-for-self-employment, but there are almost by definition no easy measurements for these objectives. Nor any indication of whether the technical skills on offer will remain relevant for those not gaining modern sector jobs.

A7. For many years schools have de facto been educating school-leavers for self-employment, even though this objective has not been explicit.

A8. It remains to be seen whether the making of 'enterprise' and self-employment' explicit objectives will alter the character of schooling or the quality and aspirations of those graduating.

A9. The education-for-self-employment message will be more acceptable where public and formal sector salaries have failed to offer a living wage.

The bulk of young people leaving school early, at the end of primary or even at junior secondary, have been obliged to find work on the family farm or on their own account in the informal sector. Now that schools and training institutions are much more explicitly targeting preparation for enterprise and self-employment, will this ease the transition from schooling or training into self-employment? In some countries, enterprise education is being made mandatory at every level of education from primary school to university, and in all training institutions. This amounts to a major recognition of the destinations of ordinary school-leavers, and an admission that the traditional modern sector orientation cannot satisfy more than a very small proportion of school graduates.

It has traditionally in Africa been difficult to commend to young people the virtues of 'terminal' primary education or of work in the rural areas. This has particularly been so where modern sector salaries have dramatically outstripped earnings from the farm or from working on one's own account. In several countries, however, the impact of the recent financial crisis has underlined the failure of formal sector salaries to offer a living wage, with the consequent need for further sources of income, either in the informal sector or in a second, part-time paid job. In such countries it is possible that the educational orientation to formal employment could begin to shift, and especially as it becomes clear to parents and students that the wages in the lower reaches of the formal sector can be bettered through trading, or other self-employed work.

What this may mean is that the struggle to become a clerk may weaken, but it is unlikely that the few better paid positions will alter their traditional attractiveness. Schooling and training are certain to continue to be influenced in a major way by the few careers for which polytechnic or university education is a necessary precondition. It is possible, however, if there develops a culture of independent, and successful business, this may begin very slowly to alter some of the orientations in schools. This could even involve some young people, as in parts of Nigeria, quitting school early in order to become trainee traders.

A10. Very little is known about the school's capacity to hold on to students, once the traditional orientation to the modern sector is clearly weakened.

A11. As the few remaining good jobs require ever longer and more competitive schooling, there will be a tendency for lower income families to rethink the value of school attendance.

A12. As structural adjustment increases the private cost of higher education, this may weaken some of the traditional reasons for low income families supporting basic education.

In some ways the late 1980s may mark the end of an era in African education. Cost-sharing, involving higher fees, is everywhere gaining ground, but especially in secondary and tertiary education and training institutions. The older tradition of virtually fee-free higher secondary and tertiary education is being dismantled, but it is quite unclear, as this proceeds, to what extent the attendance of poorer families in the basic cycle of education has been encouraged by the vision of free education further up the system. It is already clear in a number of African countries that there has arisen quite recently a dramatic problem of primary school drop-outs. It may be anticipated that these are predominantly from low income families, but what is not known is whether a contributing factor has been not only the greater competitiveness but also the greater cost of higher education. In some sense therefore universal primary education (UPE) may contain the seeds of its own destruction. If the campaigns for UPE are predicated upon increasing access to modern sector jobs, it will be soon obvious to parents that this is a mirage, and that a great deal of further, more costly education is required. And where parents have already spent heavily on educating secondary school children without their gaining paid jobs, the incentive or even the capacity to educate others may be powerfully weakened.

It is too early to do much more than speculate about the causes of this major drop-out phenomenon from primary schools, but it is just possible that it is connected with a delinking of basic education from the formal sector labour market in the minds of lower income families. In rather the same way, attendance at literacy classes has now very little connection with access to modern sector jobs.

> *A13. There is little relevant international experience onmaintain ing a universal primary education regime in a contracting formal sector labour market.*
>
> *A14. Even without the possible demotivating impact of higher education fees and shrinking opportunities for paid work, UPE needs constantly to increase its coverage to take account of popula tion growth.*
>
> *A15. In the unequal battle to maintain UPE against the tide of demographic growth, there will be even stronger pressure to in crease opportunities for access to higher education.*

There have been no detailed studies of how poorer countries have sought to maintain the momentum towards universal literacy and primary education in situations where the link to jobs - one of the original incentives to attendance - is progressively weakened. But there is no doubt that countries with a stagnant or shrinking formal sector and a massively expanding population face unique problems in both motivation and finance for basic education. There is little evidence that attendance can be maintained by the suggestion that education can be a good preparation for a marginal improvement in rural life. Indeed, it would seem that even though modern sector jobs remain very few, there is more political capital to be made out of increasing the opportunities for students to compete for these, through expansion of colleges and universities, than through investments in primary school capacity and quality.

A16. The education-for-self-employment option is unlikely to become effective through schools and training institutions alone.

A17. It is being recognised that massive support for microenter prise development in the economy generally is probably a precon dition for really effective enterprise development in schools.

A18. The experience of support to micro-enterprise and to in come-generating projects is widely scattered across several coun tries, but the lessons from this have not been accumulated.

For a number of years a large number of institutions, especially non-governmental organisations (NGOs), have been encouraging micro-enterprise development through small scale credit schemes, training, etc. Though the number of individual institutions concerned has been large, there has not been a widespread national impact. Nor is it likely that there has yet been any connection between income-generating projects out of school and the encouragement of self-employment and enterprise in schools. Major national initiatives to facilitate self-employment through interventions in the physical environment, and in financial and non-financial measures to promote self-employment will need to be dramatic, substantial and well-publicised if they are to attract and involve the millions of young people in the central and southern African region who currently enter self-employment as a last resort. Even so, it cannot be expected that governments themselves, with their own major financial problems, will be responsible for delivering small enterprise programmes; their role should be much more in the removal of current obstacles to micro-entrepreneurs in the areas of infrastructure, tax, licenses and credit, without developing a social welfare approach to enterprise development.

The sheer number of those currently involved in the informal sector and in working on their own account is so great that it cannot be anticipated that more than a tiny fraction will be the direct beneficiaries of government programmes. Very large numbers however can be assisted by a liberalisation of the environment for small and micro-enterprise. The reorientation of most of the major government and private sector institutions, including the banks, will need to be very great if there is to be a meaningful acknowledgement of the requirements of the majority of the working population. At the moment, most of the leading institutions, chambers of commerce, business development organisations are almost exclusively concerned with the needs of the small formal sector of the economy, and even the small industry development organisations tend to be dedicated to modern, small scale enterprise rather than to micro-enterprises and to the informal sector. Like the attempted reorientation of the schools towards self-employment, the realignment of such institutions towards a huge new clientele will nowhere be easy. There will be constant pressures for the traditional clienteles of institutions such as banks to take precedence over what will be seen as the higher risks of support to micro-enterprise and the informal sector.

> *A19. There will be value in reviewing the experience of such countries in Africa that have sought to address comprehensive policy change in favour of enterprise and self-employment.*

There are, we have said, considerable difficulties in learning from the experience of other countries in Africa, even when these share the same colonial history and language. The post-independence development strategies have been so diverse even within anglophone east, central and southern Africa that there are currently few indigenous regional organisations that can readily share experiences in this sphere. The external donor agencies remain one of the most potent vehicles for the encouragement of learning from other parts of the continent, or from even further afield, in India and South East Asia. There are nevertheless several examples of major initiatives which are in place or are being planned that would repay close attention. In Nigeria, over the past two years, the National Directorate for Employment (NDE), has undertaken a whole series of national programmes all of which have been designed to encourage graduates at different levels of education to explore self-employment options. Meanwhile in Kenya, following Sessional Paper no. 1 of 1986 which acknowledged the crucial role of the informal and micro-enterprise sector in job creation, there has emerged a really major concern with small enterprise development at the highest political level, and this seems likely to take the form of an action programme on small scale and informal sector enterprises. The preliminary thinking on the latter is valuable for indicating just how many financial, non-financial and infrastructural levers may need to be pulled to give such a programme national momentum.

A20. The challenge for many SADCC countries with valuable individual projects supporting self-employment will be to scale up such scattered initiatives, and move from pilot programmes to national endeavours.

There are certain to be illustrations of similar trends in many of the SADCC countries. All are bound to have a number of well known projects and programmes that appear effectively to deliver an orientation to self-employment. But in many cases, the projects and programmes are themselves small scale, linked to a particular individual, to an NGO, perhaps operating in just a handful of sites. Though successful in their own terms, such projects may have little relevance to the shape of any national initiative. The distinguishing feature of the new generation of programmes in favour of the informal or self-employment economy is that they are national in scope. In addition they seek to address at the same time both the supply side - in the education and training systems - and the demand side, in the shape of those who are already in the labour market.

A21. There is one major difference between intervening in favour of self-employment in developing countries as compared with fully industrialised countries, and that is that state-supported unemploy ment is not an option for the former.

A22. The clienteles for self-employment policy are paradoxically already self-employed, by economic necessity. The object of policy must therefore be to make that self-mployment more produc tive.

A23. Currently the bulk of the informally self-employed do not even conceive of the possibility of state or private sector support. With the development of any national programme the principal challenge will be how to target and select from the mass of the already self-employed

The fact that most people in developing countries cannot afford to be unemployed, and can at best expect some extended family support if they cannot temporarily find work does mean that the problem is not so much persuading people to be self-employed as seeking to raise the quality and productivity of that self-employment. The key issue may be how to move significant numbers of informal sector workers from what may be called 'subsistence self-employment' to some form of more entrepreneurial self-employment. Whereas enterprise allowances may be used in the industrialised countries for persuading redundant workers or the long term unemployed to consider working on their own, the problem in most developing countries is selecting from the sheer quantities of the self-employed a number who might profit from some input of business skills, flexible credit, technology support.

For the majority of the already self-employed it is almost inconceivable that the state should interest itself in their welfare; indeed, an element in the ruggedness of their self reliance has been the certainty that there would be no form of external support forthcoming. In many countries, it will take some time for the subsistence self-employed to adjust to even the possibility of external assistance. However, it is well established that programmes for credit, business training, or advisory services cannot reach more than a tiny fraction of those eligible. Hence, the objective of government must also be so to alter the environment for small scale enterprise that the bulk of the self-employed derive some direct advantage even if they are not selected for some specific programme of assistance. This implies intervention in what is sometimes termed 'the enabling environment' as much as in packages of direct aid towards individual entrepreneurs.

B. A summary review of selected past experience in education for employment and self-employment.

The reason we have given for taking the present before the past experience is that in most countries initiatives for employment or self-employment - whether in schools, training institutions, or in the labour market itself - have tended in the past to be relatively small in their scope. This is so whether the discussion is about programmes in schools, nonformal training projects, or about efforts to expand the informal economy itself. There have been a very small number of education and employment programmes that had national coverage, but in general what distinguishes thinking in what is for several African nations the third decade of independence is the desire to engineer exposure of the entire age cohort.

Typical of this latter thinking is the view in one or two countries that all university students should take compulsory enterprise courses. In another country, all senior primary school students and junior secondary must take business education. Typical also is the view that particular youth training centres should be in every village or sub-location. In reviewing some of the past experience, it must be acknowledged that not a great deal of it is directly relevant to the different terms of today's debates.

> *B1. Traditionally a number of school-based programmes concerned with encouraging self-employment have been more identified with negative messages about the modern sector than positive messages about business and enterprise.*

Historically, there have been a number of nationwide programmes encouraging school leavers to embrace agriculture, and prepare for life and service in villages rather than go to towns, but there has been a tendency for these to be interpreted by pupils as being merely hostile to secondary school expansion or to urban migration. They have seldom been associated with a programme of rural regeneration, rural electrification, improved transport, improved producer prices etc. Hence it is extremely doubtful if such programmes succeeded in reducing pupil aspirations to gain further education. The language of such initiatives which stressed 'reinsertion in the rural milieu' or 'integration of the school into ordinary village life', or, even more crudely, staying in the rural areas, did little to emphasise the scope for enterprise, income generation or success. In some instances, also, there was a quite explicit suggestion that individual enterprise was disapproved of, compared with communal or cooperative initiatives.

The difference now is that even in countries that have been more politically committed to cooperative endeavours, there is a greater tolerance of the private sector and of individual initiative. There is much more awareness now of the need for there to be an accelerated development of infrastructure and amenities in the rural areas, if the messages of the public education system are to have any meaning. To some extent there have been important admissions of incapacity in the state's ability to deliver development, and by contrast much greater faith has begun to be placed in the market and in the private, voluntary sector to take on local development issues. It may be equally worth being cautious about the extent to which NGOs and the voluntary sector can really replace some of the activities once claimed by government.

B2. In the early years of independence and with the growth of primary school leaver 'unemployment', a number of initiatives, in cluding national youth services, and rural youth training schemes were erected. Despite their national aspirations, such schemes were in practice highly selective, and absorbed only a few hundred of the hundreds of thousands of school leavers.

B3. Because of their greater cost and dependence on foreign funds, post-school vocational training schemes have remained very small as education systems have continued to expand. This very selectivity has encouraged a strong orientation to the modern sector of the economy.

There are many illustrations of these trends. 'National' apprenticeship schemes and 'National' Vocational and Industrial Training Centres, for instance, have often had just a few hundred participants for the entire country; whereas the informal sector apprenticeship has been covering tens of thousands of young learners. Equally, vocational training centres have been designed to meet the inservice needs of formal industry, and have made little acknowledgement of the needs of the informal and micro-enterprise sectors. To a much greater extent than is now appropriate, the training system is still closely wedded to industry and the needs of the sectoral ministries.

B4. Because secondary schools themselves were still highly selective in many countries of the region, it was difficult to expect a handful of technical secondary schools or industrial arts schools to develop a very different tradition and orientation to the labour market.

In many countries, the number of technical schools or of diversified secondary schools remained very small, being highly dependent on external aid for their development and maintenance. The result of their being part of a highly selective secondary system was often that their status as secondary schools was more important than their curricular orientation to particular trades or industrial arts. As the general secondary schools dramatically expanded their numbers through self-reliance and community support, the numbers of technical and thoroughly diversified schools shrank proportionately. This could actually increase the status and attractiveness of such schools, not in terms of their curricular orientation but because of an assumption about their supposedly closer links with modern sector jobs in industry. Not surprisingly the high selectivity and aspirations of such technical or industrial students did not make them particularly attractive to industry after all.

> *B5. Attempts to 'diversify' all secondary schools have not been commonplace, but where the numbers of secondary schools as a whole have remained very small, the curricular diversification has been much less important to students than the fact of their being in secondary schools at all.*

There is thus something of a 'catch 22' about introducing technical or agricultural reorientation in highly selective secondary settings. Particularly when secondary schools as a whole have not covered more than 5% or 10% of the age cohort, it was scarcely likely that diversification or technical facilities alone would succeed in communicating a quite different labour market orientation than regular secondary schools. It should not have been surprising therefore that 'vocationalisation' in highly selective settings has not been shown to produce much significant difference in labour market orientation, though it has been shown that it can be popular when well resourced and well taught. In many ways therefore the donor agency judgement about the failure of the diversification initiative has been premature. Diversification has scarcely anywhere been assessed in conditions of universal access to secondary education.

Indeed, it is worth noting that despite the agency judgement about the failure of school-based vocationalisation or diversification, policies for vocationalisation have remained almost the number one favourite of governments facing problems of educated unemployment.

> *B6. Government policies for school vocationalism may well commend themselves more when they are on offer across the whole of a relatively open access secondary system, and also when the crisis in the formal economy has become only too evident.*

B7. The very crisis in the modern sector of the economy is of course having at least two impacts on vocationalisation:increas ing popular interest in vocational alternatives, and reducing gov ernment ability to resource such provision.

This generates a further paradox of encouraging a vocational orientation in countries with a minute industrial sector and with a tradition of highly selective secondary schooling. Even when secondary schooling becomes 'ordinary', and when it becomes clear that general secondary school certification can no longer guarantee formal sector jobs, it is possible that the vocational option can become more popular. This is the very point at which government have found it difficult to find any funds for system-wide vocationalisation. There has been therefore a tendency for lowest cost (barefoot) vocationalism to be on offer in situations where it is nationally encouraged across the whole system. Such forms of vocationalism have been tempted to offer subjects which have the least dependence on equipment, materials, specialist teachers etc.

B8. Because of the contradictions in providing school-based vocationalism in both selective and open-access secondary school regimes in low income countries, it has continued to be popular for training courses to be acquired after school.

B9. The very small numbers of government training centres has had the effect of encouraging large numbers of private, 'back street' training institutions, as well as NGO-sponsored post-training centres.

There are very strong pressures still for training courses, whether public or private, to be oriented to the modern sector of the economy. The same is true for most of the large amount of training undertaken through correspondence. Very little is currently known about the changing impact of such training, once the expansion of provision makes it obvious that the course titles are unlikely to translate into modern sector jobs. The extent to which such courses begin to get used for self-employment certainly changes over time. But at the moment it seems likely that those pursuing self-employment go directly into the informal apprenticeship system, whilst those attending public or private training courses are still hoping for some opening in the formal economy.

B10. The impact of structural adjustment upon the training system both public and private is very unclear. But as public funding for training shrinks, training centres have had to go to the market to sur vive.

With the increasing cuts in materials, teachers' and instructors' salaries, and with the delinking from industry through expansion, training centres have had to become more market-oriented to survive. Lacking materials for training purposes, they have taken on 'custom jobs' and orders from outside clients, which has had the effect of combining training with production. In some cases, the temptation of contracts has taken priority over work on the theory of the trades. The result has been to move some of the training sector much closer to the world of micro-enterprise and informal training.

B11. In marked contrast, the agency-dependent training centres remain enclaves of high quality training, artificially insulated against the wider pressures affecting education and training in many countries.

In some ways, the message that training centres are defined by formal sector training requirements tends to get reinforced by the existence of very small numbers of high quality training institutions which continue to be very heavily dependent on particular donor agencies. Like many of the other training initiatives which take small numbers of students, these institutions are in one sense successful, but this success can be at the expense of a view of training that is valuable to young people entering the 'ordinary economy' of informal sector and micro-enterprise jobs.

B12. Over the decades of independence, the originally 'man power'-oriented education and training system of the colonial period has lost its very close connection with the modernsector, but at the same time, the specialness of formal sector jobs, especially in the middle and lower reaches, has been dramati cally eroded.

B13. The traditional differentials between formal and informal sector incomes have been reduced significantly, and particularly in the public sector.

As the democratisation of education (and more latterly training) has continued apace, the modern sector itself has been increasingly defferentiated. With most of the expansion in

formal sector jobs taking place in the government and parastatal segments of the economy, it is these latter whose wages and salaries have been hardest hit in recent years. One consequence has been a widening of the differential between the public and private modern sectors, and in particular the gap between a low level job in the government and self-employed work has narrowed, been eliminated, or even been reversed. This has happened, of course, not as the result of a policy to reduce income differentials, but it is nevertheless of very major significance to the functioning of education and training systems.

Conclusions on Education and Training for Employment and Self-Employment

Our analysis would suggest that for many countries in the region the already massive expansion of basic education, the subsequent expansion of training provision, and the increasing severity of the macro-economic situation are combining to produce a very different political economy of human resource development. In this respect, the old formulas are really no longer relevant. Similarly the old pilot projects and programmes of the immediate post-independence period which serviced handfuls of young people from the unexpanded secondary school systems of the time are also not likely to offer much insight now for policy.

A new logic is beginning to emerge that is seeking to see work (whether paid or own account, formal or informal) as a whole. The boundaries between formal and informal economies were always over-emphasised, but are now clearly a distraction from an understanding of the nature and rewards of work. Training systems or training institutions that continue to operate as if they could service something as separate as the formal economy are in danger of being anachronisms.

Though this logic is now apparent in the wages and income of the bulk of people, there is still a great deal of political mileage to be obtained from expanding the opportunity to compete for the very small number of jobs that are well rewarded. From one angle this expansion at the highest level of education appears like the emergence of the diploma disease at the university level, and with its inevitable links to higher fees it suggests the development of important divisions of income in society. From another angle, however, this easily criticised over-expansion of higher education is an assertion about the capacity of highly educated people to transform their working lives. There is little likelihood that the expansion of higher education will rapidly slow down, or that great attention will be given to ensuring graduates get priority in political thinking about unemployment.

Explicit promotion of the enterprise culture may help at the margins, but we have argued throughout this piece that if enterprise and self-employment is only promoted through education and training institutions, there will be little effect. A really major set of changes in the enabling environment and in the financial support of micro-enterprise will be necessary to alter the dominance of education-and-training-for-employment towards some significant measure of education-and-training-for-self-employment.

References

Commonwealth Secretariat, 'Vocationally oriented education', Tenth Conference of Commonwealth Education Ministers, Nairobi, Kenya, 20-24 July 1987

ILO, 'Training for the urban informal sector', report of a seminar, April 1987

Kenya Government, *Report of the presidential working party on education and manpower training for the next decade and beyond* March 1988, Nairobi

K. King, 'Education and Youth Unemployment', paper at Ninth Conference of Commonwealth Education Ministers, Cyprus, 23-26 July 1984
K. King 'Education, training and industry in Zimbabwe', occasional paper, Human Resource Research Centre, University of Zimbabwe, 1989, and

Centre of African Studies, Edinburgh University, January 1989

K. King 'Technical and vocational education and training in Kenya: the movement towards a comprehensive national system', policy seminar on the implementation of the sessional paper on education and manpower training, 19-22 March 1989, Mombasa, Kenya

K. King, *Aid and educational research in developing countries* Centre of African Studies, Edinburgh University

OECD/World Bank/ILO, 'The informal sector revisited', report of a seminar, September 1988

SECTION 4

CRITICAL INNOVATIONS IN EDUCATION FOR EMPLOYMENT

Patrick van Rensburg

What Employment?

If I am to talk meaningfully about education for employment and employment creation, and to suggest critical innovations in our educational systems to better serve these goals, then it is necessary first to survey the production setting and the 'world of work', as it is often called, in order to look at employment options and job-creation potentials, to which education should relate.

The Formal Sector

All our economies are of course dominated by the 'formal' or 'modern' sector of the economy with its requirements of professionals of many kinds, of technicians, of artisans and other categories of skilled labour and semi-skilled as well as unskilled, and perhaps even uneducated labour. The formal sector tends to be associated with large-scale investment, modern technology and high productivity, a well-developed infrastructure, both physical as well as economic and financial, and salaried and wage employment, at quite high levels of remuneration in its top ranks, graded downwards, of course, to fairly low earnings for those in the more menial positions. Much of the investment in the formal sector comes from outside and a substantial proportion of formal sector activities are geared to raw material exports. Usually, a much smaller part is directed towards import substitution.

Dynamics of the Formal Sector

To a large extent, the modern sector was created in the colonial era, rather as an extension of the more advanced material conditions of the colonial power than a natural outgrowth of the local society, and it was created to facilitate the extraction of raw materials, the export of capital goods by the colonising country, the recruitment of cheap labour and import of manufactures. Its dynamics of course were not to cater for and absorb the entire society; if anything, its purpose was to disrupt traditional economies and create a dependency on paid labour.

Some economists have tried to argue that a take-off point would eventually be reached in the formal sector, with internal capital accumulation and skill development at a sufficiently high level for the economy to grow and diversify fast enough to absorb the greater part of the population. In my view this is not possible. Nor are the experiences of some of the Asian newly industrialised countries, or Mauritius, replicable in this region. Other economists talk of the trickle-down effect, which we have yet to see succeed. The formal sector is predominantly, but not exclusively, urban. It comprises commercial agriculture and mining, and, therefore, estates and mining areas. It can also include tourism and services, and it certainly relates, too, to public and local government services wherever they are located.

The production systems, transport, commerce, the service industry, insurance, banking and finance are largely owned by what is euphemistically called private enterprise, although in some countries the state may participate directly or indirectly though parastatals. There may even here and there, be a small cooperative sector.

The Marginalised Population

What we today call the 'informal' sector, comprises, in reality, those people whose labour is not needed by the 'formal' sector. Given the international division of labour described by Minister Fay Chung on Monday, and given the urban-rural contradiction, there are simply not enough sufficiently profitable activities to attract enough capital to absorb them all.

Of course there are some small-scale producers in high density urban areas or in agriculture, using low-productivity technologies, who may through hard work and accumulation, and in many cases through exploitation, prosper and expand. There is a grey area around the borderlines between the formal and informal sectors, but the use of the term 'informal' can, perhaps, be construed as a way of authenticating the 'formal' sector ideologically, politically and socially. Obviously, there are a lot of vested interests there, which ruling classes and elites strongly defend. These are the most vocal and influential groups in society and they manage to capture the surpluses and most of the State revenues, which are directed to increased living standards rather than to investment in more job-creation.

Harmonising the Formal Sector and Popularly-based Development

The essence of promoting gainful production as a means of employment creation, is of course, to apply labour to the resources available, but the problem is how to do it without sufficient capital or by making better use of the available skills and capital. Now the formal sector is everywhere a reality which is not going to disappear. Personally, I prefer to speak of popularly-based development rather than the promotion of the informal sector, and I believe that it is possible to harmonise modernised development (within the formal sector) and a more popularly-based development. Let me illustrate what I mean by harmonising. My own experience of 18 years of educational and development work in rural Botswana is my guide here. I observed, for example, how traditional production activities like brewing were displaced when a Chibuku factory was built in Botswana's capital, and how thatching grass and burnt clay bricks were displaced by corrugated iron and cement blocks. I have also seen small-scale rural tanneries and other production activities collapse because they could not compete with cheaper imported products of large-scale industry. I have witnessed, too, the escalating aspirations of young people and their unwillingness to settle for jobs in rural areas - and even in urban areas - because they want very much higher salaries than their labour can produce, in many cases. These aspirations are shaped, I think, by what they see of life in the formal sector. Harmonising in the first case would mean recognising that there has to be a place for large-scale, high productivity technology, alongside a range of simpler technologies as well as a range of scale of enterprises, from very large to small. There was a stage in India's development when it was considered necessary to reserve certain products for small and medium-scale enterprises with less expensive technologies; another measure could be to institute differential sales taxes on the products of the different sized enterprises with their different technologies.

The problem of aspirations is a more difficult one to solve in the absence of generally acceptable socialist-style measures, although high taxation or compulsory savings schemes might counter the spectacular consumption that is doubtless one of the factors generating high aspirations amongst the young.

There is no doubt that in many countries in our region, small-scale peasant agriculture was neglected. Agricultural production needs to be geared primarily to the growing of food for the domestic market, with exports limited to surpluses; it needs to be geared, secondly, to the production of raw materials for manufactured goods that meet local needs; and thirdly to exports of primary non-food commodities. The system as a whole needs to be supported by land reform, the introduction of irrigation, and sound all round back-up services and infrastructure. At the same time, there should be a co-ordinated development of both light and heavy industry and mining designed to meet local demand with an emphasis on decentralisation of industries to the rural areas and in particular the establishment of small industries owned by rural and semi-urban populations on a self-reliant basis. Such industries could provide the peasants with many of the goods and services they need as well as providing implements for agriculture and maintenance and repair facilities for the rural people.

Part of the harmonisation could be achieved through linkages between the formal sector and the popular economy, between mutual exchanges of produce. It is also possible to promote shorter production and distribution cycles with a range of different product-based small enterprises supplying local markets.

Here then, are examples of different economic - and to some extent - political measures that can be applied to create a favourable environment for accelerated job-creation.

What kind of Enterprise?

Now, what kind of enterprise creation and what forms of capitalisation can we envisage being served by the educational process? Let me give some examples from both the capitalist and the socialist experience in different countries. In countries like Cuba, as I am sure we will hear later today, vocational training schemes relate to enterprises. First year students engage in production related to contracts with the enterprises and students spend an increasing amount of time actually working in the enterprises in the second and third years. By the third year, it is as much as 50% of their week. In most cases, students are guaranteed work in enterprises after training. To an extent, many of the enterprises and the vocational schools have grown and expanded symbiotically over the last 30 years.

In Spain, even under the fascist Franco regime, one of the world's largest producer cooperative complexes developed after the civil war, in Mondragon, in the Basque country. There are nearly 20 000 working members in a great many enterprises engaged in a wide range of sophisticated enterprises today. It all began quite small and simple, soon after the civil war, and amongst its most important features are the Casa Laboral Popular (the People's Bank of Labour), the Escuela Technica (the technical school), the research and development unit, and the housing, retail and social services cooperative units.

The bank mobilises funds from every quarter and it invests in securities as well as in the cooperative. Individuals can borrow the money they need to join (the equivalent of several thousand dollars) from the bank against their shares, for security. The technical school is a major training ground for the cooperative and students there spend 50% of their time learning and 50% in production, much of it related to contracts with the cooperatives. My visit to Mondragon was one of the most exciting experiences I have had.

A similar story from China concerns the Gung Ho Cooperative Movement and the Sandan Work Study School. Towards the end of the Chinese war of liberation, a New Zealander named Rewi Alley participated in a programme to set up thousands of industrial producer cooperatives in parts of China still under Kuomintang leadership but not occupied by the Japanes. Soon discovering the lack of skilled managerial and technical staff, Alley and associates then set up the Sandan work study centre to train technical and managerial cadres to lead the co-operatives. Sandan had about 30 different production units, including a coal mine, glassmaking, agriculture and small industries.

Educational Innovations

Now let us look at some of the critical innovations in education that can serve the kind of harmonisation of the formal sector and of popularly based development I have discussed here, and prepare people either for formal sector employment or for participation in the informal sector in some kind of enterprise.

Before embarking on a list of critical - crucial - innovations, some words of criticism of conventional formal education. Its pedagogy is highly abstract, theoretical and verbalised and it encourages competitive individualism. Its teacher-student relations and classroom settings encourage a somewhat passive receiving of education. With its terminal cut off point and bottlenecks between the first years of primary school and tertiary education, its selects and rejects. This is hardly the best way of educating the mass of the people. This education is intended to prepare people for modern sector jobs, but as school systems grow more rapidly than jobs in the formal sector, it is partly an education for unemployment, because the conventional school does not prepare its pupils for a life outside the formal sector, or for self-employment creation.

Education with Production

In my view, the most important of the critical innovations is work and study, the combination of education with productive work. It is the key to self-reliance, it can generate resources and it can dynamically assist the process of job-creation. It can also enhance learning in both the cognitive and affective domains. And it can promote socio-economic development quite substantially.

Let me build my arguments with reference to my own experience in Botswana. The students of Swaneng Hill and Shashe River Schools between 25 and 15 years ago, built their own schools, assisted by the Brigades, made some of their own furniture and produced some of their own food. Swaneng Hill School was a powerhouse of talents, skills and knowledge in its local community and the staff and students were involved in resource surveys, skills surveys and income and expenditure surveys which led to the expansion and diversification of the early Brigades with the introduction, amongst other things, of tanning and lime processing, using local resources.

In 1987, the 20 or so Brigades of Botswana produced goods and services to the value of Pula 11 million whilst educating and training 1000 or so Batswana. (They also, incidentially, employed around 2000 Batswana, some of whom were trained by the Brigades themselves). The goods and services produced included food and helped meet other basic needs. One centre produced P1 million in a range of goods and services last year and made a net surplus (even after allowing for depreciation) of P100 000. Twelve young Batswana, trained as printers at this Centre, have now been registered as a Producers' Cooperative. Here are examples of capital formation, profitable participation in production and the development of infrastructure through student labour, and evidence that they can succeed in running their own enterprises. There are several other examples in Botswana, and I believe many throughout the region.

All agencies in our countries concerned with development, including central and local government, need to recognise the potential role of the educational system linked to production to help promote socio-economic development and stimulate the economy as well as to create employment opportunities. If the potential of schools as powerhouses to plan and influence development is recognised, then resources and projects can be identified to fit in with local and even national development plans. Broadening objectives from education for all to education and work for all means transcending conventional economic and manpower planning, which are both today largely based on what happens in the formal sector only.

How can education with production enhance learning in both the cognitive and affective domains? In the cognitive domain, it is a case of recognising that all production has theoretical roots - as former Minister Mutumbuka once put it - in science, mathematics and other disciplines. In the affective domain, it means recognising that personal qualities, habits and attitudes, creativity and awareness, understanding and commitment, leadership and autonomy are not learned in classroom settings alone, but rather through a combination of theoretical and practical work which is what should happen in education with production.

Curriculum Transformation

This brings me to another critical innovation - that of the broadening of the curriculum. If education means that people learn to create enterprises for themselves and to manage their own enterprises, then it must provide them with the skills and knowledge, and the confidence and experience, for the purpose. It entails knowledge of the overall socio-economic and political structures and the policies that govern society's affairs, of banking and finances, of legal structures and legislation, of economics and fiscal policies. Pupils therefore need the extension of their curricula, not only to provide additional knowledge missing from current curricula, but in a way - working and learning - that offers more effective ways of learning.

A work-study college in the Southern US, which requires 15 hours of work from every student, has its own syllabus of affective learning objectives related to what it calls 'labour progressions'. The point to make is that as one becomes more skilled in work, one develops important personal habits and attitudes.

If young people are to be involved in job-creation, they will need to be good organisers and managers, to keep and understand books and records, to understand profits and losses, to know about stocktaking and sales, about ordering in time, about sources of raw materials and labour pricing. They will need initiative and courage, perseverance and good inter-personal relationships.

What Education Can Do for Job-Creation

Whilst we all recognise that education cannot by itself create employment and that this requires broader social, political and economic strategies, education can better prepare students for future productive lives within the framework of such strategies. This applies not only to productive work and curriculum transformation but also to the involvement of students in managing their own affairs, the exposure to the tasks and challenges of running not only enterprises but school affairs. Discipline must encourage responsibility and not destroy initiative and self-reliance. Even classroom design and layout need to be carefully considered because physical structures often determine processes. Do we really need students in rows with the teacher up front? Teaching methods and examinations systems both need re-thinking.

Certainly, in respect of teaching methods and even teaching aids, production provides plentiful opportunities of learning by doing. A dairy or a lime-burning, or mini-cement plant based on the availability of small pockets of limestones and clays, provide many practical instances of physical and chemical processes. Incidentally, schools can link their production to research, investigating chemical possibilities of local trees and bushes for essential oil distillation, or investigating the potential of locally available stone for monumental masonry.

Teacher Training

Coming to teacher training, we need only look at ZINTECH and SHAPE to observe important innovations that also relate, in the case of SHAPE, to preparing teachers for involvement in productive work in their schools. Distance education and in-service training are methodologies that can be linked to other innovations.

Examinations and Assessment

Our examination processes very rarely take into account assessment of characters and personal qualities which may be important in future entrepreneurs and dynamisers, and they hardly ever take account of peer evaluation. We need to give thought to both these possibilities.

Community Linkages

Schools tend to be isolated from the real life activities of their communities. Their main function is to channel young people out of the village into the formal sector, even though only a minority actually succeed. The involvement of our educational institutions at all levels, and especially, at tertiary levels, in research and productive work will establish a vital link to community life, offering many possibilities of creating work and generating resources. And members of the community can also contribute in many ways to the life of the schools, in cultural studies, in recounting orature (what was called oral literature), explaining and analysing custom, in teaching about oral history. When parents see diverse and profitable local production, they will broaden their own ideas about future careers for their children. In this respect the Brigades have played quite a useful role in Botswana.

Orientation of Production to Job-Creation

There are a variety of ways in which education can be combined with production, but one of the main factors in choosing which way relates to the extent to which the aim of the link is to prepare young people for job-creation. Within institutions like Brigades, for instance, thoughts are turning to concepts and practice like stayput (as opposed to throughput) systems, in terms of which the students place of training becomes the future workplace, as opposed to evicting the student at the end of the course to fend for him or herself. This is also found in the work of ZIMFEP and is inherent in the School Cooperative idea.

Dealing with Dualism

It is probably inevitable, given the state of economic and material progress in most of our countries, that there will be a tendency towards dualism in our educational systems - as in our economies - formal systems and popular systems. In Botswana, we have mainstream schooling alongside Brigades. In my experience, education with production can generate resources that help pay for education. Swaneng Hill School in Serowe was cheaply - and I think solidly - built. The Brigades have provided one of the cheaper forms of technical training at an acceptable first stage craft level, in our region. If we apply education with production throughout our system, and if we provide linkages that enable students from 'lower' systems like Brigades, to move upwards, then we can better level out the distinctions in dual systems, and move towards universalisation of learning and working more rapidly.

Awareness of Economic and Production Potential and Resources

One of the major objectives of education for employment must be to inculcate in students an awareness of the economic and production potential of the natural resources that surround them. That is a task of curriculum linked to productive activity. Many of our rural environments are somewhat stagnant, with limited diversification of production and limited infrastructure. One of the important points about education with production institutions is that they can create new environments with their production complexes, and this can be seen at work in several Brigade centres in Botswana. It is a reminder that education is a total social process. It is also a lifelong process which reminds us of the need for continuing education, distance education, in-service training, extension services and so on.

Technical Elements and Political Will

In this region, Mr Chairman, as we heard yesterday, there are a whole range of vital innovations - but often in isolation. We have had education with production in Tanzania for more than 20 years and in Zambia for 15. It has been pioneered in Zimbabwe by ZIMFEP for nine years. There are all kinds of innovations in curriculum, in teacher training, in community linkages all over. Today, countries are not afraid to evaluate and criticise their performance. The ultimate success of innovations is not in the brilliance of the idea or the vision but in the implementation at every level. That is why the kind of evaluation of Education for Self-Reliance that Prof. Kuhanga will comment on later today is important. How to improve implementation is as critical as the innovations themselves.

When we recognise the breadth of the innovations in our region we have also a sense of the potential of cooperation for bringing different strands together from the different countries. The important point is to try to bring together many of these innovations in a concerted way in each of our different countries. Probably we have the technical solutions at hand in our various situations. But we may lack the political will and the commitment, as Dr Machobane has put it.

REPORT ON DISCUSSIONS OF THE RECOMMENDATIONS OF THE HARARE MINI-SEMINAR

The issues which emerged from the discussion of the mini-Seminar's recommendations in the plenary session of the main Seminar, were the concentration on the 'three Rs' at the lower primary level, the definition of survival skills, and the role of education with production, community involvement in school management and in determination of the curriculum, the purposes of examinations, the length and inter-relationship of the cycles - primary and basic, junior and secondary, and the desirable primary school entry ages.

Those who had participated in the mini-Seminar made it clear, in response to questions and criticisms from other participants, that their emphasis on the 'three Rs' at lower primary level, did not constitute a return to the old style of education, to the neglect of other skills. As a shorthand, the 'three Rs' does not exclude the stimulation of concepts among children. It was meant to ensure that those pupils proceeding to upper primary education were equipped with basic skills, and were able to 'take off' in other modes of lifelong education, and - reinforced with survival skills - would be able to face the challenges of the outside world of unemployment. It was accepted that the pupils' role in the community would be emphasised together with instruction in the 'three Rs'.

For as long as primary education is terminal for the majority, 'survival skills for life' need to be imparted at the upper level and not just craft skills. It was clear from the discussion that such survival skills were intended to include some activity to organise and manage production, albeit at a low level. It was reported that a UNESCO project (NAMTANDA) was designed to establish what skills were required and could be imparted at this level and what measure of child labour was justified. "Homework is purely academic rather than helping at home", it was suggested, somewhat critically. It was important to restore education with production which was rooted in the African tradition and incorporated sound educational principles which are still valid. Education with production was potentially a valuable vehicle for imparting survival skills. One speaker believed that the low image of labour in schools was primarily the view of it of the state and the formal sector, not that of communities.

Whilst there was a general acceptance that communities needed to be involved in school management, there was less consensus about community involvement in curriculum determination. There was some feeling that different regional political and ethnic considerations could be divisive. Others were concerned that without some community say in the process, pupils could be alienated from the communities. There was a stronger measure of agreement that communities should be consulted about skills chosen for instruction and the type of production to be undertaken.

Some participants were concerned that the examination process and its pressures decided what was to be taught. This needed to be countered either by rethinking the examining process or insisting on an element of non-examinable education for self-reliance in primary schools.

The move towards a nine-year universal basic education in some countries could not be replicated in all, largely because of financial constraints. Whilst the desirable length of a full secondary education following primary education, was 12 years, there was no general agreement as to whether this should be 6:3:3 or 7:2:3. Some participants felt that an entry age of 6 years was too low, especially for those for whom primary education was terminal. It was difficult to teach life skills and involve very young people in productive work. On the other hand, it was difficult politically to raise the entry age.

REPORT ON A PANEL DISCUSSION OF ISSUES ARISING OUT OF THE WORLD BANK'S ROLE IN VOCATIONAL TRAINING, VIEWED FROM THE PERSPECTIVE OF JOB-CREATION

Chair: Cde The Hon. Fay Chung, Zimbabwe Minister of Primary and Secondary Education

Introducer: M.H. Mills, World Bank Office, Nairobi

Panelists: Dr Kenneth King
Prof. N.A. Kuhanga, Chairman, FEP
N.N.M. Munetsi, Zimbabwe Ministry of Higher Education

Mr Mills stressed at the outset that he was not an educationalist let alone a vocational educationalist, but was an economist with the World Bank, who had however in different capacities spent 8 years in the region. He was standing in for a World Bank specialist at the Seminar.

He said that the World Bank was interested in regional cooperation and in doing more with SADCC countries. It wanted to learn more about the directions in which the SADCC countries were moving. His task at the Seminar was to inform and to listen and learn, to obtain feedback.

There was increased Bank interest in human resource issues. This was reflected in a tremendous interest in training and employment especially in micro-enterprises.

He said he would begin by talking a little about the *Education in Sub-Saharan Africa Report* and the comments on it, and that he would describe the ongoing World Bank Study on vocational education. He also wanted to put some questions to the Panel and to the participants, particularly on economic perspectives.

The education report had been put together over the previous couple of years and he noted that there had been an important review of it in the new *Zimbabwe Journal of Educational Research.*

The report contained a short section dealing with training for occupation-specific skills. It argued furthermore that job-specific training is most efficiently provided after job-decisions have been made, and in institutions under (or strongly influenced by) ultimate employers. Training for occupation-specific skills categories may best be provided on the job or in specialised regional training centres. It emphasised the urgent need to establish industrial training centres and to encourage local enterprises to offer skill development programmes. It was important to use macro-economic policy instruments to raise the volume of training, e.g. investment codes, tax provisions, wage structure regulations and apprenticeship guidelines.

Mr Mills then looked at some of the criticisms received which are especially relevant to SADCC countries. One he called a 'chicken and egg' problem, noting that if training is best provided on the job, or in specialised regional training centres, how can it be substantially increased where there is a very small existing industrial base? Critics also suggested that vocational training does not need to be expensive and that the challenge was how to bring down the costs. It was also argued that the report gives far too little emphasis to the vocational skill needs of all school leavers (and indeed to those of the many who do not go to school).

Regarding the World Bank study on vocational education and training, Mr Mills said that it was being carried out by the research department of the Bank, that it was an ongoing study with results to be assembled over the following 6 to 12 months. It was based on a search of the literature, on case studies and on a process of consultation. The study was focussed on training of craftsmen, skilled workers and technicians for industrial, agricultural and commercial employment and for the informal sector. It was looking at vocational schools and technical secondary schools, at non-formal training centres, polytechnics, and training by enterprises. The study was to review a variety of issues. These included the different objectives for training, macro-economic factors (and their relevance to different economic situations) institutional issues such as financing, the linkage between training and employment and the quality of instruction.

Mr Mills then identified some of the issues being addressed which he believed that Seminar participants might wish to discuss, which he put in the form of questions. The first set of questions related to external efficiency and were generally categorised by the broad question: what types of vocational training best contribute to employment and economic productivity, and under what conditions? The specific questions were (i) how can we improve the match between the supply and demand for skilled persons? (ii) what should be the respective roles of the state and employers in providing vocational education and training, especially in poorer countries? (iii) if the training is demand-driven, with employees doing much of the training, how does one protect equity (and especially the access of women and economically disadvantaged groups, to training)? (iv) does the availability of skilled manpower attract employment-generating investment? and conversely, when economic growth rates are low, what are appropriate training strategies? and (v) what is the best way to improve the planning of training programmes?

The second set of questions related to internal efficiency and were generally categorised by the broad question: how can we improve the ratio between costs and output? The specific questions here were: (i) is it possible to reduce costs without sacrificing quality for example, through changes in staff/student ratios, utilisation of facilities, materials and equipment, and economies of scale? and (ii) can quality be improved within the cost limitations, for example through improvements in teaching materials, teacher training, integration of appropriate work experiences?

The third set of questions related to financing were generally categorised by the broad questions: how is such training best financed? The specific questions were: (i) is it possible for the costs to be financed in proportion to where the benefits accrue? As sub-questions of this: if the modern sector of the economy is to benefit, should it bear the costs? and what is the role of cost-sharing by individuals and what is the role of the state? (ii) what are the equity effects of different forms of financing, and what are the labour-market effects?

In conclusion, Mr Mills said that the appropriate strategies will depend on individual country experiences, but it was valuable to learn from each other, to identify success stories and he stressed the importance of research in this context.

Professor Kuhanga said that the match between supply and demand had to be considered not just globally but in respect of different component sectors of industry and the job-market, and especially in terms of high, middle and low technology. He said that in Tanzania there was a 'missing middle' and that most countries have major gaps within specific industries; in Tanzania, there was a lack of training for the textile and cement industries. He noted with regret a lack of central planning because, he said, there was a need to look at global issues as well as the needs of all sectors in terms of both supply and demand in training and in job-creation.

Professor Kuhanga said that whereas non-governmental organisations had previously been involved in training, the function had been increasingly taken over by governments which could no longer afford to undertake the task and were now trying to persuade NGOs to return to the field and were looking for ways of financing their own role, such as the introduction of fees for students. He felt that government's role should be rather to monitor the kind and the quality of training. Companies should also take responsibility for training. It was difficult, however, for governments to pull out once they had gone in so forcefully, he said.

Professor Kuhanga noted that the private sector gets little of its manpower from the universities because these were primarily concerned with supplying qualified personnel to governments and parastatals.

Dr Kenneth King wondered how to improve the match between training and demand, asking whether the manpower approach was the answer. He said that the private sector went its own way. It was necessary, he said, for NGOs, for the state and for employees to move towards collaboration within a national system, possibly under a QUANGO (quasi non-governmental organisation), which was dominated neither by the state nor by industry.

He said that training institutes had reacted to financial constraints in various ways including, in some cases, the creation of their own income-generating production units. He also noted that the quality of training had in some instances gone down.

Mr Munetsi said that the World Bank report and studies were posing the wrong questions. It was, of course, very difficult to plan full utilisation of available manpower, but it was necessary to make the attempt in aiming at maximum employment. The implications of the Bank studies was that more training should be undertaken closer to the workplace. Some courses can be produced entirely within institutions, but many can not. There is also the problem arising out of the narrow productive base mentioned by Mr Mills. As far as possible, employers should be encouraged to undertake and finance training for their needs, but it was important to take account of the need for equity.

A number of points were raised by the Chairperson and from the floor in subsequent discussion. One of these was that there was too much focus on top level training and not enough at lower levels. It was also pointed out that training was sometimes unnecessarily lengthy. White Rhodesian railway men were trained for 5 years, but Indian personnel now working on the National Railways of Zimbabwe had trained Zimbabweans for specific operations in 3 months. A measure of job fragmentation was possible, or training in the form of phased modules including sandwich courses, could be provided. Three months of training was adequate for many jobs.

CUBA'S EXPERIENCE IN LINKING EDUCATION AND TRAINING TO DEVELOPMENT AND JOB-CREATION

Ernesto Fernandez Rivero

In Latin America, Cuba was the last Spanish colony to obtain independence, in 1902, but independence was not totally in the hands of the majority masses of our country. During centuries of colonial oppression and many years of the first Republic, education was neglected. The people of Cuba with great faith and patriotism stood up in arms to bring the victory of the Cuban Revolution on the 1st January 1959 under the leadership of our Commander-in-Chief, Cde Fidel Castro. Thus the causes limiting the masses's access to culture and education were totally eliminated and it became possible to transform the whole system of education to benefit the masses. For the first time in history free education became the right of all citizens.

In these 30 years since the Revolution, the Government has dedicated great efforts to the continuous growth and development of the National Education System, in order to eliminate illiteracy, ignorance and underdevelopment. Education services were expanded to include the whole scholar population- no one was left without a school. The training of teachers was accelerated and favourable conditions created for qualitative development of education, in accordance with our socio-economic development characteristics.

The system of Education in Cuba is organised in the following forms: primary education of 6 years; Secondary education of 3 years, pre-university of 3 years and the University minimum of 5 years.

Briefly, we present some of our goals and successes in education, related to the training of the students for work within the National System of Education and their development in the places of life work when they complete the training.

One of the experiences was the establishment of the National Plan of Schools in the "field" or in the countryside (*Plan de las escuelas al campo*) for 4 to 6 weeks of each school year. The building of these new types of school for the secondary level of General Education made a reality of the aspirations of the revolutionary Cuban educators and public. Since the colonial era they had talked of the need for the linkage of education with production, as a fundamental factor in achieving instruction which trains men and women for life and the future.

In Medium Secondary schools and Pre-Universities, the students link education with production, by going for classes for one session followed by a session of 3 hours for production and vice versa. These rural schools are situated in areas of agricultural land and they are boarding schools. These schools also follow the national syllabus, including sports and cultural activities, like the urban schools but with a slight difference in organisation and daily timetable. Today there are more than 600 schools of the New Type with at least 300,000 Cuban students studying at them. This is three times more than the total number of students in secondary education at the time of the Revolution in 1959.

This unique Cuban experience of education is being consolidated day by day, while we are also in the process of making improvements in organisation, planning and study content. This experience is not just in theoretical design but also in practical examples such as the example of the Isle of the Youth where many schools of the new type are built to assist approximately 17,000 students from more than 30 countries of Africa, Asia and Latin America, who are receiving free education according to the Cuban principles and revolutionary practice of Internationalism.

The principle of the linkage of education with production is being applied progressively also to other levels of education. The National Education System is divided into subsystems:

Subsystem of Preschool Education
Subsystem of Polytechnic and Laboral General Education
Subsystem of Special Education
Subsystem of Technical and Professional Education
Subsystem of Training and Improvement of Pedagogical Personnel

Subsystem of Adult Education
Subsystem of Higher Education

The subsystem of Technical and Professional Education did not exist before the Revolution but has since been greatly developed. Together with the appropriate level of theory training of medium technicians and skilled workers, emphasis has been given to develop practical training, strongly linked to the Centres of Productions and Services. The State has made a great effort to offer these Centres the basic materials required and to assure the supply of raw materials for production by the students.

The subsystem of Higher Education also applies the same principles of linkage of education with production - progressively and positively. The University students link education with productive work from the beginning of the course until termination, together with their specific academic development. Production centres have been created in Cuba called Teaching Units which are integrated with the educational institutions, such as the Labour Centres with the Universities. These Centres participate in the training of new professionals, highly skilled in theory and practice.

There are many different Teaching Units and Labour Centres depending on the subjects. For Pedagogists there are schools, for doctors, hospitals, for engineers, industries etc. Successes in this objective has been possible because of the total understanding by the universities of their role in the socio-economic development of the country, and by industry of the need to participate in the training of the professionals acquainted with the goals and advances of science and technology. In fact it has been our aim to train the medium technicians and university professionals linked strongly to industrial production or services in order to acquire a solid practical preparation which really permits us to upgrade the quality of the new workers according to the demands of new technology.

The Cuban socialist State encourages the participation of the teachers of these institutions in the activities of the Labour Centre as a way of updating their practical knowledge as those tasks are considered part of their working time at the education centres they come from. In the same way, workers at the production centres are encouraged to develop their theoretical knowledge as part of their company's tasks. An essential element in order for the

Education System to respond to the needs of the economic and social development of the country is the determination by Government of the final courses and type of technicians, engineers or professionals which are required for the future development of the society.

In the concrete conditions in which we can see the construction of socialism in our country, it is necessary to train professionals with a solid and broad general technical base so that they are capable of fulfilling the various requirements of the economy and of society. In the Technical and Professional Subsystem of education, the number of courses offered have been reduced in recent years and there are now 96 courses which cater for the major demands for highly qualified manpower in the national market.

In Higher Education the courses are adjusted according to the needs of the socio-economic development of the country and actually we have 80 courses at our Universities and Higher education Institution which cover a broad field of subjects.

The State and the Party participate directly in determining the structure of technical courses at medium and higher levels to correspond with the planned development of the economy in the short and long terms. The Ministries of Education and Higher Education participate together with other Ministries to develop the policies for the Central Planning Commission. The Board so created is in charge of determining the programmes and projections of qualified manpower necessary for medium and long term and the deployment of new graduates in different teaching institutions at medium and higher levels. The Party and the State have established certain regulations for these Centres in the interests of the socio-economic development of the country and the systematic elevation of the standard of life of each citizen.

In accordance with the central objective of this seminar, we can point out, among other things:

-The policy is to ensure each trainee or graduate a place of work according to the training received somewhere within the country. The deployment is made by government in response to the needs for qualified manpower and to fulfil the requirements of the National Economic Plan.

-The State directs and controls general regulations of remuneration and the policy of employment creation in accordance with social interests.

The creation of funds to support a reserve of professionals permits the implementation of a system of upgrading in order to achieve specialisation in the profession. The reserve frees the professionals for certain periods of time from their work obligations with the objective of upgrading without affecting wages. This system has been applied for 4-5 years and primary teachers constitute one of the biggest reserves with more than 10 000 teachers freed from their teaching obligation for two years to do their post-graduate Bachelor of Primary Education. The same principle of reserve manpower is applied in Health, Medicine, Basic Industry, Sugar Industry, etc.

These experiences in our country of elevating qualitatively our National System of Education and putting its function in the service of the concrete needs of our social and economic development, have only been possible because our line of development is socialist. Our historical experience reaffirms that it is not possible to democratise the education system of a country without democratising its economy and without democratising the superstructure. And that the problems of education will not be understood in our societies in time if there is no consideration of the political, social and economic environment.

Table 1

Number of Schools according to Education Level

Education level	1958-59	1970-71	1977-78
Nursery/Creche	-	606	870
Primary	7567	15190	9617
Secondary	81	835	2148 (c)
Special	-	129	450
Adult	-	(b)	624
Higher Institutes (University)	3(a)	4	48
Others	28	775	159(d)
Total	**7679**	**17539**	**13916**

(a) Only indicates private universities, because there were no official universities.

(b) Does not reflect the number of schools (1864) because it includes independent schools and work centres.

(c) Includes 16 vocational schools in Exact Sciences, 2 Vocational schools of sports, 628 Professional and Technical Centres.

(d) Refers to 157 schools of work and 2 faculties of language.

Table 2

The 'New Type' of School built from 1970 up to 1984

Secondary Schools in the Countryside and Polytechnics	706
Pedagogical Schools	16
Primary Schools	308
Nurseries	268
Urban Basic Secondary Schools and Centres for Higher Level	402
Total	**1700**

Table 3

Percentage Structure of the Primary, Medium and Higher Education

	1959-1960	**1985-86**
Primary	89.1%	43.1%
Medium	8.5%	46.2%
Higher	2.4%	10.7%

Table 4
Number of Students by Level of Education (000's)

	1958-59	1987-88
Nursery/Creches	-	94.6
Pre-schools	91.7	136.2
Primary	625.7	936.9
Medium (2)	88.1	1114.3
Special	-	47.4
Youth School of Works	-	25.5
Adult Education	-	164.9
Higher Education	2.1	292.8
Other	3.7	1.5
Total	**811.3**	**2814.1**

Table 5
Expenditure dedicated to Education (Budget and population in millions)

Year	Budget	Population	Expenditure/per capita
1957-58	$79.4	6.9	$11
1970	$351.1	8.6	$41
1985	$1696.8	10.0	$170

THE DEVELOPMENT OF TECHNICAL AND VOCATIONAL EDUCATION AND YOUTH EMPLOYMENT IN CHINA

Yang Dong Liang

Introduction

Since the founding of the People's Republic of China in 1949, the education system in the country has undergone 40 years of development and a relatively comprehensive modern education system has gradually taken shape. At present, the system comprises 4 main parts in terms of educational structure and management modes, i.e. Basic Education (BE), Technical and Vocational Education (TAVE), Higher Education (HE), and Adult Education (AE).

What is directly related to the issue of youth employment here is TAVE, HE and AE. In this respect, the concept of employment education (EE) in China does not quite match that of vocational education or TAVE. If defined on the basis of training objectives and functions, the main tasks of TAVE are to provide specialised orientation education and technique/skill training for the large number of regular middle school leavers who are unable to enter higher education institutions for further studies, and to train and supply qualified primary and intermediate level manpower for the various sectors that serve the national economy and social development.

The main body of TAVE consists of specialised secondary schools (SSS), skill-worker schools (SWS), agricultural middle schools (AMS), vocational middle schools (VMS), a small number of short-term vocational colleges (SVC) and a large number and various forms of technical and vocational training.

In the HE sector, non-adult education institutions of higher education are also responsible for pre-employment specialised orientation education, focusing on the training of high level professionals to meet the needs of economic and social development.

AE takes in-service personnel in the society at large as its target-group. Its activities include elimination of illiteracy, qualification education, various kinds of on-job-training and practical skills training, further and social education. In a broad sense, on-job-training and practical skills training may be included in the EE norm. The difference is that they are post-employment training.

This paper mainly illustrates the current development of TAVE in China and the status and trends of youth employment.

TAVE, Economic Development and Youth Employment

With around 1.1 billion people, China has the largest population of any country in the world. The situation of manpower vis-a-vis employment is such that the human resources are vastly over-abundant. During the 1980s, there are on average 25 million people reaching the employment age (16-60) each year, of whom 21 million people are in rural areas and 4 million in urban cities and townships. After deducting those who have exceeded the working age, there is still an average net increase of 17 million per year, of whom 15 million are in rural areas and 2 million in cities and townships. It is estimated that the population in China will reach 1.25 billion by the end of the century. The annual employment population will reach 20 million during that period.

To achieve maximum employment is a common objective of all countries in the world. China is no different in this regard. In the recent decade, the Chinese government has adopted various measures to expand the employment opportunities for those who have newly reached employment age. According to statistics, the city/township unemployment rate in China was 5.9% at end of 1979 and it decreased to around 2% by the end of 1987.

On the other hand, however, the biggest problem that has been encountered during the course of economic development is that the size of the employment population is huge whereas its quality is low. With regard to the educational experiences of the labour force, in 1987 only 1.4% had university education, 12.3% had senior middle school education, 30.5% junior middle school education, 30.7% primary school education and 25.1% were illiterate or semi-illiterate. As to the quality of technical skills of the labour force, among the over 40 million skilled workers employed in the state owned enterprises, 71% were of primary level, 23% of intermediate level and only 2% were of high level. Only 15% of the annual new labour force in cities/townships had pre-employment TAVE or training; and 90% of employees in agriculture did not have systematic vocational training. This phenomenon caused high consumption of material and labour in our economic construction, making our products expensive but of low quality, and resulting in enormous waste of material resources. At the same time, the quantitative advantage of human resources could not be transformed into qualitative advantage, but rather became an enormous pressure on the society.

Under such circumstances, the Chinese government formulated a new economic development strategy in October 1987, pointing out the need for "gradually turning the basically extensive management approach into basically intensive management approach, and giving first priority to the development of science and technology (S&T) and education so as to enable the economic construction to rely on the advancement of S & T and the improvement of quality in the labour force". In terms of educational development, the State began to enforce new plans and undertook to adjust the educational structure, by enhancing TAVE in particular, to emphasise the training of primary and secondary level manpower and the upgrading of the quality of labour force. The State stressed the continuation of the policy of "walking on two legs" in the development of TAVE. In addition to developing technical and vocational schools (TVSs), the emphasis was to provide various forms of technical and vocational training for the millions of primary and secondary school leavers every year who were unable to enter a higher level of schooling, and gradually establish a youth employment training system and network that would cover the main trades of the society so as to upgrade and safeguard the quality of new labour force.

The Development Scope and Structure of TAVE

1. TAVE

The development of TVSs in China was set off in the early 1950s with the initial establishment of the SSS education system and the SWS education system. Thereafter, a large number of AMSs and VNSs were set up under the drive of regular middle school education reform. By the mid-1960s, a secondary TVS education system had taken shape. During the Cultural Revolution (1966-1976) however, TVSs were severely disrupted. In the recent 10 years, the State has adopted a series of major measures to restore and develop TAVE, and the number of TVSs as well as the student population has been growing as a result. According to the statistics of 1987, there were 16,368 TVSs of various levels and types (not including adult education establishments) with 5,668,000 students. The levels and types of TVSs may be classified as follows:

a. *Primary level vocational schools*: These schools mainly include primary level AMSs and VMSs. Their intakes may be primary school leavers and the duration of study will be 3-4 years, or they may be junior middle school leavers and the schooling period will be 1 year. Their objective is to train farmers, workers and other employees with basic vocational knowledge and skills;

b. *Secondary level vocational schools:* These schools include SSSs, SWSs and agricultural and vocational senior middle schools (ASMs and VSMs):

-**SSSs** normally take junior middle school leavers for 3/4 year courses, or admit senior middle school leavers for 2 year courses. Their task is to train intermediate level technicians and administrative personnel;

-**SWSs** admit junior middle school leavers for 3 year study programmes. Their main objective is to train intermediate level skilled workers for the industrial sector;

-**ASMSs** and **VSMSs** (including vocational classes at regular senior middle schools) offer 2-3 year study programmes for junior middle school leavers. They are responsible for the training of primary and intermediate level technical management personnel as well as a qualified labour force;

c. *Advanced level TVSs*: These institutions are mainly SVCs, which offer 2-3 year courses for leavers of secondary level TVSs and regular senior middle schools. Their aim is to train high level technicians and management personnel.

At present, secondary level TVSs comprise the main body of the three level TVS education system. Their total enrollment accounts for 91% of the total student population in all levels of TVSs or 42% of the total student population in senior secondary education.

2. Technical and Vocational Training

Technical and vocational training is a popular form of education in China, aiming at preparing youth for employment. In rural areas, regular primary or secondary school leavers who are unable to proceed with the main stream education are offered this type of education to acquire management know-how and master a particular skill for employment. According to incomplete statistics, about 150 million young farmers and junior or senior middle school leavers in rural areas have received various levels of technical training.

The Management System of TAVE

The management system of Chinese TAVE is determined by the economic management system of the country. Its main feature is that the management of TVSs is put in the charge of different levels of government departments in accordance with investment patterns. Primary level vocational schools are normally run and administered by county level education authorities or township governments. With regard to secondary level TVSs, the management system is rather complicated due to the diversity of forms and investment channels. In principle, they are administered by relevant departments at central, provincial, prefectural or county level and are jointly managed by educational and labour authorities. Advanced level TVSs are essentially accommodated in the management system for higher education institutions. Their establishment should be approved by the State Education Commission while the governance is provided by provincial or central municipalities.

In recent years, the State has undertaken, step by step and in a planned way, to adjust and reform the management system of TAVE. The guiding policy is to extend the terms of reference of local governments over the governance of schools so as to enable them to provide overall planning and coordination over the development of various levels of local TAVE and resolve such problems - scattered investment, irrational distribution of schools, repetition in courses and narrow range of student sources - as have been revealed in the running and administration of TVSs by different departments. At the same time, schools are given more decision-making independence and are encouraged to develop inter-institutional collaboration, expand the range of student sources and improve cost-effectiveness in operation. In cities, the emphasis is on enhancing the role of central municipalities in overall planning and governance of secondary level TVSs and paying more attention to the needs of adjacent rural areas in terms of manpower training. In rural areas, the focus is on strengthening the function of both county and township level governments in the overall planning of TAVE, AE and EE so that the three can integrate with each other to create more employment opportunities and vocational transferability for rural youth and to promote the development of the local economy.

Two Flexible Systems in Rural TAVE

1. '3 + x' form: This has been a fairly popular and effective form of TAVE in rural China in recent years. Its essence is that a student may receive certain technical and vocational training after completion of his/her three year regular junior middle school education. The length of training varies. Normally it is one year, but it may be six months or one or two months. The training may be provided in schools or in employing enterprises and the training contents are relevant to the needs of local employment. It is addressed as '3 +x' form because of its flexibility in length, contents and specific arrangements.

2. 'TECHNICAL AND VOCATIONAL TRAINING CENTRE (TVTC)'. This is a form of TAVE that combines rural TVS education and technical and vocational training. Its main feature is that it is multi-functional. TVTC is not only responsible for providing a regular school education to train technical and administrative personnel of a certain standard, but also offers a variety of short term technical and vocational training. In addition, it is integrated with local institutions of scientific experiment and technical transfer, forming a centre for manpower development, scientific research and technology transfer.

Two Major Measures Adopted by the State in TAVE Development

1. 'TRAINING PRECEDES EMPLOYMENT': The employment system is a key factor that constrains the development of TAVE. The Chinese government therefore formulated a policy in July 1986 to reform our labour personnel system and actively promote the principles of 'training precedes employment' and 'competitive selection', which stipulated that by 1990, a system would be enforced that the essentially technical and specialised posts in most parts of China would only be filled by those who were trained and qualified. The implementation of this policy has shown a positive effect on the development of Chinese TAVE in recent years.

2. 'RURAL EXTENSION PROGRAMME' (REP): China is still an agricultural country. However, because of the qualitative inadequacy of our agricultural labour force, 70% of existing scientific and technological achievements in agriculture can not be popularised, two thirds of farm lands are still low or medium yielding, and 10% of livestock die of diseases annually due to inadequate epidemic prevention, all of which have seriously affected the development of agriculture.

Under such circumstances, the State initiated REP in May 1988 to promote agricultural development. The essence of the programme is as follows:

-to utilise the intellectual and technical advantages of all levels of rural schools to promote education in such areas as practical skills and managerial know-how that are relevant to local development;

-to train a large rural development manpower;

-to assist agricultural and scientific bodies to undertake such activities as experimental demonstration, technical training and information services that are aimed at popularising locally adaptable technologies.

The specific objectives of the programme are:

-By 1990, 1,500 pilot townships (PT) will have been established in 500 counties all over the country. PTs will mainly be distributed among the experimental regions for agricultural resources and major state aided underdeveloped regions;

-By 1995, efforts will be made to expand the programme to most counties in this country, enabling 10,000 townships (i.e. 1/6 of the total number of townships in China) to reach PT standard.

PT standard is defined as follows:

-Nine year compulsory education achieved;

-Youth illiteracy eliminated and cultural and technical schools for farmers established;

-Effective technical training provided for most junior and senior middle school leavers in townships to enhance development in diversified local economy and increase both grain production and farmer per capita income.

The funding for the programme will mainly be raised by different levels of local government via various channels. The central government will make a 30 million special appropriation before 1990 while the People's Bank of China will provide an annual 60 million loan.

Conclusion

TAVE is an important and integral part of modern education and has increasingly revealed its vitality in the development of a modern commodity economy and in the socialisation of production. It does not only impart labour skills, but also integrates the behavioural norms of modern civilisation and cultural knowledge with technical training and the cultivation of vocational morale. It therefore has obvious economic as well as cultural and social values.

As a developing country proceeding towards modernisation, China has increasingly realised the important significance of TAVE. We may believe that rapid growth of TAVE will become a distinctive feature in the development of the Chinese education system from the end of the century till the middle of next century.

SECTION 5

REPORT ON A PANEL DISCUSSION ON COMPREHENSIVE MULTI-SECTORAL PLANNING FOR JOB-CREATION, AT NATIONAL, DISTRICT AND LOCAL LEVELS, AND THE ROLE OF EDUCATION WITHIN BROADER STRATEGIES

Chair: Cde Dr A. dos Muchangos, Mozambican Minister of Education

Panelists:

V.R. Nyathi, Chief Economist, Ministry of Finance and Development Planning, Zimbabwe
Dr M.H. Mills, World Bank Nairobi Office
Papie Moloto, ANC Department of Manpower Development
Patrick Qorro, M.P. Tanzania

Opening the discussion, V.R. Nyathi said it was important to know and understand the nature and extent of unemployment in each of the SADCC countries, and where the employed were, as well as the causes. Then it would be possible to assess how far central planning could deal with it. He believed it was necessary to readjust and restructure economies for national growth and to identify the engine of growth in each in co-ordination with other sectors, to create the conditions for job-creation. The restructuring of the economies should put emphasis on the production of intermediate and capital goods. It must be noted that the non-production of these goods within the region constrains economic expansion which is a prerequisite for the creation of job opportunities. He said that small-scale farming with middle level technology in Zimbabwe depended on imported agrochemicals, diesel engines and diesel fuels and was constrained by the shortage of foreign exchange. Indeed, the limitations of foreign exchange were felt throughout the economy and restricted growth. There was a need for industrial advancement throughout the region and this development should be based mainly on local raw materials.

Dr Mills said that given the limited availability of capital it was necessary to maximize employment per unit of capital. He stressed that the high rate of population growth required a high rate of growth in employment-creation just to 'stand still', pointing out that in Zimbabwe even a 1% population increase was 90 000 more people each year. He said that solutions lay with small scale farming and diversification into non-agricultural production in the rural areas as well as the promotion of urban informal activities. He emphasised that detailed understanding of the problem was required before appropriate solutions could be sought in planning, and action taken; it was necessary to have area, gender, age and education profiles of the unemployed, citing the Kenyan experience with the rural access roads programme which encountered labour shortages in the more productive agricultural areas. This showed that labour shortages could co-exist with an overall unemployment problem. He said that peoples' behaviour was influenced by government policies, citing minimum wages and taxation as examples and noting that in Kenya the duty free importation of tractors whilst import duties were levied on some hand tools militated against labour intensive production. He went on to say that difficult trade-offs may be necessary amongst considerations of employment, food production and exports, for instance; again quoting from Kenyan experience, he said that there was less labour intensity in wheat than in tea or coffee production giving this as an example of the choices and priorities to be faced in macro-policy formulation. There was a need he suggested also to develop appropriate technology. Kenya had a high level of mechanised production as well as of labour-intensive use of the hoe but little middle level technology in agriculture, such as ox-drawn ploughs. These, he suggested, could increase productivity, with low capital inputs, above the levels of hoe utilisation. He concluded his remarks by stressing the importance of data and applied research into the problems of unemployment, and of inter-ministerial co-operation tuned to job-creation. He said that everyone needed to 'think' employment and to work together to solve the problems.

The ANC's Papie Moloto asked whether development plans were for show or action and how realistically they were drawn up? He said that key indicators can be fictitious if inadequate data is available. What means are available from domestic and what from donor sources? Was planning just for the top of the economy and how far did it go down to rural realities? Are plans for parliamentary consumption? Do they have meaning for the ordinary people? Popular mobilisation is needed to achieve the objectives of plans that are to benefit the people as a whole. If the implementation of plan objectives is not fully thought out, then a plan is merely a projection of what might happen anyway. Questions of technology had to be resolved: new technologies are very costly, older technologies may be of better value. Perhaps technology mixes are preferable.

The Chair stressed the importance of communications between SADCC countries, to improve co-ordination and linkages of economic plans and utilisation of resources, and co-operation in SADCC sectors and in educational matters. He said that in respect of communications, the most modern technology was needed. He also agreed with panelists that sound planning was impossible without good data.

Cde Patrick Qorro assumed that development plans were based on the modernisation of agriculture to produce a surplus for the financing of industrial growth. He asked whether this justified central multi-sectoral planning, answering that it would do so provided that consultation and decision-making are not confined to the centre. He wanted the Seminar participants to recommend mechanisms to involve wider consultations both amongst all sectors involved and downwards to the producers, for planning for self-employment. He said that the planners should indentify 'profitable' fields of production, and the tools, and necessary infrastructure, including financial support, adding that there would need to be regular meetings for those charged with implementing plans to monitor progress.

A speaker from the floor said that he thought the matter under debate was on the agenda to allow for discussion of how education fitted into multi-sectoral planning and more especially how this could make education with production more effective. The panel needed to address this, he said, asking how the organisers of education with production, and the market for its products and skills could be consulted and involved in multi-sectoral planning processes. Yet another speaker rose from the floor to illustrate the possibilities in this respect from the planned participation of Cuba's 'schools in the countryside' in the development of citrus and coffee production and the planned contributions of vocational training schools to both rural and industrial development, and job-creation.

Zambia's Minister of General Education, Youth and Sports at the time of the Seminar, The Hon Kebby Musokotwane, said that the West had steam-rollered the introduction of its technology in Africa, and destroyed proven old technologies practised earlier in African countries. Calling on Ministries of Education to look into restoring and improving indigenous technologies, he urged co-operation in appropriate technology research and development programmes amongst SADCC countries to minimise unnecessary competition and duplication, citing as undesirable parallel but separate Zambian and Zimbabwean efforts to produce suitable ploughs. The Zambian Minister also complained of ideological sabotage of the policies of the politicians by civil service implementers. He noted the lack of adequate co-ordination in the educational sector amongst SADCC countries, and again urged the need to avoid wasteful duplication of efforts. Concluding his intervention, Mr Musokotwane said that 25 years after the ending of colonialism in most countries present at the Seminar, it was necessary that those in charge should take responsibility for their own weaknesses and not hide behind repeated criticisms of the colonial past.

Is multi-sectoral planning possible without a planned economy and what is a planned economy? The question was raised from the floor by a Zimbabwean participant. Another Zimbabwean, also speaking from the floor, said that planning for a mixed economy means planning the production of manpower by the state for the whole economy, adding that this needed a 'big brother' - possibly the Ministry of Finance and Development Planning.

With this intervention, the session concluded.

REPORT ON A DIALOGUE BETWEEN EMPLOYERS AND EMPLOYEES ABOUT THE ROLE OF THE FORMAL SECTOR IN EXPANDING JOB-CREATION

Chair: Ndugu Patrick Qorro
Panel:
Mr A.M.D. Humphrey, Confederation of Zimbabwe Industries
Ndugu C. Mwalongo, Tanzania Chamber of Commerce, Industry and Agriculture
Cde M. Tsavangirai, Zimbabwe Congress of Trade Unions

Mr Humphrey opened the discussion. He pointed out that in 1990 there will be 250 000 '0' level school leavers joining the ranks of the Zimbabwe unemployed. He pointed also to the high cost of job-creation in large scale industry in Zimbabwe, which he stated was Z $85 000 per job. Moreover, the establishment or expansion of large scale industries involved millions of dollars of investment, and depended on such factors as the availability of raw materials, market availability, allocations of foreign currency for imported high-tech plant, and recruitment of expensive expertise. Small industries can adapt more quickly to economic potentialities. He said that in Britain 250 000 new jobs had been created by firms with 20 employees and under over a recent period.

Mr Humphrey listed a number of factors favouring the establishment of small firms. Some 70 growth points for economic development had been officially proclaimed in Zimbabwe, which could be used for small enterprise development to generate employment. Many large industries subcontracted component manufacture to small firms. The protective barriers set up during UDI to promote import substitution had been kept up. Deregulation and the setting up of financial support institutions for small enterprises would help achieve the objectives. The speaker recommended the use of retired businessmen to help the development of small businesses.

He urged more extensive processing of raw materials currently exported, noting that two thirds of Zimbabwe's cotton crop was exported. He advocated the use in local manufacture of a greater part of this crop for clothing exports, utilising a range of technologies and of scale of enterprise, which could generate employment. He also advocated the active support of large industries in setting up employees in small firms to which component manufacture could be sub- contracted. He said that small enterprises of this kind would create 'real jobs, not the informal sector'. Mr Humphrey cited the 'white collar aspirations of school leavers' as one major constraint on school leaver involvement in small enterprise development, and recommended changes in education, commending education with production as a means to this end.

Putting the employee viewpoint, Cde Tsvangirai said that the real solutions to the unemployment problem lay more in mobilisation of national resources than in dependence on foreign aid. He went on to say that economic growth and job-creation needed basic investment. In the case of construction, for example, investment was needed in the cement industry, and this in turn would require foreign currency allocations. He argued that Zimbabwe had sufficient foreign exchange if it was properly allocated to productive industry, which he suggested it was not. He asked which Zimbabwe needed more: airplanes which consume foreign exchange continuously or cement factories which stimulate productive capacities?

Cde Tsvangirai added that an effective national transport network for freight and passengers was necessary for economic development and job-creation. Land distribution was necessary on a greater scale and at a faster pace so that many of the unemployed might be absorbed into agriculture. The people had fought for productive land during the struggle for freedom, but their demands were not being satisfied. The speaker added that producers co-operatives were also a means of self-employment generation, noting that some 300 000 Zimbabweans were members of such co-operatives presently. Even more could be so mobilised if there were adequate financial and other support. The existing laws needed to be re-thought, however, he said, and the Ministry of Co-operatives was under-funded.

Ndugu Mwalongo said that education had been left to the educators but that this Seminar had shown that it is the business of everyone. He said that it was necessary for countries to pay more attention to agriculture as the base of their economies, and that agriculture should undergo a green revolution similar to that which India recently experienced. He urged SADCC country linkages to the group of 77, more especially in trade and development promotion. He bemoaned the loss of the 'old' education with production in elementary education, adding that there was a need to focus on low-level manpower and the training of craftsmen, rather than on high-level university graduates. He said that Chambers of Commerce which until now had been the preserve of large companies had begun reaching out to involve small businesses so long as they were licenced. He noted a fear amongst them of recruiting to their employ young workers who were in established trade unions. Young people were unwilling to work on the land resulting in an ageing rural workforce and a labour shortage in rural areas. Education with production and curriculum reform was essential in primary schools. The effects of current primary schooling on the attitudes of the young was illustrated by the fact that Std 4 dropouts became craftsmen while those who went beyond to drop out at Std 7 became vagabonds. The speaker observed that agriculture-based schools often have no farms, and he urged universities and higher educational institutions to innovate and spread new ideas. Schools had lost contact with their communities and businessmen were so into money-making that they ignored their social responsibilities to help schools and to assist in career guidance. He stressed that it was the duty of employers and not just that of the state to create jobs, and urged the development of a work ethic such as prevailed in Japan and India.

A number of questions were raised from the floor, and a number of statements made by participants in response to the interventions of the panelists. Cde Tsvangirai had said in passing that the centralisation of control of apprenticeship at independence had led to a breakdown of previous manpower development programmes which had been decentralised within industries, and this prompted a questioner to ask for clarification. Another questioner asked whether employment-creation might not be better promoted through the expansion of existing large-scale industries rather than through the establishment of new ones. A third questioner expressed doubts that land distribution would automatically create new jobs and asked to whom land should be given and whether it would be given free or whether the new owners should have to pay for it in some way.

Answering the questions put to him, Cde Tsvangirai said that the mining industry has dropped 10 000 Zimbabwean workers since 1980 although production had increased. Previously, he said, mining companies had trained Zimbabwean mining apprentices whom they selected using their own, often paternalistic, criteria. For instance, preference might have been given to sons or relatives of miners already in their employ. He added that skills were now being imported. Job fragmentation had been introduced and the salaries of artisans had fallen considerably. He closed by saying that land should be allocated to those who needed it, more especially 'squatters'.

Responding for his part to questions, Mr Humphrey said that his whole paper had been about new, small industries. It is in the interests of large companies to have small, independent satellites, he added, to which they can sub-contract. His own view is that Zimbabwean industry is too dominated by conglomerates, he said, urging rationalisation along with liberalisation. In suggesting that retired white Zimbabwean industrialists be harnessed to train emergent small entrepreneurs, he was not advocating creating jobs for them, but the utilisation of their expertise for short periods rather than bringing in expensive consultants from abroad. Answering a question as to whether or not education was productive, Mr Humphrey said that it depended on the linkages between education and production. He criticised education for self-reliance, however, describing it as education for unemployment and poverty. He argued that it did not promote specialisation and that a 'do-it-yourself-economy' - as he called it - ruled out employment of others. He contrasted this with the Cuban approach which he said promoted specialisation and counteracted deskilling.

SECTION 6

POSSIBILITIES OF IMPROVING AND EXTENDING REGIONAL CO-OPERATION IN THE SECTORS OF EDUCATION AND TRAINING AND MANPOWER DEVELOPMENT WITH PARTICULAR EMPHASIS ON EMPLOYMENT-CREATION, WITHIN SADCC

Report on introductory remarks by E.S. Nebwe, Special Adviser to the Executive Secretary of SADCC, and on the discussion that followed.

In his contribution, Mr Nebwe outlined the aims and objectives of SADCC and its organisational structure and mode of operation. He highlighted the distribution of sectoral responsibilities among the nine member States. He pointed out that the responsibility for coordination of Manpower Development had been allocated to Swaziland. The Regional Training Council (RTC) was the implementing agency. The RTC was answerable to the Committee of Ministers responsible for manpower issues in member States.

Mr Nebwe observed that there was scope for cooperation in Education, Training and Manpower Development in the following areas:

(a) production of text books;

(b) harmonisation of syllabuses and curricula;

(c) utilisation of educational and training facilities;

(d) student and teacher exchange programmes.

In the discussions that ensued, a participant requested Mr Nebwe to clarify the contention of some schools of thought that SADCC and the Preferential Trade Area (PTA) had the same aims and objectives and that the two organisations were duplicating each others efforts. Mr Nebwe pointed out that the organisations made every effort to avoid overlap and/or duplication of responsibility through exchange of information on programmes and projects. He further pointed out that the PTA covered other countries which were not members of SADCC. It would not, therefore, be in order for SADCC to stop the PTA implementing projects in non SADCC member States on the pretext that those projects were on the SADCC Programme of Action.

Elaborating on the SADCC/PTA relationship in response to the question raised, Zimbabwe's Senior Minister of Finance, Economic Planning and Development, Hon Dr Bernard Chidzero, who was present to close the Seminar, said that the PTA (like ECOWAS in West Africa) was born out of the Lagos Plan of Action and its emphasis was on regional collective self-reliance. It promoted national companies and not transnationals in the region. SADCC was founded to reduce dependence among the signatory countries generally and on South Africa in particular, and grew out of the Frontline States. SADCC coordinated the search for donor aid for regionally oriented projects, more especially through annual conferences. SADCC was served by a small Secretariat and through the delegation of sector responsibility to member countries.

Another participant observed that in Swaziland, the Manpower Development Sector was being coordinated by the Ministry of Finance and Planning andnot by the Ministry of Education. He wondered whether this was not a misallocation of responsibility which SADCC should address to ensure effective coordination of the sector. Mr Nebwe pointed out that the responsibility of SADCC was allocation of sectoral responsibilities to member States, and ensuring that those member States discharged their responsibilities effectively and efficiently. It was up to individual member States to determine how best to discharge their sectoral responsibilities on behalf of all the other member States. It was, therefore, up to the member State involved to decide whether its coordination of the responsibility for Manpower Development would be better executed through the Ministry of Finance and Planning or through the Ministry of Education.

Commenting on responsibilities of member Sates for sector coordination, Hon Dr Chidzero said that the structures of SADCC provided for a Council of Ministers and the Summit of Heads of State and Government which both met regularly and received reports from officials and the Council of Ministers respectively. Therefore any country which was not satisfied with the performance of a given member State in its discharge of its sectoral responsibility could submit complaints to either or both of these organs, adding that in 1986 Zimbabwe had been criticised over its management of the Food Security sector.

One participant observed that whilst it might not always be easy to differentiate between education and training on the one hand and manpower development on the other, and whilst some aspects of education, like science teaching, had been brought under the umbrella of manpower development (though no achievements by the RTC as such were on record), the field of education was an extensive one, most aspects of which were not covered by the manpower sector; he added that the question of employment-promotion outside the formal sector of the economy, and the possible role of education within wider socio-economic strategies in job-promotion, was also not catered for under the manpower sector and a 'home' had to be found within SADCC for this concern. He further drew attention to the chapter on Manpower in the SADCC Macro-Economic Survey which had been distributed and which contained some criticism of the management of the sector. He concluded by saying that whilst the demarcation between education and manpower and the handling of manpower involved sensitive issues, they had to be faced and that it was vital to set up an education sector under SADCC.

The Special Adviser pointed out that education and manpower development were crucial to the development of the region and to the coordination of sectoral responsibilities in particular. Shortages of expertise were being experienced in all the member States in relation to sector coordination activities. Unless this constraint was addressed effectively, achievement of SADCC's goals would continue to be hampered. Further, SADCC was experiencing other problems which made the generation of employment opportunities and the attainment of the aims and objectives of SADCC difficult. These included barriers to intra-regional trade, rigid exchange control regulations which made cross border investment almost impossible, and restrictions on free movement of regional businessmen.

Zambia's Minister of General Education and Culture, Hon. Kebby S K Musokotwane, MP, MCC, noted that foreign assistance in the field of education was being given to several, if not all, SADCC member States by various international cooperating partners and suggested this aid flow needed coordination. In concurring with Hon Musokotwane, Mr Nebwe, however, observed that it was a sovereign right of individual member States to seek bilateral financial assistance from whatever source they saw fit. SADCC's efforts were, in the main, directed towards mobilisation of resources for programmes and projects which had a regional impact, but both bilateral and regional programmes were mutually supportive and re-inforcing.

Extracts from the Manpower Chapter of the 1989 SADCC Macro-Economic Survey

Introduction

The Manpower Development Sector has lagged in articulating the manpower needs of the other sectors in the SADCC Programme of Action. The exclusion of the sector from the 1985 macro-economic survey did not help the situation. The RTC Secretariat has also suffered from a shortage of skilled manpower rather than a lack of physical resources.

Two main problems were encountered in writing this review of the manpower sector:

i) The paucity of information, including the manner in which the available information is recorded, and its quality and reliability;

ii) Differences in categorisations on both the supply and the demand sides compounded the nature of the problem.

Information gathering was constrained by the sheer lack of data and the absence of centralised national data banks for manpower statistics. Where information is available, it is fragmented and scattered through different Ministries. Information was unavailable from the private sector, especially in countries like Zimbabwe where the private sector is large. The participation of expatriates, their numbers, qualifications and experience and their salaries and fringe benefits was the most difficult to obtain.

For most countries the information available is dated.

Methodology

Given these constraints, the degree of self-reliance and/or dependence in the manpower sector had to be measured by a comparison of supply and demand. Specific indicators identified on the supply side were:

i) The production of skilled labour, both locally and overseas;
ii) The existence of expatriates in local training institutions;
iii) The existing gap levels between student enrolments and available vacancies; and
iv) The degree to which shifts in training programmes have occurred from earlier needs to new needs.

Similar indicators were used on the demand side, taking into account established positions, the jobs held by expatriates and the level of vacancies. These indicators were then used to establish the degree of dependence. In other words, dependence was reduced where SADCC countries have increased their self-reliance in the field of manpower.

Despite the problems created by the scarcity of data and the problems of measurement, a good start has been made towards understanding the development of manpower in SADCC states. Impressive results have been achieved on the supply side following the rapid growth of university and tertiary education. There is evidence, too, of a shift from arts-based types of training to a greater emphasis on science-based skills. There are four main sources of supply:

a) Local training within institutions;
b) On-the-job training programmes;
c) Foreign training, and
d) The pool of expatriates.

It is emphasised that the stock of expatriates in the region is only a partial measure of needs since, given the availability of funds, there would be more expatriates than there are at present.

Main Trends

Great variations were found among the different sub-sectors, with demand exceeding supply in all sub-sectors other than mining where the supply of geologists exceeded demand by some 30%.

It appears that the majority of the skilled manpower concentrates in the leading economic sectors in each country. Most SADCC countries suffer from shortages in the productive sectors, while some have allowed the services sector to outpace their economic growth rates.

The supply of manpower is basically public, whereas the demand emanates from both private and public sector needs. The exact capacity of most training institutions is unknown. Even the SADCC inventory of institutions is incomplete and there are no reliable figures of the number of students trained, and those still training, overseas. Not a single Ministry had comprehensive data on overseas training and, with the exception of some estimates in ESRAUP's publications (Eastern and Southern African Universities Research Programme), the data on overseas training are outdated and only record information on departure.

Variations in the classifications of educational levels and/or job categories are salient features throughout. In Zimbabwe the categories are still colonial. The classification of expatriates by nationality still seems to reflect the colonial heritage.

Surprisingly, the expatriates do not seem to be affected by retirement age limits in the countries where they are working.

Training is beginning to focus on category B jobs i.e. medium-level skills such as professional degrees and diplomas. (The skills classification used in this report follows the ILO Standard Classification of Occupations 1986 where category A refers to highly-skilled and top management positions while category B covers medium-skilled personnel, and the C group refers to semi-skilled certificate holders. This changes in emphasis reflects the mushrooming of tertiary institutions offering diplomas and the opening up of specialised facilities at Sokoine (Tanzania), Zambia and Zimbabwe Universities. Industry, mining, trade and tourism tend to employ more highly qualified personnel than is the case in other sub-sectors.

It is important to recognise that the number of expatriates and their uneven distribution is not as alarming as their strong influence throughout the region. Most expatriates occupy key policy-making positions, not only in member countries, but also in the Sector Co-ordinating Units, including, for example, the mining sector in Zambia, SATCC in Mozambique and the RTC Secretariat in Swaziland.

Manpower Policy: Review and Prospects

The future of SADCC's manpower strategy will depend on the RTC Secretariat's ability to identify demand/supply imbalances. An attempt has already been made from the supply side by mounting the SADCC Inventory of Training Resources. Unfortunately, this document is incomplete in terms of capacity, enrolment, area/topical coverage, staffing and professional levels of training instructors and programmes.

Similar efforts should be made to survey the demand side, either by conducting studies in member states or by collating data available in national manpower surveys. Without knowledge of the demand situation, the impressive initial list of critical manpower shortages identified at the SADCC Second Manpower Symposium in 1986 remains speculative and baseless.

The critical manpower shortages identified by the RTC fall into five main categories: a) Engineers; b) teacher educators; c) construction personnel; d) transport personnel; and e) auditors. Except for engineers and auditors, the proposed projects seem to cater for these needs. At the same time, there are more serious deficiencies in the proposed list of SADCC manpower projects.

Manpower Projects

The present survey, though limited by data deficiencies, identifies most needs in the top managerial and professional levels requiring high technology expertise. This conclusion is underpinned by the presence of large numbers of expatriates in this crucial category.

The proposed projects are heavily dependent on foreign grants which automatically maintain the presence of expatriates as no grant comes without a 'watch-dog'. This reliance on grants from donors demonstrates the general weakness of SADCC forcing increased dependence.

The magnitude of needs in most areas of critical shortage is unknown at the sectoral, regional and national levels. Knowledge of both demand and supply aspects of manpower requirements is fundamental to an effective regional manpower strategy.

If the latest annual manpower reports for Malawi, Zambia and Zimbabwe were released and integrated with those already available for Botswana, Swaziland and Tanzania, this would provide the database for a meaningful assessment of the prevailing manpower situation.

Indeed, there are regionally-based institutions such as ESRAUP capable of conducting such a survey assessment with minimum resources.

A Complementary Programme

In the short term SADCC should make maximum use of national and regional training institutions which have spare capacity, of which there are several. Present efforts in the field of teacher, instructor and student exchange programmes should be broadened. Other policy initiatives proposed are:

i) The creation of local capacities either through building new institu tions or expanding existing ones by creating new departments and faculties. Regional and domestic training capacity will provide more relevance and on-going rather than once-off programmes. Continuing education sandwiched with working periods will reinforce learning.

ii) Training overseas as a bridging measure, even though it is expensive and continues dependence.

iii) Regrading some high level posts to replace graduates with well-pre pared and qualified technicians. Long-experienced semi-skilled personnel could be intensively trained to fill such technician positions and unemployed secondary school leavers could be given employment and on-the-job training in the place of such personnel moved upwards.

iv) Continued tolerance of high level expatriate recruitment provided that counterpart recruitment and training is thoroughly enforced.

v) Attraction of SADCC nationals back home as SADCC economies recover.

Conclusion

No single solution is likely to be adequate. Furthermore, it is wise to separate short-run solutions from long-term ones at the planning stage in order to avoid future unemployment and under-employment. Poor economic performance generates unemployment including that of skilled labour. Different economic sectors have varying growth rates while security problems and a lack of funding may delay project implementation.

Taken together, all these could result in lower demand than the more optimistic manpower forecasts predict. Thus while some of these approaches may be applicable individually, there is much to be said for a combination of two or more approaches at the implementation stage.

SECTION 7

RESOLUTIONS AND RECOMMENDATIONS OF THE SEMINAR

On the last afternoon of the Seminar, the participants in plenary session had before them the draft resolutions and recommendations of the six working groups into which they had divided earlier in the week. They had in midweek already debated and adopted with amendments the recommendations and resolutions of the mini-Seminar on The Curriculum for Employment which had been held in Harare a few days earlier between 20 and 22 April, the resolutions and recommendations of which had been collated, consolidated and presented by a group of rapporteurs appointed by delegates at the mini-Seminar for the purpose.

The six working groups each focussed on one of the following topics, all of which had also been discussed in the plenary sessions, and which had been introduced either with a paper or a panel discussion followed by questions and comments:

1. Curriculum and Skills Acquisition for Employment; in the case of this topic, the group elaborated and expanded on the consolidated recommendations and resolutions that had already been adopted;
2. Activities in Schools and Community Involvement;
3. Vocational and Technical Training;
4. Options for School Leaver Placement;
5. Multi-Sectoral Planning and Co-ordination for, and Financial Im plications of, Job-Creation; and
6. Regional Co-operation.

CURRICULUM AND SKILLS ACQUISITION FOR EMPLOYMENT

Objectives and Principles of Content

Primary Level

At the lower level, concentration should be on the basic skills of reading, numeracy and writing.
The choice of content for specific subjects should be left to individual countries, taking into account local needs. At the upper primary level, the focus should be on further developing subject areas. Emphasis should be placed on: (i) the relationship between education and production; (ii) education as a process of socialisation towards character and moral development;

Primary Schools should prepare pupils for participation in productive work. Since primary education is terminal for so many, this level should provide pupils with survival skills while at the same time preparing them for secondary and life-long education.

Secondary Level

The educational system should, by demonstrating that the concept of education with production (EwP) is rooted in African traditions, emphasize the role of EwP as a strategy for technical training and for development. Students should be introduced to locally applicable technology, making use of hands-on practical experience. As a guide to the weighting of practical work and theory, the following may be considered:
i) at general secondary level: 80% class work and 20% practical; work;
ii) at technical secondary schools: 50% in each;
iii) at vocational schools: 80% practical work and 20% class work (theory).
More effective procedures should be devised for selecting students for practical subjects, taking into account national goals as well as students' aptitudes and interests. There should be a coherent and co-ordinated transition from primary to secondary school to ensure continuity and

progression in the teaching and learning of content, theory, practical skills, aptitudes and values.

Tertiary Level

The curriculum content at this level should be dictated by individual countries according to their socio-economic needs and available resources.

Specialised Vocational and Technical Training

The objective here is to identify types of specialised vocational and technical training - technical subjects, institutional forms and approaches, and levels - appropriate to different academic levels of school leavers, as well as courses which could be offered at the different levels of general education as components of survival skills and in preparation for further technical training at different levels or direct employment. Governments should formulate appropriate policies and define appropriate programmes for these different levels.

For those who leave upper secondary schools (A levels) there are technology or agricultural institutes; for those who leave senior secondary schools (fourth form and O levels), there are formal, specialised vocational and technical training institutions and agricultural colleges, in smaller or greater numbers, in each of the countries in the region, and in different technical skills areas, which are in all cases generally directed towards preparing learners for employment in the formal sector of the economy. In these various institutions heavier emphasis should be put on vocationalisation as opposed to equipping students with general maintenance-type skills. Depending on the availability of resources, these institutions should be evenly distributed throughout each country to counter the too readily accepted disparities between urban and rural areas.

There are, or should be, a range of basic skill development centres, comprising both formal and less formal organizations, at different lower levels, supported in varying degrees by governments. These include, or should include, more formal vocational training centres and the less formal youth services, Brigades and Young Pioneers; the possibilities of gearing these various programmes to serve worthwhile small enterprises should be examined.

In addition, in some countries in the region there are various backyard and backstreet production operations offering apprenticeships, or training, requiring from their apprentices or learners substantial fees with no recognised certificates at the end of the training. Some of these are unscrupulous, get-rich-quick operations but others do offer training which can be useful to employment-creation. Governments in the countries concerned should encourage the genuine operations to improve their services by examining their facilities and aiding them where possible and appropriate.

For training programmes to succeed there is a need for correct and sufficient training, equipment, adequate maintenance of the equipment and installations, proper logistical arrangements for the transportation and storage of the equipment and materials, and adequate training as well as support staff and back-up services. All this requires adequate budget provision for recurrent expenditure, although the need for self reliance, education with production and the linkages between school and community require the maximum utilisation of the skills within training institutions to effect their own maintenance and repairs and to generate income through production of goods and services, community projects and sub-contracting to local industry.

Ideally, teachers for specific skills ought to be competent craftsmen in the skills they are to teach.

In general, vocationalisation and technical training at general schools should be reinforced by organized visits to both large and small enterprises and especially industries.

The distinction between formal and non-formal education and training should be removed: all institutions are part of a comprehensive set of provisions for job-creation. At each level youth should be able to proceed to the next level of training or re-enter the general scheme if they upgrade their academic subjects.

Skills Acquisition for Employment

The skills most needed in the promotion of production and job-creation include creative skills, artistic and design skills, financial skills, managerial and organisational skills, and various technical skills. Teaching and training for these various components of entrepreneurial skills need to be introduced at every level and in every mode of the educational systems of each country.

In skills training for school leavers all existing formal and non-formal provisions, public and private, profit-making and non profit-making, should be recognised as having a role to play. However, their number should be much increased and their facilities expanded. In rural areas many more facilities for training should be made available including schools, farmer training centres, adult education centres etc. Existing and new facilities at all levels should be more fully utilised, by conducting evening classes to train adults and school leavers.

Accordingly, all skills centres should be encouraged to broaden their scope of training; they should offer technical or vocational skills (selected in accordance with local needs and resources), and business education and general skills. They should also include opportunities for continuing education and training.

SCHOOL ORGANISATION, ACTIVITIES AND RELATIONS WITH COMMUNITIES

The school should promote self-help and prepare pupils for life and work in the immediate environment and community in which they live. The school should impart skills to the community through pilot projects which can form a solid foundation for the development of broader community projects. Teachers should be part of the communities in which they are based and should exercise the leadership role that they are expected to demonstrate in the running of national programmes at the local level.

Since the school is expected to serve the needs of the community it is important for the community to be involved in determining the ideological content, planning, organising, managing and evaluating school and vocational school programmes. Parents should be convinced that they have a role to play in the education of their children. Structures such as Parent Teacher Associations should be encouraged. Schools should draw on the expertise available in the community in order to make the implementation of the school programme more effective. The community should play an effective disciplinary role to help children develop attitudes, morals and values which enhance innovative education systems.

Education and linkage to the community, and education with production are key elements of education for employment, and are more effectively so when reinforcing each other. They are, however, not confined to schools and training places, whether formal or non-formal. They may be found in collective forms of self-employment such as co-operatives which have education, training and skill acquisition components. Local authorities should help set up small industries with an educational and training component. Such initiatives, too, must be recognised as part of the comprehensive set of provisions for job-creation. Projects engaging schools, their students and their teachers in the production of goods and services for the community and for themselves, in socially useful work and in development projects required by the community, could lead on directly or indirectly to job-creation for some of those involved. They could open the way for more coherent and more widely accepted and applied policies of integrating work and study into the curriculum in a central way. It would be easier on the basis of success in these projects to persuade parents that the aim of linking work and study is employment, and that it would be beneficial in many ways to themselves and their children.

The linking of work and study and of education and training to community life also finds expression in the Mozambican practice of placing students in workplaces (factories or farms) for one month during their holidays. Each school must, moreover, have a cycle of interest in terms of which the students go into the community and collect data on that interest. An example given related to a particular school's interest in the needs of the elderly, and the visits paid by the students of that school to old people to gather information about their conditions. In this way, the students learned about social research methodology and its value and relevance, whilst at the same time learning about the socio-economic life of the community.

Teachers, Processes and Methods, Aids to Teaching and Learning

The attitude of the teacher towards innovation is critical to its success. Education and training for employment through education for self-reliance, education with production and education and linkage to the community, need the active support of teachers to succeed. Educators must be taught to understand that schooling is to be judged not only by academic results but by the prospects their students have of becoming gainful producers. Education is not only a function of theoretical learning and but also of appropriate practice and the linking of the two. Many of the skills and character traits essential to job-creation will be learned better outside the classroom, in the linkage of education with productive work and with the community than inside it alone.

Students should be active participants in the learning process through use of simulated and real life situations.

Teacher training courses must take account of the implications of education for employment, and of the realities of current employment and economic circumstances. The teachers themselves need to be taught some of the entrepreneurial skills and character traits that are advocated for their students, and through the same approaches and methods, namely education for self-reliance, education with production, the linking of theory and practice and education and linkage with the community.

Emphasis should be placed on the production of low cost, readily available teaching materials, and teachers at different educational (and technical training) levels should, through pre-service and in-service training programmes, be trained to produce their own teaching and learning resources. The structure of schools should be improved, in terms of their buildings, workshops, grounds and other facilities, to create physical conditions conducive to education with production.

Examinations and Assessment

Limitations imposed by examinations on teaching and learning of education with production should be redressed through the reformation of the examination systems and the inclusion as an integral part of examinations, of viable methods of continuous assessment. It is important, however, that the examinations should have credibility in the eyes of the trainees, their parents and above all the employers where the training is geared to the job market.

This credibility will be best achieved if employers, parents, farmers, craftsmen and industrialists, as well as governments and curriculum experts, are involved in assessing the needs for a particular educational and training programme, and in designing the curriculum and the training project, as well as in implementing it, and in advising on the best means of examination and assessment

OPTIONS FOR SCHOOL LEAVER PLACEMENT

School leavers are defined as pupils who are unable to continue with academic education, whether at primary school level, secondary school level, or high school level. Placement is achieved through institutional sets of initiatives or options offered or available to school leavers so that they can be productive.

Whilst primary school leavers should be allowed to repeat once where possible, they should be able to proceed to basic skill development centres where they can be taught a variety of practical skills and basic business management skills with emphasis on technology related to the locality. Junior secondary school leavers should be able to proceed to trades skill training centres for comprehensive specialist areas, whilst 'O' level school leavers should be able to proceed to technician training and 'A' level school leavers to technology institutes.

The principles underlying this tiered structure, is - as already stated in relation to vocational and technical training - that the distinction between formal and non-formal education and training be removed and that all institutions be seen as part of a comprehensive set of provisions within which students can move between education and training and between the formal and non formal institutions as they qualify or mature.

While implementation and control of this structure should be decentralised, involving ngo, local authority, private industry and other appropriate bodies, governments should provide co-ordination and quality control and develop appropriate systems of assessment and progression.

Where possible, governments should supplement the budgets of organisations involved in training in this structure. In addition, all centres should give a central place to production so as to enhance the training and to ensure a degree of cost-recovery.

It is recommended that each participating country appoint a team to research at local and district levels the entire range of goods and services which have the potential for development and absorption into employment of school leavers at various levels. The team would investigate the range of manufactured goods that can be produced in any locality, and investigate the availability of skills and knowledge already available. It would do the same in respect of services that could be provided locally, and with regard to both goods and services, it should investigate transportation, markets and materials required as well as support systems. On the basis of these investigations, viable projects can be developed through the provision of training and of support, including initial loans from a special fund to be set up by governments. In general, organisations like chambers of commerce, farmers groups, and womens' groups should seek to become more involved with schools in terms of employment information, skills training and general help in careers matters. In the case of agricultural training, it is recognised that sufficient arable land must be available if self-employment in farming is to be possible.

MULTI-SECTORAL PLANNING AND CO-ORDINATION FOR, AND FINANCIAL IMPLICATIONS OF, JOB CREATION

The main causes of unemployment are seen as the lack of skills due to unavailability or inadequacy of training and the lack of capital more especially in terms of equipment and tools, as well as landlessness and the low rate of economic growth against the background of a fast growing population.

Unemployment is categorised as: rural unemployment, caused by stagnation and rural underdevelopment which over the years have resulted in low productivity in the agricultural sector; urban underemployment which is made worse by rural-urban migration; youth unemployment and the unemployment of the disabled.

Bearing in mind that the majority of the people in the region live in the rural areas and depend on subsistence agriculture to live, it is important to modernize agriculture in order to create job opportunities; here multi-sectoral planning plays a very crucial role. There are several packages that go along with modernization of agriculture, to all of which multi-sectoral planning is critical. These include:

i) lining up all industries that provide inputs into agriculture, and all industries that use agricultural produce;
ii) the improvement of infrastructure, transport,distribution and marketing and the development of irrigation potential;
iii) the provision of incentives to small farmers such as easier credit facilities tailored to their situation (with low interest rates, a grace period and longer periods in which to repay loans), low excise duties on farm implements and sales and other taxes on other inputs; management of farm produce prices to ensure profitability of production;
iv) the strengthening of supporting facilities such as adequate extension and training services and the encouragement of cooperatives;
v) the improvement of land tenure systems;
vi) the establishment of agro-based industries in the rural areas, as well as the provision of incentives to attract other types of investment in rural areas. There should be constant monitoring and evaluation of the progress of implementation of these measures.

Whilst countries may have clearly stated national (as well as district and local) development objectives, and clearly spelt out manpower requirements in terms of numbers and types of skills - both of which are to be achieved through multi-sectoral planning - there is a need to re-define the conventional concept of manpower planning and to broaden economic planning and dynamise its implementation to ensure grassroots job-creation through a variety of mechanisms including education and training for employment. This re-definition should also encompass the better utilisation of the labour power of women. The curriculum of schools and training institutions should be adapted so that they are responsive to the needs so re-defined and newly conceptualised, in ways already recognised. Thus, while training should relate to manpower needs of the labour market, it should be adaptable and responsive to future developments resulting from the constant review of economic and manpower plans.

Whilst modern and high technology will continue to be required throughout the economy, there should, wherever possible, be an emphasis on low cost projects with a preference for labour intensive technologies and the minimal use of foreign exchange. A balance should be struck between modern and traditional technologies, especially in small scale agriculture, to ensure production beyond subsistence levels.

In order to make the goal of universal education a reality, communities should be encouraged to contribute, financially or in kind, to ease the burden on governments of wholly financing the school. The involvement of educational and training institutions in production, which also has social and pedagogical goals, can ensure a degree of cost recovery, so contributing towards achieving the goal of universal education and training.

REGIONAL CO-OPERATION

The SADCC strategy of collective self-reliance through coordination is fully endorsed. Existing arrangements for manpower training under the SADCC Programme of Action are noted with approval. This applies particularly. to the development of regional cooperation in specialised higher training and research programmes, and among professional associations, to facilitate exchange and retention of high level skill within the region. The Regional Training Council and other regional and national bodies are encouraged to identify and promote further such links. Inventories of manpower needs drawn up by the Regional Training Council and other bodies are also noted with approval. In this context, particular attention is drawn to the Eastern and Southern African Universities Research Directory based in Dar es Salaam.

But concern is expressed at the inadequate representation of general education, and of the needs of education for employment creation, within the region and in national considerations of manpower training.

SADCC countries should cooperate in education at all levels and in all modes, as well as in training because of their similar environments and common problems, and because of the need for cost-effective measures avoiding unnecessary duplication of effort and expenditure, and the need to support development in the region.

There are two languages used for official and technical purposes in SADCC countries, English and Portuguese. Language training should be reinforced at all levels of education in SADCC countries, of English in Lusophone countries and Portuguese in Anglophone countries, for the purposes of official and technical communication.

There are many other languages spoken in SADCC Countries, including languages taught in primary schools and those spoken in more than one country. Coordination and cooperation between SADCC states in education and information policies, in curriculum development, research, orthography and teacher training relating to languages used in common, is strongly recommended.

A regional language institute should be established to promote those languages which will facilitate communication in the region.

Education constitutes the largest sector in SADCC economies in terms of employment, expenditure and consumption of materials; but national educational sectors are frequently too small in many respects to benefit from economies of scale and costs. Existing aspects of collaboration between national educational sectors are recognised but so is the need for further co-operation in respect particularly of:
i) the development of curricula, materials and texts, and exchanges between Curriculum Development Units within Ministries of Education or equivalent bodies, especially those relating to common SADCC interests;
ii) the printing and publishing of texts in cost-effective quantities using presently under-utilised capacity;

iii) the production of educational materials, including technical and scientific equipment, in cost-effective quantities.

The SADCC countries share a 12 year cycle of primary and secondary education to pre-university level. Coordination of syllabus content and standards of awards initially in Year 12 certification is strongly urged.

Ministries of Education and other interested bodies should promote exchange programmes between students, teachers, and other individuals concerned in SADCC countries, by correspondence, travel and the 'twinning' of educational institutions.

The development at all levels of collaboration and coordination between national research councils, research institutions including ministries and libraries and professional and technical associations in SADCC countries is endorsed.

The region has had significant experience both in production and consumption of distance education schemes. Current initiatives in distance education should be co-ordinated within the region to serve regional needs.

The region has its share of people with handicaps and disabilities, requiring special education which may not be cost-effective for the small numbers in each country. It is recommended that the needs for special education in SADCC countries be investigated with a view to collaboration in the provision of such facilities.

There should be mutual assistance and reciprocity between SADCC countries in the provision of Vocational Education and Training in particular, with the development of a common core curriculum, the setting of common technical performance standards, the achieving of equivalence of certificates, diplomas and degrees, and the coordination of, and cooperation in, staff development programmes.

Such coordination should, while taking into account national variations in curriculum, also draw on the assistance of existing African curriculum organisations.

STRATEGIES FOR IMPLEMENTING THE RECOMMENDATIONS OF THE SEMINAR

Ministries of Education of SADCC countries should maintain regular contacts and Ministers and senior officials should meet together once a year.

Zimbabwe is assigned the responsibility of coordinating the activities relating to education in SADCC countries until an Education Sector is established within SADCC.

Each country should set up a SADCC Desk in the Ministry of Education for liaising with the other relevant Ministries as well as reporting to the Zimbabwe Coordinating Officer and to the SADCC Secretariat.

The view is rejected that labels education as a non-productive sector and it is emphasised that education is a big, economically viable industry compared to other economic sectors of SADCC. It is agreed that the Government of Zimbabwe should submit a memorandum to the SADCC Council of Ministers for discussion at their forthcoming meeting in mid-1989.

SECTION 8

THE CO-DIRECTORS' OVERVIEW

A primary objective of this overview is to evaluate the Seminar, relying to some extent on the perceptions of the participants themselves. But it also has the objective of assessing the potential impact of the Seminar on educational systems in the region related to job-creation, and of defining and assessing the follow-up action that may be required to achieve this, and what the constraints are likely to be.

While Seminar participants expressed themselves on the whole as either satisfied or very satisfied with the proceedings of the Seminar, our evaluation will go further to compare its achievements with the objectives of the organisers. The first point to make here is that the objectives changed as preparations went on; the proceedings of the Seminar did not reflect the aims of the original seminar description, and perhaps it is useful to note why and what might have been lost in consequence. Then, secondly, we should assess the achievements and impact of the Seminar in terms of what we had finally been prepared to settle for when we had at last brought all the participants together.

The Seminar description had referred to an earlier generation of socio-economic and education reforms that aimed at universal education and employment and the mass satisfaction of basic needs, and observed that they were not notably successful in achieving their aims. Zambia's early economic policies and its later education reforms, Tanzania's Arusha Declaration and Ujamaa programme together with Education for Self-Reliance, and Mozambique's early drive towards socialism which included a radical transformation of education, are examples of the earlier generation of innovations. Whilst there was some discussion of the educational dimensions of these innovations, it was somewhat limited and largely confined to the mini-Seminar on the Curriculum, and the socio-economic frameworks were hardly touched upon. Zimbabwe's Minister of Primary and Secondary Education, Cde The Hon Fay Chung, presented a broad and masterful statement of many of the major international and internal constraints on implementing policies designed to serve the interests of the broad mass of the people of the region and its nine countries, and she contrasted the differing solutions represented by the Lagos Plan of Action, on one hand, and the World Bank's Agenda for Action, on the other.

The international constraints and the demands of the Third World for a new international economic order are well enough known and frequently discussed. What needs to be better aired and understood are the problems that arise out of resistances to, or misinterpretations of, innovations inside the countries of the region, and the problems of conceptualisation, planning and implementation. A frank, in-depth and detailed discussion of earlier attempts at social transformation and a more searching analysis of the related innovations in education, might have been helpful in examining the internal impediments to the success of innovations. Critical studies are available, and the organisers might not have been bold enough in ensuring exposure of these.

Studies of earlier innovations at the broad socio-economic level and in education, ascribe difficulties of implementation to a variety of internal factors including a lack of real awareness of the necessary attitudinal changes and lack of consultation, miscalculations of skill and logistical requirements, poor infrastructural arrangements, inadequate inter-sectoral and cross-sectoral linkages and provision for backup and follow-up, mismanagement, incompetence and corruption.

Cde Fay Chung was correct to point out that we have in this region both a form of capitalism without national capitalists and a form of socialism without the mass working class required to implement it. These contradictions account for some of the failures, some of the mistakes, some of the problems of policy implementation.

If there had been a fuller discussion of the earlier attempts at social change - and their outcomes - the working group on Multi-Sectoral Planning and Coordination might have given more emphasis in its conclusions to the potential of joint ventures and the mixed economy as well as of the cooperative sector (especially in production) and of shorter economic cycles (which can better link demand and diversified local production), to the necessity of various state interventions and initiatives, to the better planning of mixes of technological options and options of scale and linkages between them, to the better mobilisation of savings and of unemployed labour through various mechanisms, the harnessing of traditional exchange mechanisms in societies, to appropriate fiscal measures and to alternative forms of tax (redeemable in labour or kind), to tax incentives for job-creation and training undertaken by employers and to the incorporation into national, district and local development plans of productive functions and capacities of educational institutions. All these measures have the potential to increase job-creation and can be linked up to education and training through education for self-reliance and education with production.

The experiences of the countries represented at the Seminar (seven by their Ministers of Education) were presented by their country delegations. Country reports are traditionally uncritical and perhaps even defensive. The organisers had agreed at a late stage in the seminar preparation to sidetrack the independent evaluations of the earlier innovations in education in several of the countries of the region, originally scheduled for presentation at the main Seminar, to the mini-Seminar, and to replace these with official country reports. It is perhaps noteworthy that none of the participants declared themselves very satisfied with country reports, in their evaluation of the seminar, and that only 39% expressed satisfaction, and another 30% acknowledged they were slightly satisfied. The change of programme reflected the realities of governmental participation, which all the organisers acknowledged it was vital to secure. The discussions which took place were for all that quite vigorous, and delegations were quite prepared to ask each other very challenging questions but perhaps not so challenging as they would have been if they had been based on more critical evaluations.

Some of the resource persons who took macro-perspectives in reviewing educational perspectives in their socio-economic contexts were quite sharply cross-examined by participants, although the evaluation showed that around 60 to 70% of them showed themselves either very satisfied or satisfied with these presentations.

What the Seminar may have lost in more critical self-evaluations of the country experiences in socio-economic and educational innovations, was to some extent made up for by the inclusion among Seminar participants of resource persons from within and outside the region, and of representatives of commerce and industry, of trade unions and of non-governmental organisations in country delegations, and by the frank discussion throughout. All of this ensured that many of the issues which the organisers had intended to raise, were raised. And, so indeed, did the keynote address of Zimbabwe's Minister Fay Chung.

Most of the Seminar particpants completed the comprehensive questionnaire given to them to evaluate the proceedings, and the overwhelming majority considered the Seminar to be a very good one, which they felt should be followed up with other seminars and workshops to monitor progress and consolidate and develop the work of the Seminar.

In the final analysis the Seminar must be more widely judged in terms of the proceedings, the presentations, the discussions and the conclusions. And these are thoroughly, and we hope accurately, reflected in this book. As noted in the introduction, successful implementation of the seminar recommendations is to some degree dependent on public awareness and acceptance of the recommendations and the thinking behind them. The constraints on the implementation of innovations have already been noted; they require strong political will and hopefully public support will reinforce this.

The publication of this report on the Seminar is regarded as an important step in the follow-up, in providing a reminder to the Ministries and other organisations which had representation there of the goals and tasks agreed to, and in making the proceedings and conclusions more widely known. A major recommendation was that education and training, in particular in relation to job-creation, should be a SADCC sector to strengthen regional cooperation in education and training especially for job-creation. This is being processed through the channels of SADCC. As noted in the overview of the mini-Seminar on the Curriculum for Employment, the Foundation for Education with Production has already held workshops involving most of the participating countries, on a curriculum for education with production presented by the Director of FEP in a paper to the mini-Seminar, which is reproduced in this report. The Foundation has also invited Ministries of Education committed to this principle to use the Foundation as a vehicle for the implementation of education with production in achieving the goals of the Seminar.

Whilst the Seminar may have fallen short of the original hopes of the organisers, it marked a very important beginning of discussions at the regional level of education and training in their socio-economic context not only by educationalists but by representatives of ministries of economic development and manpower and representatives of the private and co-operative sectors and of the trade unions and voluntary organisations. This was clearly recognised by participants. Important points were raised in the comprehensive approach towards socio-economic frameworks and education adopted at this Seminar, and it is hoped that this approach will be adopted in future SADCC get-togethers on education, and that the thinking reflected in the presentations, discussions and recommendations of this Seminar will be further developed and more widely discussed.

The concept of *education for all*, which was the theme of the Baughok Conference in early March 1990, might have already been shown by the Seminar to fall short of what is required to meet the real needs of the world's young people (and a great many of its people of all ages). The need is for *education for employment for all*, and as so often reiterated in the proceedings, education with production is a critical element of that more relevant, more challenging and broader concept.

CLOSING ADDRESS BY DR BERNARD CHIDZERO, SENIOR MINISTER OF FINANCE, ECONOMIC PLANNING AND DEVELOPMENT, ZIMBABWE

I feel greatly honoured to have been invited to address this very important Seminar at its closing session, and I must at the very onset express my sincere appreciation to the sponsors and organisers. The consensus that education and training have a direct bearing on employment and that unemployment has become one of the most difficult and pressing socio-economic problems facing governments in our region is in itself already a major contribution to the sum total of national and international efforts in search of the necessary answers and solutions.

I must also at the very onset of my remarks confess that I stand before you with a great sense of hesitation to speak, even trepidation! For not only have I not been a participant at the Seminar, but I also am neither an educationist nor a Minister of Education, nor even an honorary one. Neither am I a Minister of Labour nor, obviously, am I unemployed. Rather I stand before you as representative of that species of jugglers in societal management who take away money from everybody in every conceivable way, put it into one common basket and then, in a manner peculiar to their trade, proceed to parcel it out as inequitably as possible because the demands and priorities are so many and so varied and often conflicting. Be that as it may, I can say that even Ministers of Finance know and appreciate the critical importance of that type of education and training which combines excellence with relevance and that a nation of educated and trained people in the various activities of society is bound to emerge victorious in the end, whatever the odds in the short and medium-term. But they, the Ministers of Finance and I must add Development Planning, know even better that unless a country's economy grows in material and productive terms at rates higher than the growth of services, that country courts trouble.

In saying this, I am not unaware that our governments have made concerted efforts over the years to resolve the unemployment problem and yet with visibly limited results. The fundamental causes of the problem are lack of adequate economic expansion which would absorb additional labour, high population growth rates, education systems that do not provide our youths with adequate tools to take up jobs in the modern economy and scientific farming, let alone to have the initiative to create jobs in the informal sector. The problem is, of course, aggravated by developments beyond our control, such as the prevailing state of international economic relations between our region and the developed countries, which impact adversely on our terms of trade and national revenues and aggravate debt service obligations. This is not the occasion to go into details on this matter nor do I wish to be drawn into the discussion on our vulnerable dependency on trade, such as in regard to export of primary commodities whose prices have remained low for decades, nor on imports of intermediate and finished goods whose prices have always been high and continue to rise, relative to those of primary commodities. And there are the problems of protectionism and rising interest rates and all that. The result as we are all aware is almost invariably severe balance of payments problems and an increase in the degree of human suffering. The lesson we might learn from all this is that our education and training systems should conduce to greater self-reliance (national and regional), resourcefulness, competency and diligency, and so contribute to lessening dependency on external or exogenous factors. That having been said, however, there are also certain national policies, it must be admitted, which lead to failure in economic expansion. I know that you have concerned yourselves with some aspects of these broader problems in trying to identify ways of accelerating job-creation to which education and training can relate. It is appropriate, therefore, that we remind ourselves of the nature and breadth of the problems that we face as a region.

I am glad that this Seminar is taking place on a regional basis, thus bearing testimony to the vibrant spirit of SADCC. It is only through our joint efforts that solutions to problems of the type and magnitude you have been discussing can be found. Seminars such as the present one enable us to confer together and share experiences, to make efficient use of the various kinds of talents within the region and jointly to tap external resources from a position of strength and common understanding. By focusing on the relationship and interdependence that exist between education and employment, you have underlined the fact that only when the education system and training regimes have become more responsive to development requirements can the economy and society as a whole develop. But I would suggest that we should go beyond that and formulate education systems which transcend national boundaries, which promote greater regional and continental awareness, and thus underpin regional economic and social development. Regional centres or institutes, from research to teaching and planning, can make decisive contributions in this regard.

Let me at this point turn to investment in people. There is growing consensus these days toward a design for development which emphasises economic growth involving as participants the whole population and with increasing attention to the many aspects of sustainability, i.e. in economic development, in manning the social services and in managing our physical and social environments. Investment in people is the most important enabling process of strengthening the ability of people to control their own environment or circumstances and to participate actively and creatively in the society and the economy as a whole. Hence it is said that the world's most successful economies have given high priority to educational skills and training as vital factors in economic success and social progress. In doing so, we must look at the economy as a whole, fully recognising for instance that in our circumstances the formal sector has employment limitations and the informal sector should be analysed to ascertain its requirements and enhance it because it has as yet many untapped employment possibilities.

In looking at the close link between education and training on the one hand and employment on the other, the economic evidence indicating pay-offs to education is of three principal sorts: the first one has to do with the relationship between an individual's education level and his/her productivity in the labour market as a wage employee or self-employed worker; the second links the education of individuals to important outcomes of household behaviour, i.e. attitudes and values, fertility rates, or child survival, and thirdly, macro-economic evidence relates the growth rates of national economies to prior investments in education and other factors presumed to influence growth.

Generally speaking, it has been observed that many African educational systems and curricula have been slow in adapting to the needs in agriculture, industry and science and technology. This has perpetuated serious mismatches between what is required for development and what educational institutions are able to offer. High rates of graduate unemployment alongside high vacancy rates or high rates of expatriate employment suggest skill mismatches and the irrelevance of much of what is being taught in educational institutions.

But I fear that I have, somewhat unwittingly, entered into a minefield and acted rather like a bull in a china shop! I must quickly get out and move to the relatively safer grounds for Ministers of Finance, namely that of employment.

If education is a basic right and there is no doubt it is, employment is also a right. To the extent that our policies fail to create employment opportunities we frustrate or even negate the latter. Admittedly, the magnitude of our unemployment in this region is not only the result of our success in formal education and in turning out large numbers of school leavers without requisite skills, nor only the result of our failure to generate growth and employment; it is also at least in part because our statistical methods have become more efficient and the size of unemployment has in consequence also become more transparent. This of course, should not absolve failure.

On a different plane, egalitarian objectives and policies, insofar as they have led to more equitable sharing of virtually the same amount of national wealth over the years, have to that extent also not promoted greater savings or greater capital formation. Similarly, to the extent that incomes, principally in the form of wages and salaries, have been increased disproportionately to increases in the growth of the national product or pushed up labour costs, they have also favoured in the main those already in employment, militated against new employment and accelerated resort to capital-intensive and technology-intensive forms of production as against labour-intensive methods. We need therefore to be most careful and cautious in matters of rapid income redistribution so that we avoid ending up with capital dis-accumulation or anti-labour methods of production, or simply becoming high-cost producers whose products become uncompetitive on regional or world markets and unaffordable locally.

The size of the national budget and its pattern of expenditure also have a direct bearing on employment creation. For the larger the size of the budget as a percentage of GDP, the smaller the amount of savings and the lower the level of capital formation, the more so if the expenditure is predominantly recurrent; the larger also the budget deficit is likely to be as a percentage of GDP and therefore the greater the borrowing and the greater the dangers of inflationary pressures.

There has been the tendency in many countries of the SADCC region, certainly in Zimbabwe, for the Government to spend more on the services (especially education which takes about 10% of GDP, second only to Denmark according to a recent IMF study). In consequence, employment has increased in the services, which in itself is a good thing, but at the same time resources have tended to be syphoned away from material-productive sectors i.e. from industry, agriculture, mining and construction, leading to only marginal growth in employment in these sectors, a situation which has been accentuated by such other factors as shortage of foreign currency and certain economic and labour policies which now need adjustment. Today in Zimbabwe, although we have embarked on vocationalisation of secondary education and our ZIMSCI kits programme to equip secondary school students with certain skills in gardening, building, carpentry and metal work is a success, we have nonetheless thousands of jobless school leavers, who cannot find jobs and are not equipped to 'create' jobs for themselves. Thus both the type or system of education and the pattern of government expenditure combine with other factors and policies to create or increase unemployment. The obvious conclusion to be drawn is that education, planning and manpower development must be integral parts of national economic planning and development policies and the fiscal and expenditure regimes have to be geared accordingly to stimulate growth and development. It is a matter of planned and balanced development, with defined objectives and clear priorities, not only in theory but also and more importantly in practice and over sustainable periods, long enough to produce the desired results.

I know that you have given attention to those innovations in education and training systems which link them better with job creation, including the linkage of education with productive work, curriculum transformation and closer links between schools and their communities and that you have compared country experiences in these areas. I know that you have also taken into account the valuable practical pioneering work of the Foundation for Education with Production in Botswana and our own ZIMFEP.

Turning to a different but very important matter, it is most commendable that this Seminar could benefit from the experiences of other countries outside the region. The social welfare successes and employment achievements of Sweden are no doubt as much the product of the country's economic policies as of its education and training system. We can learn a great deal from that experience. From Cuba's socialist thrust and achievements in which education and training have been matched with progressive employment opportunities for all, we can derive much inspiration, as we can also from the experience of China. We are grateful for the contributions made to this Seminar in this regard.

It would be amiss of me if I ended my address without taking full cognisance of the significant fact that this Seminar is SADCC in coverage, a fact which underscores our commitment to regionalism, our appreciation of the commonness of our problems and therefore the imperative need for common efforts and co-ordinated solutions.

There is also the very important aspect of this Seminar, the fact that it is an internationally supported event. We are indeed most grateful to our Swedish friends and supporters, the Dag Hammarskjold Foundation, with which I have been closely associated for more than 15 years, for their material support and for their contribution in ideas and in sharing their experiences with us. Theirs is a very timely and significant contribution which amply demonstrates not only their identification with our lot and destiny, but also the immense potential of the Nordic Initiative.

Our cooperation in the fields of investment and trade, in infrastructure development and cultural activities, in scientific and technological fields, will be considerably promoted and enriched by education and training systems which are founded in scientific thinking and practice, which instill and promote skills and are relevant to regional as well as national needs. Education, training and productive employment facilitate investment and promote growth and vice-versa. This in turn should widen, deepen and enhance our regional cooperation in SADCC, 'Norsad' cooperation and eventually North-South cooperation on a growing and equitable basis.

I must conclude my address here by wishing all our visitors and collaborators from abroad as well as colleagues from the SADCC area a safe return home. We are happy you came. We are grateful to you all.

Finally, to the organisers, thank you so much for giving me this welcome opportunity to close this very important seminar.

PART 2

CURRICULUM DEVELOPMENT MINI-SEMINAR, HARARE 20TH TO 22ND APRIL, 1989

INTRODUCTION

In the Introduction to the proceedings of the main Seminar at the beginning of this book, the now widely accepted point was restated that job-creation is not the function of education alone, but of broader social, political and economic policies to which appropriate educational policies may fit.

A major objective of the Seminar was to define such appropriate educational policies in their inter-relationship with more relevant and effective, broader socio-economic strategies.

Education must not only prepare people better for paid employment in the formal sector but should also prepare those who fail to find paid jobs there to be able to create their own self-employment.

The curriculum and activities of schools are two of the most crucial elements that shape the content of education and influence its capacity to achieve its objectives.

The organisers of the Seminar felt that it would be of considerable value to bring the leading curriculum development officials within SADCC together in a special mini-Seminar on The Curriculum for Employment, to review existing curriculum policies and principles in the light of the challenge of growing unemployment of the educated young, and to help formulate new approaches, as an input to the main Seminar.

To sharpen the focus on the challenge of unemployment, the sponsors also organised presentations on particular programmes and experiences within the region which had attempted to address the issue of unemployment.

These papers, together with summaries of country presentations on curriculum policies and principles, as well as the keynote address by the University of Zimbabwe's Dean of Education, Dr Chikomba, and the recommendations of the mini-Seminar, are presented in the following pages. At the end is a brief overview of the mini-Seminar by its Co-Directors.

OPENING ADDRESS
BY DR. C. CHIKOMBAH, DEAN OF EDUCATION, UNIVERSITY OF ZIMBABWE

Introduction

The world over, many curriculum specialists, developers and implementers have organised conferences to discuss invariably 'Education and Development'. There was never any need, it seems to examine the relationship between curriculum and employment, curriculum and school crime, curriculum and environment, curriculum and development. Curriculum has always been subsumed in 'education'. Yet, curriculum is an element that determines the failure or success of an education system.

This seminar has decided to punctuate 'curriculum' and its relationship to employment. This is more important now than ever before because of the escalation of unemployment figures in our region, particularly those of school leavers. I am sure that the main purpose of the seminar is to come up with a practical recipe directed at the minimisation through curriculum of the problem of unemployment.

Curriculum

What is curriculum? According to Rowntree, it is the identification of aims and objectives, planning the learning environment, exploring and structuring the subject matter, selecting appropriate teaching strategies, helping students develop new ways of learning, evaluating the effects and effectiveness of the teaching/learning system, and using the insights gained from evaluation to understand that system, and where possible, improve it.

Given this way of looking at curriculum, one can conclude that curriculum developers must be thinkers, theorists, political realists and pragmatists, developers, practitioners well versed in the needs of the learners, in economic developments and social demands, and above all they must be systems technologists.

Whatever curriculum these specialists design, it must be home based. This means that it must be based on the local needs and directed at stimulating employment.

The main reason why curricula are the same everywhere is that curriculum developers are afraid of venturing into the unknown and are afraid of criticisms. They also lack confidence in themselves. They are afraid of taking a stand in defence of their new approach to education, so they hide behind Hawes, Whitehead, Rowntree, Poignant, Castle, Entwistle, and Dunkin and Biddle. Confidence in curriculum developers grows out of research and experience. Curriculum development units should have a strong backup from research. How can curriculum developers know in which areas self-help should be emphasised in the training, unless research is done well in advance? How will curriculum developers know the new sectors in the economy which require specialised knowledge and skills unless research is undertaken?

Research

What is research? Research is the mode of enquiry involving both logic and observation (Babbie). This means a scientific understanding of the world must make sense and correspond with what we observe. Both of these elements are essential to science.

As a gross generalisation, scientific theory deals with the logical aspect of science, and research deals with the observational aspect. A scientific theory describes the logical relationships that appear to exist among parts, and research offers means for seeing whether those relationships actually exist in the real world.

The question is, how does research of this nature work and what is the purpose of research? Social research, of course, serves many purposes. Three of the most common and useful purposes are exploration, description and explanation.

Exploration

Much of social research is conducted to explore a topic, to provide a beginning familiarity with that topic. This purpose is typical when a researcher is examining a new interest or when the subject of study is itself relatively new and unstudied. Curriculum research developers can use this purpose of research.

Description

A major purpose of many social scientific studies is to describe situations and events. The researcher observes and then describes what was observed. Since scientific observation is careful and deliberate however, scientific descriptions are typically more accurate and precise than casual descriptions. If the curriculum developers use it in their day-to-day curricular activities, they are bound to develop curricula which are accurate and which will benefit the communities for which the curricula are developed.

Explanation

The third general purpose of social scientific research is to explain things.

Reporting the voting intentions of an electorate is a descriptive activity, but reporting why some people plan to vote for candidate A and others for candidate B is an explanatory activity. Reporting why Harare has higher rates than Mutare is a case of explanation. A Mathematics curriculum developer has an explanatory purpose if he/she wishes to have more calculus at lower six than at 'O' level. He/she needs an explanation why he/she thinks that it is necessary to teach more African history at 'O' level than at lower six.

The identification of aims and objectives, the planning of learning environment, the structuring of the subject matter, the selection of the appropriate teaching strategies, all of which are curriculum development activities, must be based on research.

Research, Curriculum and Employment

I am sure that the participants must be saying "what is the relationship between these two (Research and Curriculum) and employment?" Maybe I have lost sight of the topic, but the point being made here is that curriculum is needs assessment based and that needs are assessed through research (mostly action research).

A curriculum designer, who starts work at 11.00 a.m. at Belvedere, walks through Africa Unity Square everyday from the bus terminus on the corner of 4th and Manica, who sees many able bodied people lying down or just sitting or loitering around, mostly of school leaver age, will no doubt realise that these people are unemployed.

The question the curriculum specialist should ask is why are those people not working? Is it because they have been mistrained? What kind curriculum did they go through? If the curriculum did not prepare them for the world they are living in, what kind of curriculum should they follow?

This last question leads to research. Research is very vital for curriculum to change. One cannot change to something of which one has no idea. One must understand the advantages and disadvantages of the new curriculum. One should determine the needs of the people for which the curriculum is developed.

I have however, known of curriculum changes which have been based on questionnaire survey. This approach is only one way of determining needs. But observations, group dynamic and interviews need to be employed as well in order to determine the breadth and depth of the problem.

Self-Help

If curriculum is to deal with the problem of unemployment, the curriculum structure should therefore have a very strong dose of self-help. Nyerere (in Castle) states:
"Our educational system has to foster the social goals of working together and living together for the common good. It has to prepare our young people to play a dynamic and constructive part in the development of society...in which progress is measured in terms of human well-being, not prestige

building, cars or other such things whether privately or publicly owned... It must emphasise cooperative endeavour not individual advancement. It must stress concepts of quality and the responsibility to give service which goes with any special ability, whether it be in carpentry, in animal husbandry or in academic pursuits."

In short, Nyerere is saying our curriculum should emphasise the areas of self-help in order to encourage self-employment and reduction of unemployment.

Curriculum must therefore encourage the development in each citizen of three things. An enquiring mind, an ability to learn from others and a basic confidence in his own position as a free and equal member of society who can create employment for himself and others. This kind of curriculum is only possible if research and research related activities are employed.

Bibliography

Babbie, E (1986), *The Practice of Social Research* (4th Ed.), Wadsworth Publishing Co., Belmont, California

Castle, E B (1972), *Education for Self-Help*, Oxford University Press, London

Dunkin, M J and Biddle, B J (1974), *The Study of Teaching*, Holt Rinehart and Winston, New York

Enthwistle, H (1974), *Child-centred Education*, Whitstable Litho, Straker Brothers Ltd., London

Hawes, H (1982), *Curriculum and Reality in African Primary Schools*, Longman Group Limited, London

Kohl, H R (1969), *The Open Classroom: a practical guide to a new way of teaching*, The New York Review, New York

Rowntree, D (1985), *Educational Technololgy in Curriculum Development*, (2nd Ed.) Harper and Row, London

SECTION 1

CURRICULUM POLICIES: BOTSWANA

Introduction

Current policies and principles of curriculum reform in Botswana are based on the recommendations of the 1976 National Commission on Education (NCE) which conducted a broad-ranging review of the country's educational system, its goals and major constraints and submitted recommendations for improvement in both the quantitative and the qualitative aspects of education.

The National Commission on Education recommended that the aims of primary education in Botswana should be:

1) to develop in children the ability to express themselves clearly in Setswana, both orally and in writing;

2) to ensure that children acquire a basic command of written and spoken English and of mathematics. In teaching language and mathematics, schools should encourage children's sense of curiosity about the world and understanding of how to find out more about it;

3) to give children the necessary knowledge and ability to deal with the social and physical environment in which they live. This includes learning about their community and gaining basic knowledge of the laws governing the natural world around them. It also involves working with their hands and approaching simple problems in a practical way;

4) to give children an appreciation of their culture, including language, traditions, songs, ceremonies and customary behaviour;

5) to give children a range of educational experiences that will enable them to discover and develop their own special interests, talents and skills, whether these be dexterity, physical strength, intellectual ability, artistic gifts, organising and leadership skills, a special capacity for friendship or some other distinctive quality;

6) to provide children with a set of moral standards, personal convictions and loyalties that will make them good members of their family and community and responsible citizens of Botswana.

The Initial Implementation of the NCE's Recommendations and Developments During the Period of National Development Plan V

The major thrust of National Development Plan V was improvement of primary education. The Ministry of Education concentrated on the improvement of primary education through on-going curriculum review and revision. The actual process took off following the establishment of the Curriculum Development Unit under the Department of Curriculum Development and Evaluation in 1978. This Unit, as the section of the Department charged with the responsibility for on-going curriculum reform had to address the question of educational quality and relevance in the primary curriculum by coming up with instructional programmes that would relate to the environment and everyday life experiences of a Motswana child.

Following the establishment of the National Primary Subject Panels and plans for trial testing and evaluation of draft curriculum materials, the revised primary level curriculum was introduced for general implementation during the period 1981-2. Initial efforts in the review and revision of the primary curriculum concentrated on a core of six subject areas: English, mathematics, science, Setswana, social studies and religious education.

Although no detailed analysis has as yet been undertaken to ascertain the effectiveness of the revised primary curriculum, it is generally accepted that it is an improvement over the former curriculum. There is general agreement that more could still be done to give more practical orientation to the teaching of all subjects in the primary system. Secondly, there still remains a need to strive for appropriate matching between the orientation of the revised curriculum and the assessment/evaluation system. The general concern seems to be that our assessment procedures and examinations should be further refined to move away from memorisation and recall of basic facts to their application and evaluation.

Furthermore, in concluding discussion relating to developments in primary curriculum reform, it should be pointed out that the National Development

Plan V was characterised by a massive expansion of the primary education system. During the course of the plan, the government made efforts to construct as many primary schools as possible so as to ensure that primary education would be available to the vast majority of Batswana children. However, in spite of the massive expansion of primary education, recent analysis suggests that Botswana could still be about 15% short of universal primary education. It is expected that once the characteristics of the 15% out-of-school children have been determined in terms of factors such as age, settlement and socio-economic level, it will be possible to plan for their educational provision.

National Development Plan VI and Emphasis on Increased Access to Junior Secondary Education

The major focus of government's aim during National Development Plan VI has been to provide nine years of basic education for the majority of Batswana children. This policy should be seen as a logical extension of the initial emphasis given to the expansion and provision of primary education during the course of the previous plan. The National Policy on Education envisaged a form of intermediate school with standards of provision and levels of costs between the then levels of primary and secondary education to ensure reasonable levels of progression from primary to higher levels of education.

The government's policy to increase access to junior secondary education is made clear in the education chapter of National Development Plan VI where it is stated:

"It is planned that by the middle of the 1990s there will be universal access to 9 years of basic education for all Batswana children and the implementation of this policy will require the establishment of Community Junior Secondary Schools throughout the country, which will involve community participation."

However, it is important that we bear in mind what happens to children at the end of their nine years of basic education. Questions are being asked about what job or training opportunities are available following the termination of formal education at the end of the ninth year. This is a question which will assume greater significance as more Batswana children have access to junior secondary education, especially as most of these children will not proceed to senior secondary level where only a limited number of places are available. This issue will be dealt with later in this paper.

The government's intention is that eventually the nine years of basic education will consist of six years of primary schooling and three years of junior secondary schooling. The pattern that is currently followed involves a transitional stage of seven years in the primary system and two years in the junior secondary. Government policy of six years in primary school and three in junior secondary will be implemented when enough junior secondary places have been created to enable all children to progress from primary school to junior secondary. This, it is hoped, may be feasible by the mid-1990s.

The Need for an Appropriate Curriculum in the Nine Years of Basic Education Programme

The guiding principle in revising the junior secondary curriculum has been the need to develop a more practical and relevant education programme that will benefit the majority of Batswana children in terms of preparation for life and on-going personal development. Therefore, in reviewing and revising the junior secondary curriculum, an important factor taken into consideration was the need to ensure that students terminating formal education at the end of the ninth year would be equipped with the basic preparation and skills which would enable them to fit into training programmes, offered either through on-the-job training, Brigades or vocational training centres. What is more, as a result of increased access to junior secondary education, consideration had to be given to the fact that the revised curriculum had to cater for a mixed ability range of students. This is because our junior secondary education system has increasingly become open to students of different backgrounds, abilities, interests and aptitudes.

The Aims of the Nine Year Curriculum and Their Implications for Curriculum Development

The aims of the nine year curriculum present, in broad terms, the expected outcomes of the nine year basic education programme in terms of what skills, attitudes and knowledge students would be expected to demonstrate by the time they complete the junior secondary course.

The National Policy on Education states that the revised curriculum aims to provide all children with:

1) the language tools needed in either further study or work;
2) a solid foundation in mathematics skills;
3) an understanding of scientific and technical subjects, based on examples from the children's own environment;
4) a sense of the nature of their society and their role in it;
5) an orientation toward further learning, whether formal or non-formal;
6) an orientation toward work in the real world.

Implications of the Aims of the Nine Year Curriculum for the Revision of the Junior Secondary Curriculum

In order for the aims of the nine year programme to be used appropriately to lay a basis for the junior secondary curriculum, it is important that:

-An analysis be carried out, subject by subject, in order to incorporate the aims of the nine year programme into instructional objectives and activities.

-Clear objectives be developed for students in terms of knowledge, skills and attitudes that relate to the overall aims of the programmes and that are grounded in practical activities and the Botswana environment. Students should be provided with communication skills, problem-solving abilities, awareness of opportunities and basic productive skills.

-All subjects should have practical activities related to the world of work and life in Botswana. It is also important that practical subjects such as agriculture and technical studies should be related to economic opportunities and enterprise that are applicable to the Botswana environment.

-Within each subject area, units of instruction should have continuous assessment and testing which would allow students to demonstrate that they have mastered the knowledge and skills being taught. The emphasis should be on relating students' learning to competencies which are, in turn, related to life needs and opportunities.

Implementation of the Revised Junior Secondary Curriculum as an Integral Component of the Nine Years of Basic Education

The revised junior secondary curriculum is built around a core of six subjects: agriculture, English, integrated science, mathematics, Setswana and social science studies. An important point to register with regard to the revised junior secondary curriculum is a policy decision that has been taken to include agriculture in the core curriculum. Agriculture is, therefore, offered to all students in the junior secondary system as opposed to the status it previously had as an optional subject.

In addition to the core curriculum subjects, home economics, technical studies, and religious education are offered as options. According to the revised Junior Certificate Examinations regulations, students require a minimum of seven subjects (the six core subjects plus at least one optional subject) to qualify for the full Junior Certificate.

In the light of the foregoing, the major focus of curriculum reform in Botswana currently entails on-going monitoring of the revised curriculum implementation programmes so that the curriculum can be refined in the light of appropriate feedback. Besides on-going school visits and teacher in-service programmes, the Ministry of Education has recently initiated a series of National Curriculum Consultative Conferences on issues pertaining to curriculum relevance, effective communication channels in the dissemination of educational policies as well as the concerns of education and training.

Conclusion

Botswana is now three years into the implementation of the national policy to achieve nine years of basic education but it should be conceded that the introduction of a major policy change in any educational system inevitably raises issues that are not fully anticipated in the planning stages. Questions have already been raised about the availability of training and employment opportunities for Batswana children following completion of the nine years of basic education. Although the aims of the nine year curriculum represent a marked departure from past traditions, questions have already been raised as to wether this curriculum will give Batswana children adequate preparation for life in accordance with the National Development Plan VI objective of preparing Batswana children for useful and productive lives, with emphasis on training to meet the manpower needs of the country's economy as well as giving attention to rural development and employment generation.

CURRICULUM POLICIES: LESOTHO

Introduction

The Basotho nation has called upon the education professionals to provide an effective and efficient education system in relation to Lesotho's man-power and economic development needs. The Ministry of Education, in tackling this problem through curriculum revision, has taken a number of points into account. An important economic factor is that as foreign wage employment opportunities decrease, the need for self-reliance increases in two areas: firstly, food, clothing and other commodities and secondly, the growth of small businesses in the private sector demands foreign exchange earned from the sale of agricultural and other products in the foreign market.

Rethinking is needed in terms of basic education and practical studies. It is necessary to examine what basic skills are required for primary school children in the interests of the nation. Practical studies also need to be re-examined to include a more comprehensive view, allowing practical studies to be integrated into the existing education system, not as separate courses or subjects, but as a teaching technique through which a teacher emphasizes the learning of basic skill competence through practical application.

The objectives of practical studies are based on the policies recommended and adopted from the *Education Sector Survey Task Force Report* (1982). Specifically, the school graduate is expected to develop the following skills and competence levels:
Communication - oracy and literacy in Sesotho and in English as an international language.
Quantitative Reasoning - numeracy, mathematical and computing skills and the ability to draw conclusions based on quantitative thinking.
Thinking Skills - the ability to use different modes of reasoning for identifying, decoding, grouping and re-grouping information in problem-solving.
Application of Learning - the ability to apply knowledge and skills by using the skills of adapting, transferring and reasoning.
Socio-cultural and Scientific Appreciation - to develop an appreciation of the world around one and its natural and social history; to develop the ability to see oneself within one's immediate context and in a larger global context.

Self-reliance - the ability to perceive oneself and others as learners and teachers in and out of school; to care for oneself and others, physically, mentally and socially; to use the creative imagination to envision potential and utilise opportunities as they arise; to appreciate and build positive work attitudes and to develop the confidence in one's own abilities and trust in others.

Deficiencies in the education system, such as inappropriate and overly literate curricula in the secondary schools were identified in the early 1970s and, in the mid-70s, the Ministry of Education embarked on the introduction of a diversified curriculum for secondary schools. The aims of this programme were to provide students with both academic and practical studies and to create a productive and united Basotho nation.

Technical subjects were to be introduced into the schools as part of general education and for the development of basic pre-vocational skills. The subject identified for the Junior Certificate (JC) level was basic handcrafts (initially known as elementary technology). This is an integrated subject combining technical drawing and design, woodwork theory and practice and metalwork theory and practice. This syllabus was reviewed and upgraded in 1982 and reintroduced into the secondary schools in 1983.

A new mathematics course has been designed for those pupils who will not pursue a mathematically oriented programme after leaving school. It is vocationally based and provides a good foundation for occupations such as agriculture, nursing, commerce, technical training and primary school teaching. Regional Panel members have collaborated in the production of a locally written instructional book.

The home economics syllabus has also been revised and has been designed to enable boys and girls to take the subject from Standard 1-7. The main areas of this subject are food and nutrition, clothing and textiles, home management, health and hygiene and child care. This programme continues at the secondary stage.

Curriculum development in the post-secondary area has been carried out on an ad hoc basis in individual institutions, without overall coordination. This has resulted in disparity of content, standards and certification. Trade testing has been carried out by the Department of Labour at the Ministry of Labour, Social Welfare and Pensions. This proved to be unsatisfactory and the responsibility for trade testing was transferred to the Ministry of Education in 1984.

Developments

To increase awareness and competency in manual dexterity in young children, an arts and crafts syllabus has been developed for the primary curriculum and is being piloted in 22 primary schools countrywide. This syllabus is also being tested in the National Teacher Training College (NTTC). Reviews of secondary craft and technical syllabuses are also taking place.

The government introduced the Lesotho Technical and Vocational Training Act of 1984 which became law in April 1987. The Technical and Vocational Training Board was created and given overall responsibility for the improvement of technical and vocational education and training. The Board has created committees and sub-committees which attend to specific issues like curriculum, certification and standards. Trade test syllabuses in eight priority trades have been reviewed, upgraded and standardized. The syllabuses have been developed for artisan and assistant artisan levels.

A specialist committee for industrial training and specialist sub-committees have been established to advise the Technical and Vocational Training Board on all matters relating to industrial training. The terms of reference of this specialist committee are to identify training needs in the country; to determine areas of high priority and to propose plans of operation and standardized training programmes for these areas. This will be based on a modular system to allow for flexibility in enrolment, instruction and study patterns.

Curriculum Development

Curriculum development for primary and secondary schools is the responsibility of the National Curriculum Development Centre. Responsibility for technical subjects in vocational schools lies with the Department of Technical and Vocational Education and Training and its curriculum development unit. The national subject panels, which comprise subject specialists and teachers, design, implement and evaluate the curriculum. The National Curriculum Council approves curricula for implementation in the schools.

Before curricula are implemented in the schools, they must be tested in a few trial schools to determine their effectiveness. It is only after those tests have taken place that all schools will implement the curricula approved by the National Curriculum Council.

Ministry of Education Policies

Outlined below are the policy statements for technical and vocational education of the Ministry of Education. These are listed in the order of priority designated by the Department of Technical and Vocational Education (TVE):

1) The Ministry of Education will ensure that all levels of education offer technical or vocational education so that every Mosotho child, including the disabled, is provided with the opportunity to develop his/her full potential, both academically and practically.

2) The Ministry will ensure that national subject panels for technical and vocational education, at all levels, are established to develop, review and upgrade the curriculum to fully prepare the student for life in Lesotho.

3) The Ministry will establish Vocational Training and Trade Testing Centres to ensure that the existing workforce is provided with the skills and knowledge required by modern industry.

4) The Ministry will ensure that all technical and vocational courses at technical trade schools will be based on a modular system in order to accommodate short term skill upgrading programmes for employees in industry.

5) The Ministry will strengthen high schools, technical and vocational schools by offering Education with Production so that such schools become more self-reliant and students are able to reinforce the skills they have acquired in the JC Technical Education Programme.

6) The Ministry will ensure that appropriate courses at diploma level are provided for teachers of technical subjects in order that suitably qualified teachers will be available for Forms D and E technical subjects.

7) The Ministry will ensure that all instructors appointed to posts in the Vocational Training Institutes are fully qualified in order that trainees on vocational training programmes will receive a higher standard of instruction and guidance.

8) The Government of Lesotho, through the TVE Department, will establish an apprenticeship scheme so as to provide for the development of a highly skilled workforce for industry.

9) The Government of Lesotho, through the Ministry of Education, will provide training for professionals at degree level in civil engineering in order that architects and engineers are produced in Lesotho.

Curriculum at primary school level is designed to inculcate proper attitudes and work habits in our children; at secondary level, basic skills are provided to prepare the students for specialisation in the different trade subjects for employment. The alternative programme after Junior Certificate, which the Ministry is contemplating, will prepare the students for self-employment and will create a new generation for our teacher training college, technical institutes and agricultural colleges.

The Ministry of Education's major task is to pioneer educational experiments that will overcome the divisions between theory and practice, mental and manual labour and academic and practical subjects. This new approach which links schooling to real life and to the needs of society is education with production.

We believe the aims of Education with Production to be:

1) to promote a new system of education through curriculum experimentation which integrates academic and practical subjects and introduces productive income generating projects into the schools;
2) to create job opportunities for school leavers by helping them to establish industrial and agricultural income generating projects;
3) to link schools with local communities by providing community programmes which will help to improve the living standards of people and

transform the rural economy.

Education with Production as a means to prepare students for the world of work is not a new subject in our schools; what is new is the approach. Our schools run school garden projects which produce vegetables for consumption and for sale to the community. Some of our Technical and Vocational Institutions operate production units which are run by both the students and the community in an attempt to generate income for the schools and to expose students to industrial and mass production techniques.

CURRICULUM POLICIES: MALAWI

Introduction

Curriculum reform is an activity which educational systems in developed and developing countries have in common and which is on-going. The reform is, in part, related to dissatisfaction with schools geared to the needs of only some of the pupils enrolled; dissatisfaction with the focus of many schools and dissatisfaction with the irrelevance of much of the curriculum.

In developing countries, the most appropriate types of curricula and schooling have long been subjects of controversy. In place of Western models of academic schooling which are generally regarded as unsuitable for the needs of such countries, developing countries have experimented with alternative curricula to academic schooling. At Independence in 1964, Malawi, like most, if not all, African countries, found its content of education not in line with existing African conditions.

Malawi's Educational System

The formal education system of Malawi consists of eight years of primary education, four years of secondary education (two years of junior secondary and two years senior secondary) and three to five years of higher education.

Although Malawi is committed to achieving universal primary education, its net enrolment ratio is below 70% of the age group. Full-time student secondary enrolment is below 5% of the secondary school age population.

All curriculum reforms presuppose a context. In Malawi, the primary curriculum is geared to pupils for the majority of whom primary education is terminal. As for secondary education, its objective is to provide sufficient capacity to meet the manpower requirements of the economy in direct employment or as an input into tertiary education.

The Control of Curriculum in Malawi

The process of curriculum reform is linked to the whole process of curriculum control which is, in turn, linked to the overall control and organisation of Malawi's system of education. The school curriculum is dominated by the larger issues of government policies, the state of the economy and society's needs. This control results in a great deal of curriculum decision making being centralized in central government structures.

Although curriculum issues are centrally directed, various aspects are controlled at the level of defining policy, administering this policy and implementing it. Specifically the aspects of the curriculum which are under different degrees of local and central government control are as follows:

1) Subjects of the Curriculum

The Ministry of Education lays down minimum standards and competencies for every pupil. There is a common curriculum which is pursued by central government. The government ensures that every school's curriculum meets fundamental educational criteria. Stated briefly, a school's curriculum is prescribed by central government in accordance with declared needs and priorities, structured by objectives, divided into subjects and subject areas, supported by approved texts and assessed in an approved manner.

Although the policy is that all pupils should have access to the same areas or bodies of knowledge and learning, the curriculum includes options and elective areas which pupils can choose freely.

2) The Syllabus

Syllabuses are produced by subject committees. Each syllabus shows the subject objectives, learning experiences and content and approved teaching materials. No syllabus is used unless it is approved by the Ministry of Education. To accommodate changing conditions in the country and new developments in the subject matter which may require a shift in emphasis from old concepts to new ones and from knowledge studies to issue studies, the guideline is that each syllabus is due for review after it has been in use for five years. The approach to syllabus change is effected in a step-by-step fashion.

3) Timetabling

Individual institutions decide on issues regarding the timetable. However, the Ministry issues guidelines on minimum period allocation for every subject.

4) Textbooks

Only approved textbooks are used in schools. Where textbooks are written by commissioned Malawian authors, they are based on approved scope and sequence charts and teaching syllabuses. Where textbooks are written by non-Malawian authors, or written by non-commissioned Malawian authors, they are evaluated either as inspection copies or in manuscript form. Such books are either adopted as they stand or recommended subject to specified changes. The books may be recommended as pupils' textbooks (main or supplementary), a teacher's book or a library book. The task of textbook evaluation focusses on syllabus coverage and subject content; organization of topics and teaching approach; language and readability; evaluation and exercises and production; illustrations

Educational Language Policy

Language policy in Malawi, as in other countries, is determined by the government. The government sees language policy as a socio-political instrument for promoting national interests and aspirations which encompasses questions of a national culture, forging a national identity and ensuring national unity. In Malawi, it is the view of the government on language policy which prevails over that of the individual.

English and Chichewa are official and national languages respectively. The educational language policy is broadly in conformity with the overall language policy of the government. There is a language policy for each of the formal stages of education. In primary education, the medium of instruction in the first five classes is Chichewa. English is taught as a subject up to standard 5. From standard 6, English is used as the medium of instruction while Chichewa is taught as a subject. The medium of instruction at secondary level is English.

At curriculum planning and development level, all the people involved in the various aspects of curriculum work use the language policy to guide their actions. All educational documents in Malawi are in English.

The Focus of the Primary Curriculum

As in most countries, Malawi tries to relate the goals of its education system to national goals. The goals of education are articulated within the context of national development as far as possible. The Education Development Plan, 1985-1995 documents the need for the individual to advance him/herself while at the same time contributing to the development of the nation as a whole. More specifically, the document calls for the provision of opportunity for the present generation of children to achieve permanent literacy, numeracy, ethical and socio-economic knowledge as well as skills. The teaching of literacy and numeracy is the major emphasis of the new lower primary curriculum.

The upper primary level of schooling is to re-orient the primary school curriculum in the later years of the programme towards the community life which most pupils will enter, given the fact that secondary education will be available for only a limited number of pupils. In an attempt to interpret the Education Plan with regard to the upper primary curriculum, the government's Statement of Development Policies, 1987-1996 states that the emphasis is towards equipping the nation's youth with the skill and desire for self-employment. Considering that the majority of the population live in rural areas and are subsistence farmers, the primary school curriculum is being re-oriented to community life, an education which prepares pupils for productive lives in the communities from which they come and to which they will return at the end of primary education. Agriculture, mathematics, home economics, and creative arts are some of the subjects which would be included in a community oriented school.

The Focus of the Secondary Curriculum

The aims and objectives for secondary education vary in their generality and specificity but underlying most of them is the concept of a curriculum that defines universally valid skills and knowledge for a given type of education, regardless of student interest or local interest. As in most developing countries, the emphasis is on the preparatory function which accords with student aspirations to high level positions and the expansion of the modern economic sector. The main objective of secondary education in Malawi is to meet the needs of the labour market and to serve economic needs rather than social demand.

Conclusion

The curriculum in Malawi is centrally prescribed and made uniform throughout the country. The vehicles for curriculum and syllabus development are the various syllabus committees. Each committee designs the syllabus, prepares teachers' guides, sets suitable books for use with examination syllabuses and develops teaching and learning materials as well as teacher support services. The Inspectorate Division of the Ministry seeks ministerial approval for any changes in syllabus and accompanying examinations as well as new textbooks intended for use with any syllabus.

CURRICULUM POLICIES: MOZAMBIQUE

Curriculum and Textbook Development

1. 1975-1979

In 1975, all colonial curricula and textbooks were replaced by new curricula drawn up over the following two years by the respective National Directorates of the MEC (General, Adult and Technical Education). However, textbooks were not available in the initial stages. In 1977, the full primary course programmes were printed in three volumes; for higher levels, each teacher received a stencilled document containing the programme for his/her subject.

By 1978, the General Education Directorate (DNE) had produced Portuguese readers for the primary and lower secondary level followed by readers for the middle secondary level. Prior to this, there had been no experience of editing school books in Mozambique, the work having been done in Portugal before Independence. In 1978, with the beginning of the planned literacy campaigns, a Portuguese reader and a literacy teachers' manual were produced by the Adult Education Directorate (DNAEA). Between 1979 and 1980, books were produced for the Adult Education post-literacy campaigns while the literacy service produced a revised teachers' manual, a mathematics book and manual and a supplementary exercises book for Portuguese.

In 1978, the newly founded National Institute for Education Development (INDE) took over the production of general education textbooks. The period 1978-82 is characterized by the rapid production of essential textbooks by dispersed groups, often without sufficient experience and with few guidelines as to what learning rates and teaching methods should be demanded. The results were often over-ambitious curricula, especially with regard to content and methodology; an absence of a method for the teaching of Portuguese as a second language; the development of serious gaps and imbalance between and within sub-systems, grades and subject areas; and a continuing absence of textbooks for many grades and subjects (most importantly, primary level mathematics textbooks).

2. 1980-1983

In 1980, the INDE was charged with co-ordinating the planning, development and introduction of the new National Education System on the basis of acquired experience and with a tight timetable. The INDE convened an Education System Board (GSE) composed of representatives of all the National Directorates of MEC to undertake this work. The following work method was selected:

1) definition by the GSE of the general aims of the National Educa tion System;
2) proposal of the general objectives of each subsystem by the respective Directorates of the GSE, followed by making these ob jectives compatible;
3) composition of subject groups in the General and Adult Education areas to define the general objectives per level and per subject area, firstly, to achieve compatibility between subjects, levels and sub-systems and secondly, for approval by the GSE;
4) continuation by the subject groups of the definition of the specific educational objectives per grade and the planning, drafting and writing of the objectives, contents, means and methods to be applied;
5) practical testing and subsequent revision of the work produced, approval by the GSE and the Minister and, finally, production of definitive textbooks and teachers' guides for each grade on schedule in accordance with the demands of the progressive time table for the introduction of each stage of the National Education System.

Through these developments, in 1981-2, eight Adult Education textbooks for the literacy phase were prepared and printed and, in 1983 another ten books were produced.

Some other previously prepared books were to be published in 1983 to cover lacunae in the existing education system, as well as some ten books for the Adult Education fourth year, bringing the planned total up to some 39 books for that year.

3. 1984-1990

At each stage of the timetable for the introduction of the National Education. System, it is planned that the required programmes and textbooks will be produced at least one year before the introduction of each grade or level. This implies a steady rise in the number of books needed each year, rising to around fifty new books in 1985 and to nearly one hundred in 1990. At this stage, not only will books be needed for the General and Adult Education sub-systems but also for the technical subsystem. Publishing of new textbooks for parts of the old system and for the proposed distance education programme will be needed, as well as the substitution of textbooks produced for the National Education System and the reprinting(often with revisions) of other books. On this basis, the INDE has proposed the establishment of a publishing house.

In terms of the manpower needed for all this work, it must be stated that a lack of curriculum planners and textbook writers with experience has been felt from the very beginning of the process, even for the initial levels. As the introduction of the National Education System reaches higher levels and grades, the existing subgroups will have difficulty in meeting the capacity required. For curriculum development to follow the desired timetable, extensive reinforcement in quality and quantity will be needed with trained and experienced personnel in all subject areas for all sub-systems.

Textbook Layout, Publishing and Printing

Since Independence, the overwhelming majority of textbooks have been printed and published in Mozambique. In 1980, an Editorial Nucleus was created in the INDE in order to edit, lay out and publish textbooks. Currently the nucleus has a staff of 12 including editors, layout personnel, illustrators, photographers and typists. The Editorial Nucleus receives the draft material from the subject groups after it has been approved by the Ministry, lays it out, does the illustrating, type sets the originals, edits and prepares the finished pages for photo-litho in the printing houses.

After book originals have been prepared, they are distributed to the ten or so printing houses in Maputo on the basis of a plan agreed between the INDE and the Institute for Books and Records of the Ministry of Information. In 1980 and again in 1981, over three and a half million school books were printed. According to the SIDA editor working for the Editorial Nucleus, future printing demands will require further extension of the printing and layout facilities available. In 1982, two first grade textbooks had to be printed in Portugal, at foreign exchange cost, owing to the lack of local printing capacity and behind schedule production.

Distribution of Textbooks and Other Didactic Material

Printed textbooks and other materials like pencils, pens, rulers, rubbers and exercise books are delivered to the MEC Maputo warehouse for countrywide distribution according to a central plan which takes into account numbers per province and the relative time priority for arrival. Breakdowns often occur in the system. These include:
-delays in initial delivery of material to the MEC warehouse;
-delays in boat departures and arrivals;
-damage to books en route;
-enemy action preventing transport of, or destroying books and material;
-lack of access to inland provinces and various districts, owing to enemy activity, to the weather destroying roads and bridges or to lack of land transport or truck breakdown;
-various problems such as whether to provide credit to the impecunious, how to distribute to distant parts of a district on foot and how to recuperate the selling price.

Given these problems, the system works surprisingly well. Transport at district level has always been a very severe problem; the state of the roads requires distribution to start before the rainy season commences in October, especially in the north. The land transport fleet is always in a precarious state owing to lack of vehicles and of spare parts and accessories. The state of the roads and enemy destruction of vehicles have exacerbated the situation.

CURRICULUM POLICIES: NAMIBIA

Background

Education for the African majority in Namibia was in the hands of the different missionary societies from 1884 to 1962. The major aim of these societies was to convert the African to Christianity as a means of taming and disarming the African people. Misionary education did much to destroy African culture which has a lot of practical elements in its traditional educational activities. In African culture, the young learn from their parents and other adults all that is worth knowing and doing.

Missionary education introduced in Namibia the dichotomy between theory and practice. The theorists were the preachers and the teachers while the practitioners were the nurses, carpenters, masons and manual labourers. It should not, therefore, surprise us that many Africans set their sights on theoretical studies. However, to a small but important extent, missionary education introduced an awakening in the thinking of Africans, so that the South African regime could no longer allow this type of education to continue.

The Introduction of the Bantu Education System in Namibia

Bantu Education simply means that education for African children will be tailored to prepare them to do only those things that the white people want them to do. It is, therefore, an education system which does not allow independent thinking and does not encourage scientific inquiry. It does not value mathematical skills, technical drawing or technological training. Bantu Education attempts to produce perfect slaves.

We need to ask what causes Bantu Education to fail. Clearly, Bantu Education was introduced at the wrong historical time. The 1960s were the years of Independence in Africa and the spirit of freedom and African dignity dominated that decade. Bantu Education is too crude both in its theoretical foundation and its implementation.

Education for Liberation

Education for Liberation was born in the bushes of Zambia and Angola during the protracted armed liberation struggle. By 1973, SWAPO had a large following of school age children who could not fit into Zambian or other education systems. Thus the Namibia Education and Health Centre was established in Zambia's Western Province.

By 1976, the Namibian population in Angola had swelled to thousands of people, including children, and another Namibian Education and Health Centre had to be created. This was in Kasinga and, tragically, it was destroyed during the Kasinga Massacre of 4 May 1978. The survivors were later transferred to Kwanga Sul Province in Central Angola. A large number of students were sent to Cuba where they continued their primary, secondary and university education.

The physical establishment of schools is difficult and demanding but more difficult is the creation of curriculum content that is in line with the aspirations of our people. With the help of international organisations, we have been able to produce relevant learning materials. UNESCO helped us in the field of curriculum development; Finnida assisted us with textbook publication and the University of Bremen's Namibia Project worked with us to produce Namibian history and geography textbooks for our secondary schools.

The SWAPO Schools in Zambia and Angola

These are basically primary schools, although they also allow junior secondary training. The subjects covered include: mother tongue, English, mathematics, development studies, science, technical training, agriculture and sports and culture. There is also provision for clubs for languages (French, German) and other special interests.

Within these schools, adult training programmes are carried out. The adult programmes cover literacy, distance education, secretarial courses, weaving and tailoring, carpentry and shoe-making, bricklaying and kindergarten teacher training. There is also a school for trade union activities and the transport department has courses in mechanics and car driving. All these activities are programmed to make the adult Namibian a useful member of his/her society. The physically handicapped and war victims have their own programme of training in useful work. Agriculture workers are trained and practise in SWAPO gardens.

The United Nations Institute for Namibia

The Institute was established in 1976 and is located in Lusaka in Zambia. Its objective is the training of managerial and administrative cadres who will carry on with the work left by South African whites who may depart from Namibia after Independence. It has a three year course which offers a Diploma in Development Studies and Management. After this basic diploma course, two year diploma courses are offered in magistrate training; teacher training; business administration; public administration and international relations and agriculture studies. The Institute also offers a course in secretarial training. Up to now, the Institute has trained over 1,200 cadres in development studies and management, over 100 teachers and over 60 magistrates.

An important area of the Institute's work is the publication of research papers by Institute lecturers on relevant socio-economic topics on Namibia. These research topics include: constitutional affairs, language policy, education, mining, trade, the electoral process and transport.

The United Nations Vocational Training Centre, Sumbe, Angola

This Centre was established with the financial assistance of the International Labour Organisation. It trains cadres in carpentry, building construction, car mechanics, agriculture, plumbing, electricity and other trades. Many war victims and former combatants have benefited from this programme. What is more, women have been dominant in fields such as car mechanics, car driving and electricity.

Namibia Secondary Technical School, Loundima, Congo

This is our most ambitious educational programme. Although constructed with Norwegian, Swedish, Finnish and Danish financial assistance, it is solely a SWAPO school. It aims to introduce and firmly establish the principle of marrying theory and practice, education and production. As the name indicates, it has a strong bias towards science and agriculture, the latter being a core subject for all students. Carpentry and metalwork are also offered and both boys and girls are encouraged to study home economics. The school is a model for the type of school we would like to introduce in Namibia after Independence. It has also been the testing ground for our curriculum development activities.

We expect this school to produce students able to study medicine, engineering, science and technology. Since the school is in the Congo, French is taught as a subject. Competency in both English and French may help those who want to study public administration and international relations.

Future Prospects

Implementation of the SWAPO education policy will be difficult and slow. Some of the reasons for the anticipated difficulties are:

-the official language is not yet widely spoken;
-national disunity as a result of ethnicity being over emphasised;
-it will take time before complete peace and harmony are restored throughout Namibia;
-the shortage of trained teachers and other educationists;
-lack of school facilities, especially in rural areas, and lack of equipment and textbooks;
-anticipated student population explosion;
-integration of all educational programmes at home and abroad will be necessary in order to create a unitary national education system;
-it will be necessary to create institutions and programmes to care for ex-combatants, war victims,,etc.;
-the need to make educational opportunities democratic and universal for all our students;
-the need for finance for all these essential educational programmes.

In conclusion, we look forward to Independence, knowing well that the struggle for national reconstruction will then just have started. During these many years in exile, we have established valuable contacts and programmes. It is our hope that our colleagues and friends will continue to support us, even increasing their assistance. Major educational issues still remain to be decided by the government of the new Namibia. Among these issues are: the creation of a national university; the establishment of a curriculum centre and the creation of an effective nationwide technical and vocational training programme. With the genuine support we have received, we are encouraged to continue the educational struggle, confident of the final victory in educating our youth for employment and citizenship.

CURRICULUM POLICIES: SWAZILAND

Introduction

The population of Swaziland is approximately three-quarters of a million. Of this population, 47% is said to be of the 0-14 age range. About 80% of the population live in the rural areas and the rest in urban and industrial areas. The majority of the population depends on subsistence farming for a living.

The economy is a free enterprise system which encourages local and foreign investment. Since the country is naturally endowed with fertile soil, an abundance of water and a conducive climate, agriculture constitutes the backbone of the country's economy. The major cash crops include sugar cane, citrus fruits and cotton. Despite the fact that the largest section of the population is in the rural areas and depends on agricultural farming for subsistence, the country still has a long way to go before it reaches self-sufficiency in food supply, including maize, which is the staple food.

The Education System

The education system has three cycles: primary, secondary and tertiary education.

Primary education takes seven years to complete and is usually completed at about the age of 12. The results of the examination written at grade 7 serve as a criterion for selection for Form I.

Secondary education spans over a period of five years from Form I to 5. The graduates at this level complete at the age of about 17. Of the total number of children who begin Form I, only 20% proceed to the fifth form. The children who complete Form V with a first or second class proceed to the University which offers four year degree programmes or to colleges which offer three year diploma programmes. Some of the remaining completers find employment of one kind or another and the others go into vocational education.

After Independence, steps were taken to introduce education reforms at both primary and secondary levels in order to better prepare the graduates of the system for effective participation in the development of the country. The national goals of education guiding curriculum development strategies and classroom practice from primary to secondary can be summarised as follows:

1) understanding of the child's own culture and respect for cultures which are different from his/hers;
2) respect for authorities and the rights of others;
3) ability not only to benefit from what society can offer but also to contribute to that society;
4) ability to use scientific methods of enquiry to solve problems;
5) ability to give scientific explanations for natural phenomena;
6) creativity and resourcefulness in life situations.

In order to achieve the above, the curriculum and teaching strategies had to be revised. Practical arts (an integration of agriculture, home economics, art and crafts, business education, physical education and music) had to be introduced in primary schools in order to equip children with survival skills. At secondary level, practically oriented subjects including agriculture, home economics and technical subjects had to be introduced. What is more, secondary education had to be highly practically oriented and geared to the needs of self-employment and also had to provide a broad enough training to enable the more able students to continue to Form IV and V. It was also important that the syllabuses for primary and secondary education were constructed with the local situation in mind.

The teaching approach had to change from the traditional one of 'chalk and talk' to that where a child learns by doing. The approach can be summarized in the following points:

1) using the environment as a learning resource and allowing the child to interact with it;
2) introducing a practical bias to learning where the child is actively involved in his/her own learning process;
3) encouraging a problem-solving approach to learning;
4) encouraging field trips to expose children to the outside world and especially to industries and business;
5) encouraging the use of resource persons in the community as instructors in their area of specialisation to bring the community

closer to the school.

These education reforms were to be accomplished through systematic curriculum development processes. This necessitated the establishment of the National Curriculum Centre. Institutionalising curriculum development meant that the school curriculum would continually be reviewed and kept in line with constantly changing needs. The curriculum reforms had implications for teacher training procedures. The pre-service programmes had to be revised and brought in line with the new curriculum and in-service programmes had to be launched for serving teachers.

At present, there are plans to restructure the primary and secondary education phases. Firstly, it has been observed that children complete primary education at the age of 12. Given that a large number of students, 34%, do not proceed to secondary education, 12 is considered a very tender age for children to terminate formal schooling. Furthermore, it is considered that however useful the skills they have acquired at primary level are, they may not be much use to children who are still too small either to join the labour market or to set themselves up in self-employment. It is proposed that a nine year basic education be introduced. This will necessitate the phasing out of the Primary Certificate Examination, taken at the end of Grade 7 and the Junior Certificate Examination taken at Form III. At the end of the ninth grade, children will be about 15 years old and should be able to fend for themselves or develop themselves through the available non-formal and vocational programmes.

With the introduction of a nine year basic education system, it is expected that the guidance and counselling programme of the Ministry will be strengthened to help direct children according to their natural abilities and inclinations. Furthermore, since examinations will be phased out throughout the nine years of basic education, it is planned that a systematic programme of continuous assessment will be introduced.

Secondly, there are plans to introduce pre-vocational education. The reason for this move is that provision needs to be made for the different talents and abilities of children. The aim is to enable all children to pursue programmes for which they are suited. In the light of the high rate of unemployment, it is hoped that on completion of secondary education, children will be able to develop or set themselves up in some form of income generating project. It is envisaged that the pre-vocational streams will follow the same secondary school curriculum; except that in the case of practical subjects, the weighting between theory and practicals will be in favour of practicals.

Vocational Education

At Independence, there was one vocational institution. It has since been expanded to offer both craft and technician courses. The last ten years have witnessed an expansion in terms of the vocational course offerings and of the number of vocational institutions. At present, there are four vocational institutions, with three more in the pipeline.

The vocational institutions are a government priority because there is a need to meet the manpower requirements of the country's fast expanding economy and there is a need to equip the youth with the necessary skills not only to be competent job seekers but job creators as well.

Non-Formal Education

Non-formal education is a strong component of the Ministry of Education; it attempts to cater for people, young and old, who did not have the opportunity to go to school and attend a formal vocational institution. This form of education also attempts to improve the quality of life of the majority of the population living in both urban and rural areas by equipping them with skills which enable them to start income generating projects. The courses offered include basic literacy; agricultural farming; upholstery; dressmaking; printing; panel beating; leatherwork; tailoring; welding; motor mechanics; pottery; handicrafts; woodwork; secretarial courses and business education.

Constraints

Though the country has tried to diversify the education offered to both young and old to overcome the problem of unemployment, this attempt has not been without difficulties. The problems are numerous and solutions are not easy, especially as some of them lie outside the realm of education. The following are examples of the problems we encounter:

1) lack of teachers to teach technical and vocational subjects;
2) lack of funds to provide adequate facilities for special subjects;
3) lack of capital for graduates of vocational and non-formal education to

set up small businesses;

4) a land tenure system which makes it difficult for those who would like to do agricultural farming;
5) the conservative attitude of graduates expecting to be employed rather than use their skills to create jobs for themselves;
6) lack of proper guidance for graduates resulting in the majority of them doing the same thing, hence saturating the market with their commodities;
7) lack of a market for the commodities produced;
8) lack of business management skills among graduates of vocational institutions.

Possible Solutions

The solution to the problem of unemployment is not simple and the possible solutions suggested below should by no means be regarded as a panacea to this complex problem.

The tendency in industry is to recruit unqualified personnel and then train them. Since the graduates of vocational institutions cannot be sure of getting employment on completion of their programmes, an attempt should be made to emphasise the importance of self-employment rather than preparing them for employment. There is also a need to set up a machinery for assisting graduates of vocational institutions in setting themselves up. This could be done by establishing a department for this task or having it built in as part of the training institutions' follow-up programme. It is also essential to help graduates find markets for their commodities.

The attitude of society towards vocational subjects has to be changed. Part of the solution lies in giving good remuneration to people with vocational skills to make this type of training attractive. A business management component has to be part of vocational/technical training if graduates are to be able to set up and manage their own businesses. Lastly, there is a need to establish a loan system for graduates of vocational education to enable them to obtain the needed capital to start projects.

CURRICULUM POLICIES: TANZANIA

The Experience of Tanzania

The work of curriculum development or reform in any society requires that the new curriculum be based not only on the philosophy and goals of development of that society but even more on the society based educational objectives. Tanzania, as a nation, has based its development philosophy on Ujamaa and self-reliance as elaborated in the Arusha Declaration of 1967.

Tanzania aspires to develop its people along the lines of Ujamaa socialism in which every able-bodied person is required to do productive work; in which the major sources of production of national income and general economy are owned, managed and controlled by the people through their cooperatives or other public institutions and in which the welfare of the people is the central focus in all development planning.

In the 1982 Report of the Presidential Commission on Education, the twenty year old practices and performance in education have been reviewed and evaluated and , based on its findings, recommendations for the future have been made. In that report, a whole chapter calls for reforms in curriculum across the spectrum of education. This recommendation reflects, on the one hand, upon the possible conservatism of curriculum developers in their delay in proposing the reforms needed since 1967 and, on the other hand, the unpreparedness of the society to equip itself for implementation of the new curriculum for lack of the necessary inputs.

The Role of the Institute of Curriculum Development

The Tanzania Institute of Curriculum Development is an independent parastatal under the Ministry of Education. It reports to the Commissioner of Education who is the ministry's chief of educational and academic practices in schools and colleges. The Institute is charged with the legal responsibilities of developing and, where necessary, reviewing the curricula; developing educational materials, teaching aids and equipment; in-servicing teachers and conducting research in curriculum matters and using the results to advise the government on the improvements which are needed.

The Process of Curriculum Development

In drawing up educational goals relevant to the political, socio-economic and cultural needs of the country, Tanzania's practice has been to work through subject panels composed of interest groups such as subject specialists to establish the relevance of different subjects in development; educational psychologists to establish the learnability of prescribed concepts, ideas, skills and attitudes; and philosophers, including politicians, sociologists and religious leaders. The panels work together to translate and put into operation national broad aims of education which are put into curriculum and instructional objectives, learning experiences, selected and organised content, development of instructional materials and evaluation of the effectiveness of the resulting curricula.

The broad aims of education in Tanzania can be deduced from the concept of Education for Self-Reliance and have been explicitly spelt out in the 1982 Report of the Presidential Commission on Education. Most curriculum materials produced by the Institute are tabled for consideration by the primary, secondary, teacher training and technical education programme committees before they are piloted, adjusted and recommended to the Commissioner for Education for endorsement and adoption. The Institute also produces instructional materials in the form of textbooks, teachers' guides, teaching aids, charts and other instructional devices.

Education Packages

In response to the recommendations of the Report of the Presidential Commission on Education at the primary, secondary, technical and teacher education levels, the Institute is presently preparing research for fieldwork in which a cross-section of people will be interviewed in an effort to identify the kinds of content that are considered appropriate, suitable and relevant to the needs of Tanzania and its learners.

This research has been prompted by the complaint that schools are offering too many subjects; that some of the content is irrelevant and that there is more relevant content which has not been included in the existing curricula.

The research will also respond to the need to streamline diversification and vocationalisation of the curriculum in line with the demands and spirit of Education for Self-Reliance. The reviewed educational packages will give students curricula that are appropriate and suitable to their needs.

In order for a country to have timely responses to the calls for reviews and reforms in the curricula, there is a need for trained curriculum developers. When the policy of Education for Self-Reliance was pronounced, ministry officials and school administrators responded by expressing their readiness. However, there were no trained curriculum developers to do systematic curriculum evaluation of past practices and so to recommend new educational packages. The Institute has now embarked on a programme of identifying and meeting training needs and ensuring that all teachers, especially those appointed to curriculum reform work, are properly trained through in-house seminars, short or long courses.

Diversification and Vocationalisation of Curricula

At the primary education level, the emphasis is to ensure permanent literacy, numeracy and the ability to communicate effectively through writing and proper use of language. Other academic subjects are offered in order for the students to understand and appreciate the rich potential in their environment and to develop their mental capabilities for formal or non-formal higher education.

In order to prepare the young people for the realities of real life where most of them will not get paid jobs in the formal sector, uncertificated practical skills of agriculture are offered in the hope that many of the young people will engage in agriculture for survival. Post-primary training wings have also been established in different primary schools where skills training programmes are offered in carpentry, metalwork, masonry, home crafts etc. However, no trade/ test certificates are offered.

At the secondary level, the curriculum is diversified and vocationalised. Academic and vocational subjects are offered by each school. Emphasis is directed to four broad vocational areas: agriculture, technical, commerce and home economics. Every secondary school is expected to follow one of these broad vocational areas up to '0' level.

For the young people who leave primary or secondary school, there is room for vocational training under the National Vocational Training Department (NVTD) of the Ministry of Labour. Such NVTCs offer trade test certificates.

Problems of Skills Training in Schools

Whereas the government is hopeful and the young people are anxious to come out of primary and secondary school equipped with both academic and employable skills in one or more trades, this aspiration is frustrated by a number of factors.

There has been the problem of not developing in time an appropriate vocational curriculum for schools. This deficiency has been caused mainly by lack of training on the part of curriculum developers. Assumptions often made are that teachers in schools can implement educational ideas without a clearly spelt out curriculum supported by essential inputs.

Where a vocational curriculum has been made available, some conservatism has surfaced about the place of the new subject in the already overloaded school timetable. What is more, parents resist vocationalisation of primary and secondary education for fear that the academic and white collar future of their children will be interfered with by such vocational involvements.

In many cases, there has not been adequate preparation or supply of vocational teachers and guidance career personnel in the vocationalised schools. Those expected to teach vocations turned into theorists, giving 'chalk and talk' lessons without practicals for lack of the necessary materials such as timber for carpentry practicals, metal for metalwork practicals, wires for practicals in electricity and electronics and even the basic ingredients for the home economics practical classes. The lack of local manufacturing industries for many work tools and the shortage of foreign currency to import equipment and tools continue to make vocational training in Tanzanian schools a dream rather than a reality.

For those young people who might be lucky enough to obtain some vocational training in primary or secondary schools, possible employing industries do not recognise their qualification. Some industries claim that schools are not the right places for skills teaching; rather they are academic centres. From academic schools, it is claimed, young people should then proceed to join vocational training centres where they are trained, trade tested and certified as fit to operate machinery in industry and elsewhere. On the other hand, young people who want and actually strive to learn vocations in the formal schools would like to be given certificates of competence in these vocational skills in order for them to have the potential for employment in the modern sector.

Vocationalisation of the school curriculum is also frustrated by the unpreparedness of society and the economy to absorb and utilize the vocationally trained pool of young people. Schools do not offer career counselling and guidance services. Graduates from schools are not given advice on the use and application of the skills they have learnt.

It is often rightfully claimed that vocationally trained young people should be able to create employment for themselves. This may be possible on rare occasions but, in many cases, the young people need a variety of predetermined projects they can take up, identify with or modify, according to their interests or needs. In order to be able to obtain a bank loan to start a project, the need arises for the young people to develop project proposals, project justification and anticipated management and accounting procedures.

Furthermore, the rural areas of the country may not be at all attractive to young people. There may not be good roads, transport facilities and other infrastructure, such as electricity, in the villages. This may make one wonder whether to establish one's productive project in a place where it will not be possible to sell or transport the product to the consumers or to establish the product in the urban centres. It is the lack of basic services which causes rural-urban youth migration.

Conclusion

Vocationalisation of the curriculum for skills development and job creation is necessary. It reflects the practical interpretation and aspiration of the spirit of Education for Self-Reliance. It needs well trained curriculum developers to re-examine the selection and content of the disciplines to be taught in schools and to integrate content in an effort to produce academically sobre yet skilful young people with an appreciation of the realities of the world of work, production and service. The need to standardise and certify one's readiness and potential on graduation also needs reflection.

The society and the general economy have to accept that vocationalising schools is in the interest of young people and benefits them, their parents and society as a whole. Existing financial institutions could be a great help to young people if they were more forthcoming in making known the procedures and conditions for loans to people who want to establish small, individual or cooperative economic projects.

There is a need for educationalists, trainers, economists and welfare experts in Africa to exchange ideas, to deliberate on issues and to draw up effective and workable strategies to link education, training and employment, especially for young people.

CURRICULUM POLICIES: ZAMBIA

The education system of Zambia is divided into three stages.

First Stage

The first stage, the Basic Education stage, has two levels, grades 1-7 and grades 8-9. The goal for the first level, generally known as primary level, is to assist the child to master essential learning skills which s/he can build on as s/he proceeds with further education or enters the world of work.

All the subjects offered at this level are compulsory and the list comprises mathematics, English, Zambian languages, creative arts, practical subjects and production work, physical education, political education, spiritual and moral education, environmental science, social studies and music.

At grades 8 and 9 the curriculum and other activities are more diverse. The programmes are not too specialized because of the variety of routes the student may follow after graduating from grade 9. They consist of general academic education and practical subjects. In the practical subjects emphasis is laid on the applied approach so that the pupils are at some stage during the learning process engaged in actually making useful products rather than token items in their productive activities.

All students are required to cover a common core area of the curriculum with options which include practical subjects. The core subjects offered are English, mathematics, general science, political education, social studies, physical education, spiritual and moral education, Zambian languages and production work. Optional subjects fall into two broad areas. The cultural/ creative group contains French, Zambian languages, art and craft and music. The practical subjects group contains industrial arts, agricultural science, commercial subjects and home economics. Pupils are required to choose one subject from the cultural/creative group and one subject from the practical subjects group. The industrial arts subjects are woodwork, metalwork, technical drawing and related subjects, depending on the facilities in the school. The subjects included in commercial subjects are office practice, typing and book-keeping. Guidance and counselling is included among school activities and is generally practised in the form of careers guidance.

In developing the relevant curricula for this stage, the general principles in curriculum development are observed. Measures are taken to avoid overloading of the programmes, to ensure continuity within a subject and integration between subjects and to ensure relevance by making the curriculum development process a participatory endeavour among relevant parties.

With regard to out of school training programmes, the party and government, in conjunction with local authorities and other agencies, including the Ministry of General Education, Youth and Sport and the Department of Technical Education and Vocational Training, have devised skills training programmes in a variety of occupational fields.

Second Stage

This stage is comprised of many varied programmes including grades 10-12 and training programmes like the Zambia Enrolled Nurse Course. Here we shall be concerned with grades 10-12.

Grades 10-12 are a preparatory stage to prepare students for entry to the third stage education programme. The curricula, therefore, are developed in close consultation and co-ordination with institutions offering courses and general education programmes in which the graduates of this stage may enrol. There is consultation between the Ministry of General Education and the tertiary institutions to, which some of the graduates will gain entry.

The curriculum at this stage consists of common core subjects which give students a general education and optional subjects, including practical subjects, which may be studied in greater depth. The subjects in the core group are English, mathematics, a science subject, political education, physical education and production work. At least one mathematics syllabus and one science subject are taken as part of the core course; other mathematical syllabuses, e.g. additional mathematics, and those science subjects not taken as part of the core course may be taken as options. There are five categories of optional subjects: humanities, science, mathematics, commercial subjects, technical and practical subjects.

Agricultural science is included among the sciences; the commercial subjects are commerce, economics, principles of accounts, shorthand and typing; the list of technical and practical subjects is comprised of food and nutrition, general housecraft, needlework and dressmaking, woodwork, metalwork, engineering, art and craft, music and geometrical and mechanical drawing.

The minimum number of optional subjects a student can take is four from at least two groups and the maximum number of optional subjects which can be taken is seven. Adequate guidance and counselling is provided to help students to select their optional subjects.

Vocational Training and Third Stage Education

Programmes in the Department of Technical Education and Vocational Training are planned to satisfy the manpower needs in the technical, commercial, agricultural and industrial sectors of the economy and also to facilitate meaningful Zambianization in critical areas of technology and economic activity. Institutions under the Department concentrate on full time pre-employment training and give in-depth theoretical knowledge integrated with practical programmes.

For trades and crafts training programmes the minimum entry requirement is grade 9. In general, these courses have three components: a six month basic training programme, a two year technical training programme and one year of practical work experience in the relevant industry or field. On graduation the trainees are awarded crafts certificates in fields such as agricultural mechanics, automotive mechanics and carpentry and joinery.

The entry requirement for technicians, technologists and air service training and other areas of vocational, business and commercial training is set at grade 12, school certificate level. Technician courses generally take three and a half years, including one year of industrial experience. Examples of technical courses are building, mine ventilation and refrigeration and air conditioning. The technologists' programmes, which lead to diplomas in fields such as industrial science, electronics and town and country planning, are of four years duration.

Education and Training for Self-Reliance

As much emphasis is put on education and training for self-reliance as is put on education and training for employment. The term employment also implies self-employment. A problem which has increased in recent years is that of unemployment. We are now faced with a surplus of fairly well educated and trained people chasing very few jobs. Two of the causes of this phenomenon are the negative attitude towards settling in the rural areas among school leavers and the near stagnation in economic growth in the country. There has also been a massive urban drift by rural people, particularly young men and women.

The government is trying to redress this situation through education by incorporating the teaching of skills for self-employment which school leavers can rely upon as a source of generating income for themselves. As a result of this initiative, numerous small scale industries have mushroomed in urban and rural areas. The skills and knowledge pupils acquire through learning practical subjects have helped to create more positive attitudes towards working and living in rural areas.

Our educational policies provide for equal access to education for all Zambians, regardless of gender. The government is trying to balance the number of girls and the number of boys in schools, particularly at secondary level, by having different cut off points for the sexes when selecting pupils for grade 8. The cut off point for girls is usually lower because, in general, there are fewer girls in school than boys. Tradition is the main cause of this imbalance; parents, especially in rural areas, do not consider the education of girls to be as necessary as the education of boys. For this reason, efforts to change attitudes have been aimed at parents.

CURRICULUM POLICIES: ZIMBABWE

Background

Since Independence, Zimbabwe has consistently argued that education, apart from being a human right and a basic human need, is an economic investment in human beings who are the means and end of all economic activity. In its first economic policy statement *Growth with Equity*, published in February 1981, the Government declared that education "will enable Zimbabweans to acquire a broad base of knowledge which will influence their attitudes, values and skills and on which they can build in later life . . . . Without the output of the educational system it will be impossible to sustain, let alone accelerate, economic growth and development."

In pursuit of these principles, the government introduced free primary education and it regards the introduction of universal primary education as its next goal. Running side by side with this development has been the dramatic expansion of secondary and tertiary institutions.

However, this increase in educational provision has not been matched by a comparable growth in the economy. On the contrary, the economy has largely remained static and maintained its 1979 absorptive capacity. In fact, viewed against the background of an increased population growth rate, it can be argued that the number of jobs available in the formal sector in 1989 has declined, in real terms, compared to the number of jobs in 1979. Since the formal employment sector has maintained its 1979 absorptive capacity, there are more jobless school leavers on the streets. Far reaching strategies have been adopted to cope with the increasing number of school leavers in a situation of a static economy. All sectors have been challenged to come up with a job creation programme.

On a formal level, technical-vocational institutions have been established throughout the country to provide the skills needed in all sectors of the economy. The programmes address manpower needs and turn out skilled artisans and journeymen ready to take up an active productive role. As part of the same package, upgrading programmes have been run to give skilled status to experienced workers who were dubbed semi-skilled or unskilled to suit the purposes of successive colonial administrations.

Another orientation of these institutions is to provide technical-managerial know-how to peasant farmers, small enterprises and co-operative groups. These programmes have also encouraged school leavers to form production orientated co-operatives in order to make a living for themselves.

Curriculum Policies and Principles

The colonial system of education Zimbabwe inherited was designed to create a cadre of clerical and administrative staff and teachers and nurses to service the colonial administration while that administration depended on expatriates. The system fostered attitudes which looked down on manual productive work. In fact, education was regarded as an escape route from this kind of work.

When, as a result of contradictions within the system, the colonial administration was persuaded to introduce production oriented strands into the curriculum, the level was geared to produce operatives devoid of initiative. At Independence, this curriculum was discarded and new principles and policies were introduced to ensure that it would serve socio-economic needs and be a vehicle for employment creation.

While accepting that primary education should provide a broad general education, the need to use it for the purpose of establishing a firm mathematical and scientific foundation was confirmed. It was also felt that it should be used for creating positive attitudes to work through engagement in simple production activities. Schools were directed to introduce Education with Production to primary school children.

At the secondary school level, the employment-related approach has found full expression. The mathematical and scientific input is intensified and technology is taught across the curriculum. The technical-vocational subjects of woodwork, metalwork, building, technical drawing, graphic art, food and nutrition, fashion and fabrics, home management, art and craft, commerce, principles of accounts and economics are offered throughout the system with individual schools offering at least two subjects.

The concept of Education with Production was introduced in eight pilot schools by the Zimbabwe Foundation for Education with Production

(ZIMFEP). While it has not been possible to replicate ZIMFEP schools on a national scale, serious attempts have been made to integrate theory and practice in all schools.

In 1984 technical kits were introduced to beef up the teaching of technical subjects at the Zimbabwe Junior Certificate level. The following year, this programme was extended to '0' level. The result of this has been the widespread introduction of technical-vocational subjects across the curriculum as kits freed the teaching of these subjects from a dependence on workshops. What is more, the teaching of accounting-managerial subjects has given students entrepreneurial skills which enable them to run their production enterprises on sound business lines.

Perhaps the most promising innovation has been the vocationalisation of secondary school education through the introduction of technical-vocational subjects at the Zimbabwe National Craft Certificate (ZNCC) level. To date, 29 schools have introduced the programme, offering one subject each at ZNCC level. The subjects offered are machine shop engineering, motor mechanics, bricklaying/blocklaying, cabinet making and carpentry and joinery. Another 48 schools have started offering typewriting at Pitman's intermediate level. It is intended to include specialist areas in agriculture and home economics. The programme is heavily dependent on expensive machinery and specially trained teachers and its diffusion through the system, therefore, will necessarily be slow.

In the field of technical colleges, rapid expansion followed Independence. In 1979 there were two technical colleges; by 1989, the number had increased to seven with a total enrolment of 11,577 students. There are also three Vocational Training Centres (VTC), one in Bulawayo and two in Harare; these cater for apprenticeship programmes. Vocational Training Schools (VTS) were also created to produce graduates who either work individually or in cooperatives. These graduates have found a ready market at growth points and in rural schools which they supply with vegetables, furniture and school uniforms. Some of these schools belong to private groups and NGOs. Subjects offered in these schools include metalwork, building, automotive mechanics, leather work and tailoring. Because of the co-operative nature of this scheme, the Curriculum Research and Development Unit (CRADU) has introduced such subjects as business studies, social studies, business language and accounts to cater for the entrepreneurship aspects in the programme.

A problem that has plagued our technical colleges is the shortage of appropriately qualified lecturers which has made us rely on expatriate expertise. To correct this, we started a Staff Development Programme of sending some of our college lecturers overseas to train in various courses.

The University is now offering B.Ed. programmes in a number of technical-vocational subjects. A recent development is the intention to establish a second university which will be development oriented and which will boost the number of technically trained teachers who are needed to make our vocationalisation programmes succeed.

Challenges

These programmes pose a number of serious challenges which it will take time to overcome. These are:

1) Inadequate supply of suitably qualified and experienced teachers for practical subjects.

2) Lack of facilities and equipment which are expensive and need foreign currency.

3) Lack of financial resources for raw materials.

4) Poor organisational methods within schools trying to introduce technical vocational subjects, especially in relation to timetabling.

5) Lack of supportive attitudes from parents and pupils who associate good education with academic subjects.

6) Inadequate hands-on experience which, in some cases, involves twinning schools to factories and farms.

7) Lack of credit facilities for co-operating school leavers who do not meet the collateral requirement of finance houses.

SECTION 2

THE BOTSWANA BRIGADES: BOTSWANA'S EXPERIENCE OF EDUCATION FOR EMPLOYMENT, 1965-89

Q.N. Parsons

Introduction

The Brigades movement in Botswana provides an instructive test case of a practical scheme of education for employment in a Southern African country, over nearly a quarter of a century. It is a case history that shows that the development of such a scheme is determined more by the changing political economy of a country, than by the internal dynamics and personalities within the scheme. But at the same time, by setting the agenda of the movement, the basic questions posed by its founders have still to be confronted by those who have taken over the movement.

The Brigades movement began as a semi-formal response to the 'school-leaver problem', as seen around one particular secondary school run on progressive lines. One brigade proliferated into many, and spread to other centres, becoming a movement. But while the ideology of the movement developed through cooperative ideas into ideas of total communal transformation, the actual institutions of the movement were coopted by government and gradually formalised into the lowest level of national post-primary vocational education.

In order to understand this case history, one must look at its three phases. But first one must understand the changing context of national political economy in which it was set.

Botswana's development

The modern economic history of Botswana is well known: from a per capita income around US$50 in the mid-1960s to around US$1000 by the early 1980s. The concomitant social effects of such economic growth are less well known. On the one hand, the familiar litany of the rich growing richer, and a new rich class growing out of the national bureaucracy; massive export of investible surplus through an export-oriented economy dominated by multi-national corporations, and lack of internally-generated development of production. But, on the other hand, a general consensus that the poor for the most part have not grown poorer, but on the contrary a general rise in living standards - water, medical services, education and roads extended to the majority of the population. Economic growth also bolstered a relatively open political system, under a political elite that grew out of the contradictions of local politics, more or less responsible to a national electorate of which the numerical majority were older rural women.

First Phase 1965-71

The first Botswana Brigade was founded when the country was very poor. It was founded in 1965 in the rural town of Serowe, then the biggest population centre and the most important political centre within colonial Botswana. (The new capital, Gaborone, built out of virgin bush, had only just opened in 1964-65).

The founder of the Brigades was Patrick van Rensburg, a South African exile who was to become a Botswana citizen. His personal viewpoint of the painful step-by-step growth of Brigades can be read about in his sequence of publications with overlapping content, each reflecting a new stage of progressively changing thought - notably the books *Report from Swaneng Hill* (Uppsala, 1974), *The Serowe Brigades* (The Hague/ Basingstoke & London, 1978), and *Looking Forward from Serowe* (Gaborone, 1984). In these publications we can see how ad hoc responses to circumstances, and crises in particular, were transformed into ideological virtues - virtues, such as the principle of 'cost-covering', which had to be deconstructed and reformulated with each phase of growth of the Brigades movement.

Van Rensburg had founded a secondary school at Serowe in 1962-63, in response to local political demand after a Christian mission had failed to fulfil its earlier promise. The school, Swaneng Hill, soon found the number of applicants overwhelming. So the first Brigade was formed in 1965 to give general building skills to young men who, unlike their younger and more academically suited brothers and sisters, could not be admitted to the secondary school. This first Brigade supplemented and then largely replaced the building efforts of regular students within a school based on a self-help philosophy. In effect, Swaneng Hill became a two stream school: an academic stream with 80 per cent class work and 20 per cent manual work; and a vocational steam with 80 per cent manual work and 20 per cent class work. The Brigade covered its training and equipment costs by income from its production, at first for the school and then for outside contracts in Serowe - a figure around US$30 000 by 1968.

The first Brigade proved to be a great success in answering local building needs and the skills shortage in a large country town recovering from the economic effects of prolonged drought. It made a start in providing local employment for a male labour force that had been reduced to massive out-migration since the 1930s; and it opened eyes to the problem of what to do with the 88 per cent of primary school leavers for whom there were no secondary school places. The Brigade also fitted in with local traditions of community service and education under the leadership of local traditional authorities, as well as with lapsed ideals of industrial education once espoused by the formal educational sector in Botswana prior to 1945.

Over a decade, from 1967 onwards, the successful Brigade formula was extended at Serowe from builders to farmers, weavers and dress-makers and mechanics, with long-term plans for brick-makers, lime-burners, even iron-smelters and smiths, glass-makers and beer-makers. Swaneng Hill was to be a city built on a hill that would spread its light to the wider rural society, as a model modernised self-sufficient rural community. This was a utopian ideal which was actually realised, so far as it could be, by 1976-79 when the Serowe Brigades had 510 trainees, 125 salaried staff, and 226 other employees, with an annual turnover in excess of US $1 000 000.

The Brigades initiative in education led to a Brigades initiative in employment. The first cohort of building trainees posed the question: after training, what? The impoverished economy of central Botswana had very limited formal employment, and the trainees as graduates lacked business skills and capital to become self-employed. The answer was to develop the cooperative ideal of self-employment on a group basis. A construction cooperative, known as Con-Coop, was set up as a limited company in 1966-67, moving north to Shashe and Francistown, and finally collapsing in 1972. There were two obvious problems which made Con-Coop 'uncompetitive' in the open market: first was financial management, second was dilution of work pace and standards by taking on too many unskilled and trainee workers. A third, less obvious problem was to prove more fundamental: the conflict between the general building skills provided by Brigades against the demands for specialised skills in the formal building sector.

The question of 'after training, what?' was answered by the 1969-71 building boom, with increasing demand for semi-skilled labour in formal employment in central Botswana, brought on by the start of diamond and copper-nickel mining. Without the Builders Brigades, the development of Botswana's infrastructure would have been even more dependent on the import of foreign labour. (The vocational training school set up by government at Gaborone in 1962 concentrated almost entirely on clerical training after 1964).

There was, however, no such simple solution for the second type of Brigade at Swaneng Hill, the Farmers Brigade. Attempts to settle Brigade graduates in farming cooperatives near Serowe and Mochudi were unsuccessful. Besides difficulty in getting land allocated to youth by the traditional gerontocracy, the farms lacked the capital and management skills for modernised farming. Most basic of all, the youths proved to be too feckless to live off low initial shared income, and expected formal wages as from a formal employer. Commercial farms on the borders of Botswana, however, were the least likely to employ ambitious young men demanding good wages.

The Brigades were a successful penetration into the political economy of Botswana, which eventually won conversion of the political establishment. At first the Brigades saw themselves, and came to be seen, as a threat to the late colonial political economy - by promoting ideals and practicalities of economic and social self-sufficiency away from previous South African and Southern Rhodesian dominance. The office of the British High Commissioner in South Africa attempted to nip Swaneng Hill in the bud by feeding the Bechuanaland authorities with scare stories of a 'commie' hotbed. This failed to persuade the new political elite, otherwise cautiously conservative, which saw the future if only vaguely in terms of a cooperative movement to lift rural areas by the bootstraps - this being before the prospect of future mineral wealth opened up slowly in 1967-69.

Botswana became independent towards the end of 1966. By the next year the new Department of Community Development had taken up the Brigades idea to set up three new Builders Brigades elsewhere in the country. By 1968 the Ministry of Education was won round to seeing Brigades as the revival of the old idea of 'industrial' departments attached to secondary schools. Such was the openness to ideas of self-help in government circles before the mineral boom opened the floodgates for offers of foreign 'aid'.

Second Phase 1971-80

The Brigades movement was fed by and helped to feed the economic boom of the 1970s. But in helping to transform Botswana, it was itself transformed in line with developments in the political economy. Self-help cooperative ideals gave way to ideas of competition in a monopoly-dominated 'free' market.

Other Brigades centres, with at least a Builders Brigade, were founded in imitation of, or in contrast to, the Swaneng Hill model at Serowe - thirteen more Brigades centres by the mid-1970s. Each had a different fate. A few collapsed, the main reason being that the Department of Community Development decentralised itself from Gaborone to the districts and thereby lost its dynamism and vitality as a national movement. But most of these lapsed centres subsequently revived, and some centres split into two centres, so that by the early 1980s there were more than twenty centres. The 1970s also saw the growth of rival self-help community development projects outside of, and consciously contrasting with, the Brigades movement - such as the Lentswe-la-Odi Weavers Cooperative, Pelegano Village Industries at Gabane, Southern Rural Development Association and Rural Industries Innovation Centre at Kanye - all heavily dependent on the new streams of foreign 'aid' being offered Botswana, which had now become respectable in the world community in contrast to South Africa and Southern Rhodesia.

From 1970-71 the Brigades movement was brought under the wing of the Ministry of Education, in the National Brigades Coordinating Committee (NBCC). The NBCC, initially dominated by van Rensburg, started by calling the tune for the formulation of future rural development policies, based on government mineral revenues, through the setting up of a

National Rural Development Council. However, this initiative was quickly taken over by advisers and planning officers funded through British, American, Scandinavian, and eventually West German, 'aid'. The national economy expanded, government revenues rose, and economic growth did 'trickle down' to the rural towns where most Brigades were centred.

Increased government income pulled government policy in two contrary directions. On the one hand to talk about rural development as the way in which the masses would share in the mineral wealth. On the other hand, in a world of increasing inflation following the oil price hike, being forced to concede higher and higher wages in the formal sector of the economy - thus widening the gap with rural incomes.

Within Brigade centres there was a growing diversity of production and community activities, aimed at uplifting the lives of poorer members of the community either through direct employment or extension activities and adult education. In government eyes the model Brigades centre was Molepolole rather than Serowe, with its emphasis on commercial viability rather than on building an alternative socialist society. At a time of increasing international tension and insecurity on the part of the Botswana government, as the Rhodesian war drew to its climax, Serowe Brigades embarked on a breakneck plan of autonomous expansion, and threw in its lot with socialist opposition to government. Government responded by throwing the legal book at Serowe Brigades, insisting that it must not be run by an internal democracy but must follow the Molepolole model - under a board of trustees elected at an open meeting of the community outside the Brigades.

Deprived of power, the Serowe managers opted for pay. Salary hikes put Serowe Brigades into bankruptcy. Van Rensburg resigned and left Serowe. The obvious clash of policies and personalities makes a good story, but Serowe was not alone in suffering crisis. Runaway inflation of costs, increasing failure to recover costs, and covering of recurrent losses by pouring in new capital from foreign donors, proved to be beyond the limited managerial capacity of Brigades. When the biggest Brigade centre, Serowe, began to teeter and collapse, the second biggest, Molepolole, began to have financial woes as well, and smaller Brigades centres followed in quick succession.

Third Phase 1980-89

The economy of Botswana suffered a temporary levelling off in 1980-82, due to a diamond glut in the world market and cattle disease at home in the north and centre. This gave government a time for reflection and evaluation at the same time as foreign donors went wild for project evaluation. The Brigades centres at Serowe, Molepolole, Mochudi, Shashe, and in a lesser way elsewhere, were all drastically evaluated and forced to curtail their activities - and to render separate accounts for each activity so that one did not unconsciously cross-subsidise another. The Brigades centres that survived best were the small 'development trusts' with little or no training activities and few staff - concentrating on a few viable production schemes to finance community development extension work.

There was a hiatus in government support for Brigades between August 1980 and June 1983, a period of reflection and indecision which spread to foreign donors and to the Brigades movement as a whole. Serowe Brigades centre petered out and actually closed in 1983-84. Government planners were given the brief of reconsidering the movement in the light of the fifth (1979-85) National Development Plan goal of employment creation - constrained by government insistence on 'deregulating' the economy by withdrawal of any direct state participation in production.

The neatest solution was for government to take over the training brigades as the lowest level of a new national technical and vocational education system, and to set the production and development Brigades free as autonomous 'development trusts'. But this neat dichotomy, for the bureaucratic convenience of government would have torn the heart out of the Brigades movement - the combination of education with production. Birds cannot fly on one wing. The Brigades movement itself, meanwhile, wanted to combine autonomy with government subsidy by converting its central support and training body BRIDEC (the Brigades development centre under the ministry of education's technical and vocational department) into a National Brigades Trust.

Action was eventually forced by a popular outcry in the districts, at the collapse of the most visible form of rural development promotion in the major rural centres - an outcry channelled to central government through the annual gathering of district development officials. The compromise solution achieved was for government to save the training Brigades by higher subsidy and thus to free the non-training units of Brigades for autonomous expansion. BRIDEC was upgraded within the ministry of education to provide support for production and community service as well as education within the Brigades. Government was now free to concentrate its resources on developing second and third level technical and vocational education, content with leaving most first level TVE with the Brigades movement. Conversion of all training Brigades centres into district trade schools would have been prohibitively expensive, as well as counter-productive in destroying the Brigades movement. (The second level institutions are four Vocational Training Centres, three of which opened in 1988; while the third level is a Polytechnic in Gaborone).

The end result is that Botswana has lost ten years in the momentum of technical and vocational education for the formal sector of the economy. Not until 1989 has the number of trainees in Brigades recovered to the 1978 level of around 1200. Meanwhile the formal sector has doubled in number of employees - the 1979 and 1986 figures being 75 000 and 130 000 respectively. Even the projected figure of 1800 Brigades trainees in 1991 will still be falling behind the 1970s trend. (The trough of trainee enrolment was 683 in 1982).

It is not so easy to be categoric about the fate of non-training Brigades in passing through the fire of the late 70s and early 80s. The number of employees in Brigades tumbled from 1282 in 1980 to 796 in 1983, of whom 669 were production workers (and 60 were foreign volunteers in staff positions). But the success of production Brigades and of 'development trusts' cannot solely be measured in terms of direct ('stay-put') employment, but also by the 'through-put' elements of education and extension to the adult community around the centre.

How did the Brigades movement react? It is fair to say that while those centres engaged primarily in training suffered, the ones primarily engaged in production and community service on a small scale did not suffer. The later exponents of the 'development trust' idea even rejoiced at the movement being rid of youth training, supplying the needs of the rich formal sector, and being free to attend to the wants and needs of the rural poor. The Brigades movement can indeed be divided into two wings, private trade schools and 'development trusts', but the main body combines both functions, and the wings relate strongly to the main body.

The main concern of the Brigades movement in relation to government has been to make sure that it does not simply become a surrogate of the ministry of education, doing the ministry's work in technical and vocational education in return for only partial subsidy, and become diverted from its tasks of production and development "to improve the quality of life of rural people in Botswana". To this end the Brigades movement returned to the quest for some kind of National Brigades Trust, created out of the National Brigades Coordinating Committee, autonomous but financed by government as a thanks gesture for the movement's work in meeting national objectives of rural development and employment creation. Such claims were incorporated in a so-called Francistown Document of the NBCC, which was still being discussed with the ministry of education even in the week of this present conference.

There are two other concerns of the Brigades movement which are outstanding and perennial. One is community relations; the other is localisation of staff. The standard deed of trust, on the Molepolole model, states that the Brigades centre shall be governed by elected trustees. This precludes staff, workers and trainees in having a say in how the centre runs (though they may have a say in their own Brigade). But it also makes for difficulties in meeting the objectives of the Brigades movement. Put quite plainly, the rural poor (mostly women) tend to defer to successful men in elections who better represent their own interests than those of their constituents. The other question - localisation of staff - also suffers from the hierarchy of 'success' in society. Though there has recently been some success in retaining Batswana managers and staff on the basis of commitment to Brigades objectives, there is an inevitable tendency for many people to regard a Brigades staff job as a step-up, with training provided, into the more lucrative formal sector of the economy. They leave for a 'better' job.

Education and employment in Botswana today

The Brigades movement is of course but one part of wider attempts to "improve the quality of life of rural people in Botswana" through education with production. As participants in this conference will know, van Rensburg went on from Serowe to found the Foundation for Education with Production, an international body, whose two most famous daughters are ZIMFEP and BOTFEP. The latter's concerns cover work-study institutions such as training Brigades, as well as production cooperative activities (work-teams) and the incorporation of production in formal education.

The magnitude of the employment 'problem' in Botswana, with a small population and some significant economic growth, may not seem dramatic by other African standards. Nor is it yet generally realised by people, since the growth of education and the raising of the educational levels of unemployment, have lagged ten to fifteen years behind other African countries such as Zambia or Kenya. The size of the problem in Botswana is expressed by the size of the labour force, and the growth of output into the labour market by schools. In 1984-85, using new international standards of comparison, the labour force was put at just under 400 000 out of a population of more than a million; 22 per cent in formal employment and 5 per cent employed abroad; 9 per cent still in school; 10 per cent in 'self-employment' (peri-urban informal activities) and 4 per cent periodically employed; 28 per cent employed in traditional communal areas agriculture; and 22 per cent 'unemployed' but seeking work in the formal economy. Other estimates makes the size of the labour force larger, and the numbers of people (especially older women) in traditional agriculture much greater. Meanwhile most observers agree that 10 000 more school-leavers come onto the job market every year than can be employed in the formal sector, while popular expectations are that education to school leaving level (recently primary and now junior secondary) means inevitable employment in the formal sector.

The Botswana Brigades are therefore only a small, though significant, bite out of the unemployment apple. Tracer studies have shown that Brigades graduates are the most likely 'school-leavers' to get jobs in the formal sector. Ironically, few go into self-employment; though tracer studies chasing graduates of 20 years ago might give a different picture. A recent tracer did however find that plumbers from Maun were an exception in finding employment; but it may be retorted that the formal market for plumbing is small in such a remote town. All this underlines the fact that Brigades are the major supplier of lower level skills to skills-hungry employers in the towns of the east. The cost of equivalent level graduates from the government's Polytechnic or new VTC's is several times higher than Brigades. The effectiveness of the 1983 Apprenticeship Act, recently put into operation, remains to be seen in terms of overall cost. Present indications are that the scheme will not become widespread, beyond a few big employers with conscious interests in promoting the whole political economy, without a certain amount of coercion by government on private employers.

Possibly the long-term more effective future for Botswana's Brigades in tackling 'unemployment' lies in the 'development trust' wing of the movement, rather than in its private trade schools. A number of these development trusts and production units of Brigades have joined CORDE (Cooperation for Research Development and Education). CORDE grew out of the experience of previous attempts to create self-managed production cooperatives parallel to the Brigades, such as Boiteko the adult women's cooperative at Serowe and the more recent youth cooperative at Gaborone called Tshwaragano Enterprises. CORDE gives advice and support to 21 self-managed enterprises across the country, as a more modest version of government's BRIDEC towards the Brigades. It has its own programmes of stimulating food processing from local production, of encouraging low-cost housing building cooperatives in villages, and a programme in the Kgalagadi in conjunction with local authorities to raise the level of participation in development by people in the remotest areas. CORDE also holds workshops and workcamps on the sites of its members, to spread cooperative ideas of self-management. Maybe a hundred people will live together for five weeks, learning by their mistakes, to divide their labour as well as to combine their labour efficiently - with CORDE providing tools and ideas but only three days food before the group provides for itself. As elsewhere, progress with production coops is slow and painful.

Brigades have of course been pioneers for 25 years of ways in which to incorporate productive activities and understanding of production in the formal school curriculum. BOTFEP assisted some community junior secondary schools in productive activities, but such schools have looked forward to being taken over by government with the formal curriculum and facilities. Development Studies as a school subject fell from favour in Botswana during the recriminations of the late 1970s, but has come back in the 1980s - not least as an increasingly important element in curriculum development for Social Studies based on the contradictions between environment and development. One can also detect a corresponding emphasis on environment and development emerging in Integrated Science courses.

Select Bibliography

Botswana, Republic of. Ministry of Education, Brigades Development Centre. *Annual Report 1987/88 for Brigades Development Centre* (Gaborone: BRIDEC, 1988) 50 pp

Emanuelsson, A-C, E Franzen & A. Narman. *A Tracer Study Evaluation of the Botswana Brigades March-April 1988* (Goteborg: University of Gothenburg, Department of Human and Economic Geography, 1988) 51 pp

Gustafsson, I. *Schools and the Transformation of Work, a Comparative Study of Four Productive Work Programmes in Southern Africa* (Stockholm: University of Stockholm, 1987)

Hinchcliffe, K. *The Cost Effectiveness of Technical and Vocational Education in Botswana* (Gaborone: British Council & University of Botswana, for Ministry of Education, April 1988) 203 pp

Kann, U. *Education and Employment in Botswana* (Gaborone: British Council & University of Botswana, for Ministry of Education, June 1988) 167 pp

Kgathi, D.L. & Q.N. Parsons. *The Brigade Movement in Botswana: Annotated Bibliography* (Gaborone: National Institute for Research, Working Bibliographies No. 3, 1982)

Lockhart, L. (comp.) *Towards a New Relationship between Brigades and Government* (Gaborone: Ministry of Education, Brigades Review Working Group, 1982)

Narman, A. *The Botswana Brigades - Some Preliminary Notes* (Edinburgh: University of Edingburgh, Centre of African Studies, Botswana Seminar, December 1988) 14 pp

Parsons, Q.N. *Report on the Botswana Brigades 1965-83* (Gaborone: National Institute for Research, October 1983) 99 pp

Van Rensburg, P. *Looking Forward from Serowe* (Gaborone: Foundation for Education with Production, 1983)

Workteam (Nhimbe/Letsema/Ilima) No. 6, 1988 (Gaborone: CORDE) 41pp

EDUCATION FOR SELF-RELIANCE: THE TANZANIA EXPERIENCE

Professor N.A. Kuhanga (Chairman of the Committee for the Open University and Chairman of FEP)

Introduction

I have been asked to present to this august Seminar a critical review of Tanzania's experience in the implementation of its policy of Education for Self-Reliance (ESR). I find this to be a difficult task, for although the topic itself sounds simple, it is in fact a complex one as it has many aspects including political, economic, sociological and attitudinal ones. Thus, a critical review of it demands an indepth study of these aspects because without such a study it is difficult to do justice to the subject since conclusions may be based on incomplete truth.

I have not made such a study and therefore, what is presented in this paper is inevitably limited in scope, and is based on what I have been able to get from the available literature on the subject, and on my own limited experience.

The paper is divided into three parts. The first part deals with general views about ESR. It looks briefly at the introduction of the policy, the planning (or lack of planning) of implementation strategies and how it was interpreted by implementers at the various levels of the educational system. The second part deals with the implementation performance by educational institutions at the various levels of education, that is primary, secondary, tertiary and adult education. And the final part presents some of the lessons which can be learnt from the survey and which need to be studied carefully by all those concerned with the implementation of, and the challenges posed by the policy of Education for Self-Reliance.

General Views

Twenty years after the pronouncement of Education for Self-Reliance policy Mwalimu Nyerere (1989) reiterates that,

".... Education for Self-Reliance is not only the best, but also the only strategy by which this country can provide a good education for its young people; yet we have not been implementing it in its fullness. Educationalists seem to be a little afraid of its implications, and many members of the society - including some leaders - have been unable to free themselves from the mental attitudes to education inherited from colonialism." From this statement one notes three things. The first is that, after re-examining the policy for twenty years, Mwalimu Nyerere is more convinced that Tanzania took the right course in adopting Education for Self-Reliance, because, as Komba (1988) puts it, it is developmental and realistic. Komba adds that:

"It is based on the realism that man is born almost completely dependent on others for all his basic needs, and yet with a seed of self-reliance which is clearly noticeable almost from birth. Education should thus help him to grow less and less dependent on others and more and more dependent on his own abilities. "

The second thing which one notes is that there has been some success in implementing ESR but more efforts need to be exerted in order to implement it in its fulness. The third thing noted from the statement is that there are certain forces which militate against implementing in full a policy which has won acclaim even beyond Tanzania's borders. The question then is, which are these forces and what can be done to eliminate them or at least minimize their impact and gradually overcome them? According to available literature there are a number of forces and bottlenecks which impede smooth implementation of ESR but only a few of the most important ones will be discussed here.

Policy Formulations and Pronouncements

The policy of Education for Self-Reliance was formulated and pronounced within one month of the Arusha Declaration in March 1967. It was intended to be an elaboration on the implications of the Arusha Declaration and to give guidance to policy-implementers in the education system. It was also meant to clarify to the general public why there was need to reform the existing education system. The immediate response of the Ministry of Education was to organize a conference in Dar es Salaam "to study, understand and draw strategies to implement the message," (*Mmari, 1988)*

The Conference was attended by delegates from the Ministry Headquarters, Regional Education Officers, Principals of Teachers Colleges, Headmasters and Headmistresses of Secondary Schools, Representatives of Educational Agencies and other invitees from schools, colleges and the University of Dar es Salaam. According to Mmari, the "conference endorsed whole-heartedly the aims of education as outlined in the President's paper on Education for Self-Reliance and adopted several recommendations aimed at facilitating implementation of the new policy".

The recommendations covered the following areas:

1) The need for teachers, tutors and heads of institutions to study and understand the two documents, that is, the Arusha Declaration and Education for Self-Reliance;

2) The importance of re-orienting teachers and tutors to enable them to cope with the new challenge;

3) The need to review curricula at all levels of the education system so as to accommodate changes dictated by the new policy;

4) The need to review the examination system so that the examinations reflect all aspects of learning - cognitive, affective, psycho-motor - and the experience gained in carrying out economic and other self-reliant activities.

The conference was particularly concerned about the training of teachers and tutors and urged that the teacher-education curriculum should be reviewed in order to incorporate topics which should ensure that the training produced teachers and tutors with the right attitudes, understanding, knowledge and skills necessary for the implementation of ESR.

Furthermore, the conference recognized the importance of integrating the school with the community in which it is situated. It recommended therefore, students, teachers and other workers in the school should participate fully in all self-reliance activities carried out in the school and in the larger community.

Action by the Ministry of Education

It is evident from the above that the participants had studied the policy document adequately and contributed concrete ideas to facilitate the formulation of strategies for the implementation of ESR. However, the Ministry of Education did not act on the recommendations systematically with the expedience shown in organising the conference. It started acting two years later - in 1969 - by introducing an amendment to the existing Education Act in order to accommodate changes that were necessary for the implementation of ESR. In fact major reforms of the education system were not made until 1978 when a Committee for the Consolidation of Education was established to investigate possible ways of improving the quality of education at all levels; whose recommendations resulted in passing a new law thereby repealing the old one. In the intervening period between 1969 and 1978 another policy statement was issued by the ruling Party, TANU, in November 1974, directing the Government to introduce Universal Primary Education in 1977, that is, three years later; and to change admission procedures governing entry into universities. The directive required that from then on there would be no direct entry into universities after 'A' level. All aspiring students were to acquire working experience for two years after serving in the National Service for one year. Thus, the review carried out in 1978 was not only dealing with one policy issue but with several.

In addition, another important event in the chain of reforms of the educational system of Tanzania was the establishment in 1982 of a Presidential Commission on Education in response to a public cry that the standard of education throughout the system was falling. Its task was to review the entire system and come up with recommendations aimed at improving the provision of education up to the year 2000.

From the above paragraphs three points stand out clearly. The first is the fact that there has been a long gap between the pronouncement of policies and the actual implementation of such policies. This kind of a delay no doubt has serious consequences as we shall see in the next paragraphs. The second point relates to the frequency of policy pronouncements. On the average there is a policy issued every seven years which might necessitate a review of the curriculum. Which means not enough time is allowed for implementation and evaluation of the substantial policies. And finally, the question of curricular review. It becomes extremely difficult for the curriculum developers to keep up with the changes in terms of review of content, production of teaching materials and review of examinations, etc. when policy pronouncements are so frequent.

Planning

From studies on ESR it is evident that there has been no comprehensive planning for the implementation of the policy. The early responses to the challenges of ESR were spontaneous and not planned actions. Individual schools embarked on economic and other self-reliance activities on their own initiative. In many instances it was the push from the head of the school or college which led to self-reliance activities being introduced in a particular institution.

Thus, lack of timely guidance meant that there was no common understanding of the policy, and even more important was the fact that there was lack of direction from the centre. Consequently, the most important aspects of ESR have not been taken care of fully in the school curricula: integration of classroom learning with self-reliance work outside the classroom; making primary and secondary education terminal; integrating the school into the larger community; and making the school a place for training in democracy and leadership.

Mwalimu Nyerere saw the need for including these in the curriculum of each level of education and directed that:

"...farm work and products should be integrated into school life; thus the properties of fertilizers can be explained in science classes, and their use and limitations experienced by the pupils as they see them in use."

He continued thus:

"One difficulty in the way of this kind of re-organisation is the present examination system; if pupils spend more of their time on learning to do practical work, and on the contribution to their own upkeep and the development of the community, they will not be able to take the present kind of examinations - at least within the same time period. It is, however, difficult to see why the present examination system should be regarded as sacrosanct. There is no reason why Tanzania should not combine an examination which is based on the things we teach with a teacher and pupil assessment of the work done for the school and the community." (*Nyerere*).

To be fair, some changes have taken place in the curriculum of each level, to reflect at least in theory, the requirements of ESR, both in content and the method of evaluating academic and practical work of students. With regard to content, the primary school syllabus has been re-organised so that in the first three years emphasis is placed on the teaching of the 3Rs to ensure permanence of the skills learnt. For the remaining four years pupils are introduced to additional skills in art and crafts, home economics and, in rural areas agriculture and animal husbandry, over and above the regular academic subjects.

The same is true about the secondary school syllabus. Subject biases have been introduced to provide for the different interests of students. Thus, the syllabus now includes agriculture, technical and business education and home economics in addition to the traditional subjects. However, these biases are to be found only in designated schools. Moreover, the choice of a bias is not completely by an individual's preference. Rather, a student is selected to join a school and after joining it he chooses from the biases offered by the school.

Continuous assessment has also been introduced since the early seventies at both primary and secondary levels. However, two things need to be pointed out here; first, that these changes are grossly inadequate, and secondly, that one needs to examine how they are actually put into practice in order to appreciate the problems inherent in the process of implementing ESR.

Studies have revealed a number of weaknesses, among which are:

1) Real curricular reform in response to the demands of ESR in primary education has yet to take place. What has been done so far has only touched the periphery, although the experiments going on now are in the right direction. At the secondary school level, however, the change came later; and hence, the present state of affairs in which self-reliance activities are divorced from classwork, making them almost completely economic ventures and not moments of learning functional knowledge, skills, values and useful school community relations. (*Komba and Temu*). The Ministry of

Education confirms this in its combined annual report for 1976 - 1981 in the statement that,

"…. production took place outside the academic curriculum and hardly were scientific methods employed in the production process" (*Education, 1987:8*).

2) Examinations do not reflect the concept of terminality of education at each level as they are still being used as a means for selecting the few who will move to the next level higher up. (*Komba and Temu; Omari and Mosha; Kweka; Nyerere*).

3) Very little of what is taught in school can be related by students in practical terms, to what is actually going on in their homes (*Unesco; 1982:37*).

4) Curricular change has not gone hand in hand with preparations of teachers' guides, textbooks, charts and other materials needed to support implementation.

This situation cannot be left to continue uncorrected. It calls for an immediate joint effort of the Ministry of Education and curriculum developers toward completing the curricular reform while at the same time rectifying the various shortcomings revealed by research findings.

Interpretation of the ESR Policy

The delay in providing operational guidelines to implementers in the field has contributed greatly to the misconception about the meaning of ESR. It has meant that the chief actors - the teachers, students/pupils, parents, education administrators and planners did not have the right information before they started performing. As a result there has been a misinterpretation of the objectives and meaning of education for self-reliance.

Studies carried out so far on the implementation of ESR have shown that in practice, in many cases ESR has come to mean farm production work Because of this misinterpretation schools in rural and urban areas alike have looked around for land for agricultural activities such as the growing of food crops, fruit and in some cases cash crops as well. Sometimes urban schools have obtained land many miles away outside the towns, thus necessitating long hours of travelling and little time for actual work. This has rendered the whole exercise uneconomically non-productive. Instead it has inculcated negative attitudes in the pupils, teachers and parents.

There have also been vigorous competitions among schools in different parts of the country for first position in production because those schools which have produced more and earned a bigger income from the sale of their farm produce have received publicity from the administrators because they should be considered as having responded well to the challenge of ESR that:

"Each school should have as an integral part of it, a farm or workshop which provides the food eaten by the community, and makes some contribution to total national income". (*Nyerere*).

Unfortunately, the administrators have not taken the trouble to find out whether the process involved in achieving high production is in conformity with the requirements of ESR. They have not asked themselves, for example, whether the planning of the activities, the production process and the selling of products, etc. were all learning processes; or whether the whole process of producing food on the farm or goods in the workshop has indeed made the students more self-reliant. Has it produced an individual who relates work to comfort, who has learned the meaning of working together for the common good of all, an individual who has self-confidence and has acquired the skills and knowledge he requires to enable him to lead a happy life in his community and at the same time make a positive contribution to its development? These are the things which have yet to be taken seriously.

Performance by Educational Institutions

In the preceding section the focus has been on the examination of the preparations which were made for the implementation of ESR. The conclusion is that there was no central planning immediately after the pronouncement of the policy. Whatever guidelines and directives were prepared at the centre came out late so that they did not have much impact on the implementers since they had already begun implementing the policy in their own way. Of greater importance is the fact that the curricular reform has yet to be realized in full, thus indicating that there is a big gap between pronouncement of policies and their actual implementation.

However, implementation of ESR is taking place despite this anomaly, and good results can be seen in many of the educational institutions. That is why Mwalimu Nyerere complains of not being able to implement the policy in its fullness, rather than of not having implemented it at all. The Ministry of Education states in its report for 1977-1981:

"Concerning the training of students in practical skills and to make them respect manual work, appreciable success was scored both in the vocation-alisation of secondary school curriculum and in the involvement of schools in productive and cost-saving activities". (*Education, 1987:11*).

Research findings also confirm that, despite the short-comings in the understanding and implementation of the policy which have been seen at all levels, the future of the economic activities is bright especially if corrective measures are taken to improve management, integration of the activities in the curriculum in an unambiguous manner and to reflect them clearly in the national assessment procedures.

A similar positive picture is painted about the attitudes of both teachers and students towards productive work and other cost-saving activities carried out in schools. Studies show that participation in economic activities by all sections of the communities of the schools concerned has been accepted as a matter of course.

What is even more encouraging is the fact that the lead has been taken by the institutions themselves, of course,with some guidance from the centre. However, this has depended to a large extent, on the leadership of the school. Where there is dynamic leadership with management skills, economic projects have been conceived, planned and implemented in accordance with the spirit of ESR. Thus, management committees have been formed with representation from all sections of the community. Students are given the opportunity to learn through participation in the whole process of executing projects including making decisions on how to disburse the money earned from the projects.

At the primary school level there has been some experimentation on the idea of community schools. The basic objective has been to make the school a meeting point where both the villagers and the school community learned from each other through joint activities. Through this type of integration the school would not operate in isolation. The experiment which started in one village in 1971 with assistance from UNICEF and UNESCO, was extended to 34 villages in 1974. And in 1981 the Government decided to extend the experiment to include all schools in two regions (*Mwajombe)* as a first step toward making all schools community based. However, Mwajombe who was the first co-ordinator of the project reports that present features of the first project in Kwamsisi village in Tanga region have been adopted "in varying degree in primary schools all over the country and have served as an inspiration for community participation and productive work..." in the Universal Primary Education Programme.

In community schools the common feature is that there are joint management committees which plan and supervise the implementation programmes which take place in both communities, the school and the village. Economic ventures like agriculture take place on the village farm in which the school is given a portion to take care of. Expertise comes from both communities and where necessary it is requested from relevant bodies outside the village.

Participation in self-help projects has been very high from both communities. Schools, dispensaries, toilets, daycare centres and the like have been constructed through joint efforts. In some cases the higher classes in the school have been responsible for the running of day-care centres under the joint supervision of teachers and parents. Some members of the village have been involved in teaching in schools the skills they have while the pupils have rendered whatever services they are able to offer.

Unfortunately, community schools are still at the stage of an experiment. It is not known when the results of this experiment will be officially integrated in the national system as it was originally envisaged. This is not the only experiment going on currently, and maybe many more are on the way, since normally, these experiments are brought in by those with dangling carrots. It is time we learned to have time perspective in all the experiments we carry out so that the end result benefits the system.

In terms of actual production and financial gain it is difficult to make an accurate assessment. Research reports reveal that records kept on economic activities are not always complete. Probably this explains why in reporting the income generated by self-reliance activities, the Ministry of Education gives a total picture only for all primary schools, or secondary schools or colleges. For example, it has been indicated that between 1976 and 1981 there was an increase in revenue from economic activities from Tsh. 9.8 million to Tsh. 20.8 million in primary schools. But for secondary schools the Ministry talks of surplus rather than gross income. It is reported the surplus generated in the same period increased from Tsh. 0.84 million to Tsh. 3.3 million. However, measured against the directive that schools and colleges should contribute up to 25% of the total bill of maintaining them, one may say that the achievement has been minimal. The Ministry reports that in the period mentioned above, on the average secondary schools met about 5 per cent of their catering bill.

The overall impression given by research findings is that schools are able to off-set total expenditure by only about 2.5% (*Maliyamkono, 1979:37 - 38*). One may consider this to be a good beginning since this was not the case before the introduction ESR; nevertheless it is too small a contribution when one takes into account the time it has taken to achieve this level of contribution. The encouraging thing is that many individual schools have performed extremely well all round - character formation, inculcation of the right attitudes and values in the students, integrating academic work with practical work, integrating school into the larger community and running profitable economic projects which have earned them substantial incomes. These incomes have been usefully utilized in the construction of class-rooms, assembly halls, teachers' houses; in re-investing in new projects and for feeding students or buying them stationery. In fact many schools have projected such a good image that parents fight for places for their children knowing fully that they (children) will have to undertake economic activities in which they would not normally allow their children to participate.

In financial terms, it seems Folk Development Colleges (FDCs) have excelled the rest of the institutions as can be seen from the following table.

INCOME GENERATION IN FDC's IN THE YEARS 1981/82 TO 1987/88
INCOME, EXPENDITURE AND PROFIT

YEAR	INCOME SHS.	EXPENDITURE SHS.	PROFIT SHS.
1981/82	5,483,634	4,086,085	1,397,540
1982/83	9,542,960	6,621,209	2,921,751
1983/84	18,375,111	13,692,801	4,682,310
1984/85	23,001,086	15,668,862	7,332,324
1985/86	36,002,395	27,641,011	8,361,384
1986/87	54,361,529	40,554,802	13,806,727
1987/88	70,873,139	51,036,161	19,836,978
TOTAL	**217,639,954**	**159,300,931**	**58,339,023**

Source : Department of Adult Education, Ministry of Education

There are 52 FDCs spread throughout the country. These are tertiary institutions for adult students who have gone through the functional literacy programmes and are ready to take advanced educational programmes.

Their achievement is attributable to good management and planning in most of the colleges. FDCs usually have trained personnel for each line of activity introduced in the programme. It is also noted from departmental reports that there is a close follow-up and monitoring by the centre. This has enabled FDCs to get çonstant guidance and other assistance. As a result, it is reported that in the majority of cases achievement is 50% above the 25% prescribed by the Centre.

Conclusion

I shall end the paper by repeating what I said at the beginning; that the topic under discussion is a complex one and as such it is not easy to review it critically without an indepth study. However, the short-comings notwithstanding I have tried to reveal some of the salient points which deserve greater consideration if we are to improve implementation of Education for

Self-Reliance in its fullness. It is evident from the account given in the preceding paragraphs that there are many problems which have hindered the smooth implementation of ESR and which need to be addressed immediately. Most of these are fundamental, relating to planning and curriculum reforms. These two areas are central to the success of the whole policy. In fact it has been pointed out that it is the absence of these elements in the implementation approach which has led to the present state of affairs.

Hyden (in *Omari and Mosha)* is of the opinion that in Tanzania there is a deliberate refusal in the policy-making circles rationally to analyse the adequacy of the available resource potential as a pre-condition for policy making. Supporting this argument, Omari and Mosha suggest that the state of confusion which prevailed at the beginning and still prevails to some extent at the present time, in terms of interpretation of the concept of ESR, lack of central direction through a comprehensive plan, etc. is a result of the way the policy was formulated and later on pronounced to the public. They contend that it was all done in a rush and presented with political pressure so that no allowance was made for public debates or opposition. They finally conclude that implementers could not avoid acting in a state of anxiety when examining a policy. As a result, implementation of policies has been haphazardly done.

With this note in mind perhaps it is time to look at some of the lessons one can learn from research studies. These are listed below not in any specific order of gravity.

1) *Reform of the curriculum*: Practically all studies point to the need to have an immediate curriculum reform. This is considered crucial because properly worked out curricula will answer many of the current questions directed toward integration of all types, content of syllabuses, interpretation of the concept of ESR etc. It has taken too long to effect the reform and it should not be delayed any more.

2) *Co-ordinated Planning*: It is clear from studies on implementation of ESR that ministries, departments and institutions outside the education system are not fully involved in conceiving, planning and implementing ESR activities in schools and colleges. As a result rarely do schools make use of experts from these organs despite the fact that most schools lack trained personnel to supervise their economic activities. This is because there is no machinery that brings all relevant organs together at any of the

levels. This calls for planning which recognises the importances of these organs in the success of ESR.

3) *Training of Teachers and Tutors*: It has been pointed out elsewhere that the training of teachers needs to be re-examined if they are to carry out responsibilities as spelt out by ESR. The content of the syllabus in Teacher Training Colleges needs to be improved so that training in making (or improvising) teaching materials using locally available resources is introduced. Teachers should be able to solve some of the problems themselves instead of waiting for solutions to come from higher up.

4) *Financing ESR Activities*: Studies have revealed that there is very little money given to schools as capital for starting economic activities and other self-reliance projects. In fact the Ministry of Education confirms this and states that the little that there is, is given to those schools which do well. This means that Cinderella schools will not even be able to start.

5) *ESR Activities in Private Schools*: It seems that so far the government has focused its attention only on public schools. Private schools have been left alone. That is why production activities in these schools is at the lowest level. The tendency of the Government to leave the private schools unmonitored is bound to create a class distinction between the labouring and the small masters contrary to the spirit of ESR. Some of these schools are owned by a group that had a privileged status before independence. We now seem to negate the idea of integration of education systems thus going back to the colonial period. This is a dangerous move which needs to be checked.

6) *Management of Projects*: Management is a science and can be taught; but studies have revealed that ESR projects are rarely well managed because those responsible for them lack the skills of management. It is important to consider the inclusion of management training in all teacher-training colleges so as to prepare teachers for their future role in the implementation of ESR activities.

This list is by no means exhaustive but it can be added to as time goes on and serious study is done on research findings. However, in the light of the experience narrated in this paper it might be advisable to have only a few in the hope that they may be acted upon.

References

Komba, D. "Philosophical Concepts of Education for Self-Reliance: Interpretations and Misinterpretations". A Paper presented at the National Symposium on Twenty Years of Education for Self-Reliance organised by the Tanzania Professional Teachers Association, at Marangu College, September 12-17, 1988

Komba, D. and Temu, E.B. *Education with Production in Tanzania: Implementation of Education for Self-Reliance in 1985*. A Report of a FEP/ Ministry of Education co-sponsored Research Project, 1987, Dar es Salaam

Kweka, A.N. "Problems of preparing students for society in a dependent economy: the case of Tanzania", in *Some Important Issues in Education in Tanzania*. The Convocation. University of Dar es Salaam

Maliyamkono, T.L. *The Unproductive School*. Africana Publishers, 1982, Dar es Salaam

Ministry of Education, *Combined Report for years 1976-1981*. Adult Education Press, March 1987, Dar es Salaam

Mmari, G.R.V. *Education for Self-Reliance; Preparation of Teachers for ESR*. Chakiwata, Education Service Centre Ltd., 1988, Dar es Salaam

Mwajombe, R.S. "Education for Self-Reliance in Practice: Elementary Education since 1967". Paper presented at a National Symposium on Twenty Years of Education for Self-Reliance, organised by Tanzania Professional Teachers' Association at Marangu Teachers' College, September 12-17, 1988

Nyerere, J.K. An address delivered at the National Symposium on Twenty Years of Education for Self-Reliance, Marangu Teachers' College, September 12-17, 1988

Nyerere J.K. *Education for Self-Reliance.* Government Printer, Dar es Salaam 1967

Omari, I.M. and Mosha, H.J. *The Quality of Primary Education in Tanzania.* Mau Graphics Ltd. Nairobi, 1987

UNESCO *A Study on Strategies for Rural Development and the Role of Education.* Paris, 1982

UNESCO, *Integration of Education and Productive Work in Zanzibar.* Paris, September, 1982

THE FEP CURRICULUM: AN ANATOMY OF EDUCATION WITH PRODUCTION

Patrick van Rensburg

Education and Work for All

Education for all has for long been a well understood and accepted goal of African governments, but as the number of youth in schools has increased, economic expansion has not kept pace and we are witnessing the emergence of large-scale unemployment of educated youth. We need now to back up the call for education for all with the call for work for all. Education cannot by itself create mass employment. That needs new and different strategies at the broader socio-economic level. But there is a role for education, and with crucial innovations it can serve better the goal of work for all.

Mass-Based Pedagogy

Education for work for all requires a mass-based pedagogy. It must be the opposite of the abstract, highly verbalised and excessively theoretical pedagogy of the inherited model of formal school which basically serves to filter a minority through the upper reaches of education and to prepare them for mental labour, while it rejects the majority at its various cut-off points. It must link theory and practice, and particularly work and study and it must introduce into the curriculum vital content - currently missing - relevant to the all-round development of individuals as responsible members of society. It must ensure that educational institutions are closely linked to their communities and that both staff, students and communities are involved in their democratic organisation and management.

Forms and Types of Production

Education with Production manifests itself across the world in a very wide range of forms and types of activities. It might involve students at primary and secondary schools or even universities in timetabled work in production units, or workteams attached to the school, farms, factories and workshops - engaged in producing a variety of goods and services either for own consumption or sale to the public, or in the construction of physical infrastructure for the school or the surrounding community. It might involve students working in cooperative, community or collectively owned enterprises outside the school. Or it might operate in out-of-school programmes where mainly young people produce and learn at the same time, acquiring particular vocational skills. Another form is to be found within vocational training institutions in which students engage in production of goods and services for public sale, or in which (as in socialist countries) they work under supervision in collective enterprises. Here, student engagement in production increases progressively as they proceed through their courses. And there are also school-cooperatives or cooperatives-in-formation where young people study, acquire skills and together learn co-operative management in the expectation that they will remain together and create their own employment after completing studies.

There is also production with education, namely the education of the direct producers whether in town and countryside, whilst they are working. It is an important application of the principle of lifelong education, and recognises that education is a total social process, in which consciousness is shaped as much by our social and material conditions as by what we learn intellectually.

Economic, Social and Pedagogical Benefits

In any progressive conception (and practice) of it, education with production should offer a minimum of economic, social and pedagogical benefits in some or other balance, depending on the level of social, cultural, political and material development in a particular society.

Economic Benefits

The economic benefits can be assessed in terms of income generated through sales of goods and services, or savings on the schools' budget where produce is used for internal consumption; it can also be assessed in terms of the value added through student labour to school and community facilities where the school takes part in building infrastructure.

The Brigades in Serowe, Botswana, in 1979, with 400 students in 30 different productive activities, acquiring skills and knowledge, produced P1 million of goods and services (worth at least US $2.5 million at today's values) and contributed almost 70% to all their costs - of administration, education and training.

A special case is that of work and study in a socialist country like Cuba, where the 'schools in the countryside' have provided the labour for the citrus industry and for introducing coffee production to certain areas. Here, the school plays a major role in economic development.

Swaneng Hill School in Botswana in the sixties gave practical effect to the thesis that the school was a powerhouse of talents in its community and could serve development and the setting up of enterprises. Science and Development Studies classes combined to undertake resource surveys and to examine the possibilities of using certain local resources like limestone, beer wastes, roots, pods and barks in production of building lime in one case and tanning in another. As a result, new Brigade activities were established and the students found a local material with which to build their school.

An important economic benefit is the contribution of education with production to employment-creation. Institutions like Sandan in China and the Mondragon Escuela Technica, at both of which work and study were combined, were training grounds for technicians and, in some cases, managers of the huge production cooperatives to which they were related. The ZIMFEP School Cooperatives are also trying to prepare young people for employment by training them in technical management skills within production enterprises which they help run whilst at school. The Tshwaragano Enterprises project of FEP in Gaborone trained young people in technical and cooperative management skills whilst producing, on the understanding that their place of training would become their future workplace, and that when earning they would collectively buy the assets - a process now under way.

Social Benefits

The main potential social benefit of work and study is lessening the division between mental and manual labour and reducing the division between privileged student and exploited workers. This seems to be one of the main objectives of the 'school in the countryside' in Cuba. This aim is achieved by worker and farmer/peasant education as much as by student labour.

Pedagogical Benefits

Perhaps the pedagogical benefits are best assessed in terms of the cognitive, affective and psycho-motor domains of learning.

The benefits for cognitive learning can be seen in terms of the practical basis provided within production by the application of scientific and mathematical principles, or in observing the practical effect on production of particular working relationships, to cite random examples.

Textile trainees in Brigades in Serowe in the late seventies learnt symmetry whilst pattern cutting. Agricultural students learnt about contours when ploughing, and reinforced their biology lessons when treating cows for mastitis, or pasteurising milk. Building trainees applied the theorem that the square of the hypotenuse was equal to the sum of the squares of the other two sides of a right-angled triangle, in setting out for building foundations. They also learnt about roof angles in relation to water run-off, or wind-lift, through practice.

Whilst the theoretical roots of production in mathematics and natural science, and its scientific and mathematical structures, are readily identifiable, it is not only to these branches of knowledge that production is related. Workplaces of schools are microcosms of workplaces in society, and require, inter alia, investment, management, and diverse social, economic, financial and cultural relationships with communities; involve working relationships, and improved and directed use of language.

Issues arise in a practical way that make investigation of principles embedded in social science and studies meaningful. To be sure, the skills of management, and self-confidence cannot be learned from books alone, but through experience gained from practice linked to theory.

So it is with the affective domain of learning. Behavioural traits and attitudes are not learnt from theory alone, but from a combination of theory and practice, from constant exposure to real life situations, especially in production, where appropriate attitudes and behaviour, like care of materials, equipment and tools, can be seen to be socially and economically beneficial.

Berea College, one of five work-study colleges in the USA, where 15 hours of productive work a week are compulsory for every student, has developed a 'syllabus' of affective learning related to work, which outlines learning progressions related to functional levels. Learning objectives start with basic work habits and attitudes, proceeding to responsibility and skills development, creativity and awareness, understanding and commitment, and leadership and autonomy.

The psychomotor domain recognises not only the learning of manual skills, finger skills and dexterity, but also perceptions of interrelationships of time, space and movement, for example, related to the mechanical operation of a lathe, that can only be learned from reality.

Maximising the Benefits of Work-Study

The full benefits of the linkage of education with production will be achieved only when it is supported by the other crucial innovations already cited, namely, the linking of theory and practice, curriculum transformation, closer ties between school and community and the democratic organisation of both school and its associated workplaces.

Existing curricula of conventional schools do not readily and easily lend themselves to the linking of theory and practice related to the full realities of the world of work, and particularly to the combining of education with production. The high levels of abstraction, theorisation and verbalisation that are inherent in an elitist pedagogy related so strongly to the mental/manual division of labour; the associated compartmentalisation of curricula; and the omission of large areas of knowledge seen as potentially subversive of the conventional pedagogical objectives and functions (which also include socialisation and custody) are examples of the fundamental incompatibility of most of what is in these curricula with work and study.

It is no wonder that evaluations of Education for Self-Reliance in Tanzania, of the production units in Zambian schools, and of the ZIMFEP schools in Zimbabwe, find a poor linkage between the productive work and academic study. It requires a supreme effort and considerable experience, and is like sifting bodies of ore to find grains of gold, to find linkages between work and the substance of conventional curricula.

Important and vital elements missing from conventional curricula include a comprehensive knowledge of culture, what it is and how it relates to material life; of technology, its links to science and mathematics, its diversity, and complexity; of development and of production, and of the social, cultural, political, economic, financial and material issues that relate to both; of management and all its complex and diverse functions, and its linkages to social stratification; of the historical interrelationship and interaction between human society and the environment (at present compartmentalised as history and geography); and of the real-world, direct linkage between mathematics and science and production and development.

Here, of course, are the basic areas of knowledge which precisely do link theory and real practice, and education with production. This is why the Foundation for Education with Production is proposing a curriculum that broadens and reinterprets the bodies of information in the existing curriculum and relates them to the broad realities of life, not just the experiences, lifestyles, perceptions and consciousness of an elite.

The FEP curriculum comprises Cultural Studies, Development Studies, Environmental and Social Studies, Fundamentals of Production, Modern Communication in English and in African Languages, Applied Mathematics and Applied Science.

Whilst FEP acknowledges that there is some overlap of areas of knowledge within this curriculum it is also felt, that these over-lapping areas have an integral relationship with each of the different wider bodies of knowledge under which they fall, and which can be studied in the sequence of each, and that they are also starting points for integrating the broader curriculum. It is quite possible to select a number of common topics and teach these separately in terms of their inherent logic, as well as to touch upon them again in the context of the other subjects to which they relate.

The importance of closer ties with the community, as a supportive innovation to education with production, is evidenced by the potential of these closer ties for cultural development, for collaborative economic and social development and the establishment of productive enterprises that promote collective job-creation. Presently, schools are ivory towers separated and divorced from their communities and playing little role in the life of the communities. It is in the community and in the neighbourhood of the school, that a wide variety of knowledge, skills and natural resources are to be found, that markets are to be found and development opportunities seized. Community-linked development, and productive and other activities, initiated from schools, may help change conservative and ingrained attitudes about youth and education, that are inimical to socially just development.

Finally, in this context, the democratic organisation and management of schools and their associated workplaces, and the participation of parents, teachers and students in these processes, is important to the realisation of the school's educational role as well as its developmental and social roles. If students are to become entrepreneurs or organisers of production, then their initiative must be encouraged, not stifled, as it is under present conservative systems of school management and discipline, reinforced by parental attitudes at home. Young people are part of society and are not to be treated as enemies. They must be encouraged to question, to solve problems, and to learn from their elders the best they have to give, and to build thereon in an environment conducive to real education.

The Syllabuses of the Core Curriculum

Cultural Studies, for its part, asks what is culture?, and looks at basic aspects of culture in terms of material culture, concept formation, logic, organised systems of thought, custom and tradition. It examines the conscious production of culture as art, and shows how cultures differ. It looks at continuity and change in culture and contact between cultures. The syllabus then focusses on the culture of Southern Africa, briefly surveying pre-colonial culture, imperialist culture, and the emerging culture of independent Southern Africa. Having looked generally at the framework within which culture is produced, the course then allows students to specialise in both study and cultural production relating to two fields amongst five, comprising writing, music, graphics, visual arts and performing arts.

Development Studies, which is already examined by Cambridge, and is offered in schools in Botswana, Lesotho and Zimbabwe, looks at production, changing societies, Britain's Industrial Revolution, Imperialism in Southern Africa, Government's role in development, international trade, strategies for development and development in Southern Africa.

Environmental and Social Studies, looks at humanity and its physical environment in terms of the origins of both, and their mutual interaction and inter-relationships. The course then, surveys different epochs and stages of historical development and identifies and discusses principles of historical and sociological analysis. The course includes a survey of Southern African history and focusses on the national history of the country where the student lives. It introduces the concept of Social Geography - the transformation of natural landscapes into cultural landscapes, historically - and also has a section on Demography. It looks at environmental and ecological issues and conservation in depth; and it requires students to undertake practical activities (group and individual), suggestions for which place strong emphasis on environmental issues.

Fundamentals of Production looks at science and technology in production, the inter-relationship of production and social change, the historical growth and diversification of skills and the development of training systems, and surveys different branches of production on an international and national scale. It then examines the initiation, organisation, ownership and management of production and contrasts the different structures for these in different socio-economic systems. It then looks at finance, economics and production, politics, the State and law and production, and the quality of life and production.

Applied Mathematics and *Applied Science* will not only enable students to study formulae, principles and other mathematical and scientific abstractions but to learn the application of these in everyday life and more especially in relation to actual production processes.

Language as Communication will promote improved reading, writing and speaking of official languages of the student's country. It aims to develop the ability to use language effectively for the purpose of practical communication so that students will be enabled to play a more effective role in their communities and places of work to develop their intellectual and critical faculties; to help them to understand and use effectively the language and terminology appropriate to technical and other work-related concepts; understand information from a variety of public sources, including the media, and communicate effectively and appropriately in a variety of real life situations and in various social contexts.

THE CORE CURRICULUM FOR EDUCATION WITH PRODUCTION

S.B. Matsvai

Introduction

We have addressed the above topic with the hope of giving insights into the thinking behind our programmes of Education with Production vis-a-vis the theme of this seminar: Education and Training for Employment in the SADCC countries.

However in looking at the purpose of education as defined by the theme of this seminar i.e. Education and Training for Employment, we have taken a broader definition of the purpose of Education to include the objective of 'employment creation' as opposed to employment per se.

The reason for this is that if we say education for employment, we are consciously or subconsciously assuming there is employment somewhere and the products of education and training are simply going to be inputs into that sector or pool of employment opportunities.

The reality in most, if not all, SADCC countries today is that there is less and less incidence of automatic output-input relations between the education and training and the employment sectors of our economies.

The Core

Thus when we talk of the core curriculum for Education with Production, in our own context, we are defining, moulding and putting into practice a curriculum that seeks to prepare school leavers for both the employment opportunities that exist in the economy and the lack of those opportunities. The second part of the object of this curriculum i.e. helping to overcome the problem of lack of employment has meant that education with production also seeks to prepare students for employment creation.

Employment and employment creation revolve around the core process which sustains every human society i.e. the process of production. Irrespective of where one is employed or what career path any student chooses to take, in the end, they have to have some form of relationship with the 'productive base' of their society in order to live and sustain whatever else they may be doing.

The productive process in any country, whatever form and character that process assumes depends on the level and stage of social and political development of that country. The education process is one of the essential processes that supports that process of production by producing the human capital which must be injected into that process and sustain it.

In our own reality, and I believe the reality of many of us gathered here today, there have been serious distortions of the output-input relationship that should exist between these two processes. This has led, in many instances, to a manpower gap in our economies which we have all tried to address with differing approaches and degrees of success. This manpower or human capital deficiency in our economies has manifested itself both in terms of quality and numbers. Against this scenario, we have had to grapple with the need to develop our economies using educational reforms and innovations as some of the options available.

In Education with Production therefore, the following constitute the core of our curriculum:-

The Technical Component

Given the human capital gap that has been inherited from our colonial past, Zimbabwe has had to import skilled manpower since independence in almost all the sectors of the economy, including the education sector. There is inadequate wo/manpower to support our economy. The colonial education system we inherited had at its heart academic subjects which sought to create minds that sought the white collar jobs of clerks and messengers not technicians and scientists. The productive base was manned by whites, and blacks were found at the level of spanner boys, drivers, messengers, foremen, etc. not mechanics, managers and engineers.

Therefore as I mentioned above, to sustain the productive base to maintain our bigger post independence society, we have had to embark on curriculum changes which put technical subjects and the relevant theme of production at the centre of the education process. We had had to offer a curriculum which trains students in the skills of construction; metalwork, as a basis for future training in related engineering trades; agriculture as an obvious basis on which we can develop manpower to sustain our agriculture based economy; textile design and technology, as a base for building up local expertise to enter into one of the most significant industrial sectors of the economy. Related subjects such as science and language subjects have also been offered to enable the students to see and appreciate the scientific concepts behind these seemingly just 'practical-technical' subjects and to be able to communicate, respectively.

At the heart of this core curriculum is the all important aspect of the methodology of delivering it. Since we are grappling with the problem of employment and employment creation it has been imperative for us in education with production to ensure that production is central in the delivery of this curriculum. But what form of production? The production we have emphasised is that which permits the students to explore further, with the guidance of their teachers initially, what potential there is to transform the knowledge they will have gained during their lessons in the classrooms and workshops into tangible products or services which are of value to themselves, the school and the community.

Thus an essential component of the core process of education with production has been the setting up of what we call 'productive activities and production units'. At the former level, the students are under the guidance and active leadership of their teachers in doing productive activities related to the disciplines they are involved in.

At the latter level, the production units stage, the students take up the leadership and organisational roles of the teacher and venture out on their own to try out their knowledge. This is a crucial stage in the process of delivering the core education with production curriculum because the students will have not only an opportunity to test out the acquired knowledge but also to *create new knowledge through practice* - through the mistakes they make, through the successes they achieve and through the experiences of management, organisation, and marketing and also the sharing of funds (and the misuse of funds and relevant safeguards and corrective measures), all of which they would otherwise not experience had they been restricted to the confines of the four walls of a classroom with the teacher as the all-knowing expert.

The width and depth of this experience of our students as a learning process has proved invaluable at the stage these students become school leavers and seek *non-existent employment* - they have been able to take up the challenge to create their own employment opportunities.

Without seeming to de-emphasise the need to provide 'education and training for employment', the above core curriculum and the methodology of its delivery has also addressed this issue; with students who have undergone training of the nature described above, taking cognisance of the fact that we are not training them in 'nuclear technology' but in areas that are relevant to our level of production, these students obviously become *better and cheaper candidates* for either tertiary training or on-the-job-training. They already know at least the basics of workshop practice and managing people or working together in an enterprise from the production units and industrial attachments organised while they are still at school. In this manner we can optimise the use of our resources in training and manpower development nationally.

The Ideological Component

Inseparable from the core of the education with production curriculum is the ideological aspect of education with production. We believe there is no country which has an education system which is ideologically neutral - the process of education is loaded with values that are representative of what the policy-makers or ruling class believe to be acceptable ways of thinking, behaving, working etc. Our own colonial system of education was overloaded with values which were incompatible with the values and aspirations of the new Zimbabwean society. Some people might think this has no link to employment and the economy! However our own experience in Zimbabwe of a massive white *'human capital flight'* to Europe, South Africa, New Zealand, Australia and other countries at independence taught us that just preparing students technically for their roles in the national economy is not enough. The human capital flight I have mentioned above happened because the skilled Rhodesians could not serve an independent Zimbabwe.

Thus even though our countries are independent, unless our school leavers have received adequate exposure while at school as to the realities of our economies, the historical factors that have affected them, and what our respective roles should be in order to change the socio-economic reality of our Third World economies, then after training, these same nationals of our own countries can 'fly off' to work elsewhere because of the disparity in our economic realities.

Thus as part of the education with production core curriculum, we place a lot of emphasis on creating an understanding of the social and economic reality around the school and the pupil so that when the school leaver faces *the world of work and no work*, she/he does not revolt against it helplessly but seeks to change it. For employment creation, not only skills are required but also the right kind of emotional disposition of the school leaver and above all an environment which supports whatever initiative the school leavers can come up with.

Conclusion

Finally it is difficult to separate all the component parts of the education with production programme as we are carrying it out into core and periphery especially because we regard education as a process and education with production is also a process with several components integrated together.

What we have therefore defined above as the core of education with production is the basis of a process which takes in what the productive base of our economy needs, what the parent and pupil want, what the policy-makers prefer and finally what our resource base can permit.

SECTION 3

RECOMMENDATIONS OF THE MINI-SEMINAR

The mini-Seminar on The Curriculum for Employment had divided into working groups to focus on different aspects of its work, such as primary education, secondary education, tertiary vocational training, teaching methods and activities, teaching and learning materials, school organisation and relationships with communities, and regional co-operation. The mini-Seminar concluded by appointing a resolutions sub-committee to collate the recommendations of the working groups and present the product of their work as an input to the main Seminar. A report on the main Seminar's discussions of the recommendations appears in Section 4 of the proceedings of the main Seminar.

RECOMMENDATIONS

Curriculum Content

(a) *Primary Level*

1. At the lower primary level, concentration should be on the basic skills of reading, numeracy and writing.

2. The choice of content for specific subjects should be left to individual countries, taking into account local needs.

3. At the upper primary level, the focus should be on further developing subject areas. Emphasis should be placed on:

(i) the relationship between education and production;

(ii) education as a process of socialisation towards character and moral development.

4. Primary schools should prepare pupils for participation in productive work especially since primary education is terminal for some pupils. This level should provide pupils with survival skills and prepare them for secondary and life-long education.

(b) *Secondary level*

5. The education system should, by demonstrating that the concept of Education with Production (EWP) is rooted in African traditions, emphasize the role of EWP as a strategy for technical training and development.

6. Students should be introduced to locally applicable technology making use of hands-on practical experience. As a guide to the weighting of practical work and theory, the following may be considered:

(a) at general secondary level: 80% classwork and 20% practical work
(b) at technical secondary schools: 50% each
(c) at vocational schools: 80% practical work and 20% classwork (theory)

7. More effective procedures should be devised for selecting students for practical subjects, taking into account national goals as well as students' aptitudes and interests.

8. There should be a coherent and co-ordinated transition from primary to secondary school to ensure continuity and progression in the teaching and learning of content, theory, practical skills, aptitudes and values.

(c) *Tertiary Level*

9. The curriculum content at this level should be dictated by individual countries according to their socio-economic needs and available resources.

Teaching Methods

10. Students should be active participants in the learning process through use of simulated and real life situations.

11. Limitations imposed by examinations on the teaching and learning of Education with Production should be redressed through the reformation of the examination system and the inclusion of viable methods of continuous

assessment.

Teaching/Learning Materials

12. Emphasis should be placed on the production of low cost, readily available materials.

13. SADCC states should set up a network of national resource centres for the production and distribution of teaching/learning materials for national education systems.

14. Teachers at different educational levels should through pre-service and in-service training programmes, be trained to produce their own teaching and learning resources.

School Organisation and Relations with Communities

15. The school should promote self-help and prepare pupils for life and work in the immediate environment and community in which they live.

16. The structure of the school should be improved i.e. in terms of its buildings, workshops, grounds etc. to create physical conditions conducive to education with production.

17. Since the school is expected to serve the needs of the community it is important for the community to be involved in determining the ideological content, planning, organising, managing and evaluating vocationalised school programmes.

18. Parents should be convinced that they have a role to play in the education of their children. Structures such as Parent-Teacher Associations should be encouraged.

19. In order to make the goal of universal education a reality, communities should be encouraged to contribute, financially or in kind, to ease the Government's burden of wholly financing the school.

20. Schools should draw on the expertise available in the community in order to make the implementation of the school programme more effective.

21. Teachers should be part of the communities in which they are based and should exercise the leadership role that they are expected to demonstrate in the running of national programmes at the local level.

22. The school should impart skills to the community through pilot projects which can form a solid foundation for the development of larger community projects.

23. The community should play an effective disciplinary role to help children develop attitudes, morals and values which enhance innovative education systems.

Regional Cooperation in Vocational Education and Training

24. There should be regional cooperation among SADCC countries at all levels of education in order to establish common curricula and standards. The purpose of such cooperation should be mutual assistance and reciprocity between SADCC countries in the provision of Vocational Education and Training (VET) and in the technical facilitation of development through the use of:

(a) a common core curriculum for VET;

(b) common technical performance standards;

(c) equaivalence of certificates, diploma and degrees.

However, alternative curriculum offerings desirable in individual SADCC countries should be taken into consideration in setting up the above.

25. A regional language institute should be established to promote those languages which will facilitate communication in the region.

26. Existing African curriculum organisations should be involved and mobilised in the formulation and implementation of VET programmes.

27. SADCC countries should set up regional staff development and student exchange programmes in the area of VET to enable technical cooperation and development to take place.

28. There should be more coordination among manpower planning bodies within the region. The concept of 'manpower' itself should be redefined on both sexist and conceptual grounds.

SECTION 4

CO-DIRECTORS' OVERVIEW

The participants in the mini-Seminar on the Curriculum for Employment were asked to evaluate it by completing a quite comprehensive questionnaire. A very substantial majority of them expressed themselves as satisfied or very satisfied with the selection of topics and with the coverage. They were also satisfied with the methodology of the Seminar, namely presentations followed by questions, answers and discussion and group work followed by plenary discussions.

The general view of participants was that the seminar was informative and facilitated the exchange of ideas, and that it fostered regional co-operation in education and training. It helped educational planners keep abreast of international curriculum changes and trends and gave curriculum activities clearer direction and purpose. Some 90% of the participants thought the Seminar was good or very good overall and that there was a good rapport among participants in a free and friendly atmosphere. They were united by common issues of concern, shared ideas and experiences and made constructive proposals.

Criticisms from individual participants were that discussions of teaching aids and materials were inadequate and that there was not enough focus on the problems facing SADCC countries in education and training, particularly in relation to job-creation. Some participants felt that inadequate time was given for discussion and that papers should have been made available well in advance of presentations. There was also a suggestion that an opportunity should have been provided for a visit to the Zimbabwean Curriculum Development Centre.

Despite the criticism on this score coming from one or two participants, it was clear from the presentations of the various country representatives about their curriculum principles and policies that the challenge to address unemployment and promote self-employment creation was very much on their agendas.

It was also clear that most of them are aware of the problems, both those facing educators in preparing students for self-employment, and those that would face young people themselves, in this effort, once they left school.

Educators needed not only to provide vocational skills but also management skills, several argued, and they needed to counter conservative attitudes amongst students themselves whose expectations were of paid employment. The school entry age needed to be raised as school-leavers were too young to create their own production opportunities.

Problems facing the students themselves include the lack of capital, land tenure systems which make it difficult for young farmers to get land and the lack of institutional support, in terms of management and marketing advice and assistance in setting themselves up in production.

One country representative reported that a small scale industrial organisation had been set up to offer financial and consultative support to young people starting projects. Others saw the solution in terms of absorption by young people within their own communities.

There was strong support in the recommendations of the mini-Seminar for education with production and for improvements of the linkages between theory and practice and the relationship between academic content and productive activities. A major stimulus to this undoubtedly came from support for the presentations by resource persons on programmes and experiences both within and outside the region which attempted to address the issue of unemployment, and to all of which education with production was central.

The presentations by the Foundation for Education with Production (FEP) and its sister organisation ZIMFEP, on curriculum proposals linked to education with production focussed sharply on the content of curriculum for employment and have since resulted in six follow-up workshops (in which six of the SADCC countries and one Liberation Movement participated) on the syllabuses presented by FEP. One result is that the University of Cambridge Local Schools Examinations Syndicate is likely to offer examinations on the revised syllabuses.

In his closing speech, Mr Arthur Bagunywa, the UNESCO representative in Southern Africa, requested the sponsors to arrange follow-up Seminars to work out concrete strategies to ensure that education becomes the productive occupation that it has for so long been urged to be. He strongly called for greater regional co-operation in this effort and in the vocationalisation of curricula.

A start has been made with the FEP curriculum workshops.

ANNEXURES

Annexure 1

THE SEMINAR DESCRIPTION

The 'Time-Bomb'

"Unemployment - or more accurately, low productivity non-wage employment - is emerging as one of the major problems confronting the SADCC Member States and a major challenge to the region as a whole", according to a 1986 Macro-Economic Survey commissioned by the SADCC Secretariat.

Unemployment of young people leaving school is especially high and is a source of great concern to every Government in the region, considered by many to be a 'time-bomb'.

Seminar Proposal

The proposed Seminar on Education and Employment for SADCC Countries will be held in Zimbabwe in the first quarter of 1989, to be attended by multi-sectoral delegations representative of governments and popular organisations (NGOs) and drawn from ministries and agencies concerned with development and job-creation and with education and training. Ministers of Education will be invited to head the delegations.

The proposed seminar will be jointly organised by the Dag Hammarskjold Foundation (DHF), the Ministry of Higher Education and the Ministry of Primary and Secondary Education of Zimbabwe, the Zimbabwe Foundation for Education and Production (ZIMFEP), and the Foundation for Education with Production International (FEP).

The Seminar's Co-directors, appointed by the joint organisers, are Ms Heather Benoy, of the Zimbabwe Ministry of Higher Education and Mr Patrick van Rensburg, Director of FEP.

Countries to be invited to participate in the Seminar will be Angola, Botswana, Lesotho, Malawi, Mozambique, Swaziland, Tanzania, Zambia and Zimbabwe. Each of the major liberation movements of Namibia and South Africa will be invited to send two delegates. The participating countries will each be invited to send five delegates, of whom at least one should be a member of the teaching profession and another a representative of a popular association with practical experience in addressing the question before the seminar. The host country, Zimbabwe, will be represented by 20 participants. The Secretariat of SADCC will also be invited to be represented.

In addition, UNESCO, the ILO and the Commonwealth Secretariat will be offered an opportunity to participate at their own expense by designating one representative each who can comment meaningfully on the question of education for employment by virtue of having been closely associated with successful programmes in this area. One representative of each of two other Third World countries with a successful record in gearing education to job-creation will be invited. And finally, a few independent resource persons with relevant experience will be invited.

Background: The Problem

According to the SADCC Macro-Economic Survey, only two of the SADCC countries have more than 20% of their labour force in the 'formal' wage sector of their economies. These are Botswana and Zimbabwe. In all the other countries, the percentages are well below 20% and vary from country to country.

The 'formal' or 'modern' sector is an extension of the industrialised world rather than a natural outgrowth of local societies. It is a colonial legacy, perpetuated by continuing dependency relationships, which has been accompanied by a continuing process of breakdown of traditional societies and economies, rural under-development and stagnation, accelerated urban-rural migration, and increasing unemployment.

An overview of the problem and an analysis of its origins and causes will be presented to the Seminar.

The problem has arisen acutely among young people who leave school because school systems grow more quickly under popular pressure than the 'formal' or 'modern' sector of the economy. The problem is also seen by many as being the result of inappropriate, predominantly academic, conventional schooling which is geared towards producing employees for the limited number of jobs in the 'formal' sector. A critical analysis of the existing educational systems and how they exacerbate the problem will be presented.

Background: The Role of the Dag Hammarskjold Foundation in Identifying the Problem and Formulating Appropriate Education Strategies.

Since 1974, the Dag Hammarskjold Foundation has been closely involved in a number of seminars which have helped define the nature and process of education for liberation and education for development, and the mutually interacting relationship between education and society.

The 1974 Dar es Salaam Institute of Development Studies/Dag Hammarskjold Seminar was opened by President Nyerere, who said that "Our peoples do have a conception of what education is; and although it might be wrong and contrary to their real needs, this conception cannot be wished away".

The President invited the Seminar to "think about how we can move away from what is, to what should be".

That seminar attempted to formulate some of the criteria of the education that "should be", but in response to Mwalimu's invitation, it recognised that changes in the educational system cannot by themselves remedy the various deficiencies in it, which we have noted. "A change in society was a necessary pre-requisite".

Subsequent seminars in Maputo 1978, in Harare 1981 and in Lusaka 1982 were to suggest that this was too mechanistic a view of the relationship between education and society; they defined education as a total social process in which there were close and direct linkages between educational changes and innovations on the one hand and social transformation on the other, which mutually interacted.

Another Development for SADCC

The 1985 DHF Seminar on Another Development for SADCC in Maseru, Lesotho, adopted an *Agenda for Action*, which noted that the actual conditions prevailing in the SADCC countries reflected their continued heavy dependence, and recognised that, above all, the problems of dependency cannot be solved by the more intensive application of conventional development strategies, which created the problems in the first place.

The thirteen point *Agenda* recognised furthermore that collective self-reliance at all levels, nationally and internationally, provides the key to the solutions, and it presented a comprehensive, integrated and inter-connected, multi-sectoral approach to Another Development.

The *Agenda* was, moreover, postulated on the extension of cooperation and collective action within SADCC to several vital sectors, in addition to those already agreed on, and most notably Education and Culture, Health, Habitat, Science and Technology, Political and Human Rights and Information. And finally, the *Agenda* saw its success as being dependent not only on the cooperation of Governments, but also of the private sector and the 'third system'.

Education and Employment in the Agenda for Action

The *Agenda for Action* noted that Another Development, "as part of its commitment to mobilisation of the whole population, pursues the twin goals of education for all **and** productive, gainful employment for all.

"Broadening objectives from education for all to education and work for all, means transcending conventional education planning, but also transcending both conventional economic and manpower planning, which are based on what happens in the formal sector only.

"All development agencies need to recognise the potential role of the educational system linked to production to help create employment, and to promote development and stimulate the economy in a number of ways.

"A positive and determined effort is needed by the educational authorities and the development and economic agencies to link, coordinate and integrate their plans and activities and to provide regular and practical support on a mutual and organised basis."

Applying the Findings of the Seminars to the Realities of SADCC

The signal achievement of this series of DHF Seminars has been in defining the main characteristics of education for liberation and education for development and in identifying levers for change in going from what 'is' to what 'should be' (applying Mwalimu's terminology) in the mutually interacting process of educational and social transformation.

In all the countries of the region, there are 'cracks' in the educational systems in which to apply the critical 'levers of change'. The concerns felt everywhere about unemployment and the widespread faith that education can contribute to solving the problem of unemployment, provide some of the most important ' open spaces' in which to introduce key innovations.

Regional cooperation at both governmental and 'third system' levels can be very important in spreading innovations, which have been shown in some countries to have helped to increase job opportunities through new educational strategies.

An opportunity should be provided early in the Seminar programme to review the deliberations and findings on education of the series of DHF Seminars.

Tackling the Problem

It is generally recognised that the educational system is not able by itself to solve the problem of unemployment and to meet the challenge of job-creation, and that this requires the coordination of policies, plans and measures of implementation involving a number of agencies, an approach recommended in the *Agenda for Action.* Possible strategies for such coordination related to the roles of the various agencies will be looked at on the basis of proposals to be put forward in papers in this context.

But although solutions require comprehensive multi-sectoral action, nevertheless, schooling and training can play an important role in helping to shape the attitudes of young people and in preparing them to meet the challenges of development and job-creation. But many would feel that this would require far-reaching action throughout the educational system as a whole.

As a first step, therefore, it would be valuable to undertake a critical examination of the system as a whole, of schooling, of training, of apprenticeship and of 'non-formal' education at all levels. It would be valuable to take note of innovations in the various components of the educational system which have been aimed at better linkages to job-creation, and to have evaluations of these. Papers will be presented addressing these questions.

Critical Innovations

One option, which finds a measure of support in several countries, is based on the belief that educational institutions can better prepare young people to create their own gainful production opportunities for themselves than conventional schooling does today. Supporters of this approach believe that far-reaching changes in the curriculum, activities, funding, management, and teaching methods of the school, and its relationship with its surrounding community are necessary. It also, they argue, requires new attitudes and skills in teachers. Such people feel that a scientific outlook and economic insights which are essential to entrepreneurship need to be backed up by knowledge and confidence which can only really be built up through practical experience.

Education with production, curriculum reform, participation in decision-making and closer links between schools and communities are seen as critical areas for innovations in this connection.

Papers to be presented will look closely at these critical innovations.

Vocational and Technical Training

The experience of many reformers and innovators suggests that vocational and technical training by themselves are no guarantees that students will find jobs. Like the school system generally, current programmes are geared towards the manpower requirements of the 'formal' sector, but there are similar pressures to expand beyond the area of wage employment to absorb the output. Critical innovations in this mode of education would aim at providing, alongside technical training for self-employment in a wide range of new skills related to diversification of production, education for entrepreneurship, either in formal or 'non-formal' programmes. A paper will be presented on this question.

Vocational Training and Employment

The linkage between vocational training and employment will be surveyed not only in the Third World and in a selected industrialised country, but also in socialist countries.

The socialist experience includes linking enterprises with vocational training institutions so that students, while being trained and educated, take part in productive work linked to sub-contracts from 'parent' enterprises, and subsequently spend an increasing amount of time working in the enterprises which eventually offer them employment.

In Cuba, the linking of education with production has been successfully used to create new enterprises which provide full-time employment for many students after they leave school.

Regional Cooperation

At present, Manpower is one of the SADCC sectors of cooperation. This tends to be confined to training of manpower for the 'formal' sector of the economy, in formal institutions and usually specialised institutions. A Regional Training Council has been set up to carry out the objectives of manpower development in SADCC, responsibility for which was assigned to Swaziland.

To help meet these needs, a number of critical factors have been identified for incorporation into the manpower sector programme. These are scholarship funding, language training, scientific and vocational resources, harmonising and coordinating levels of certification, and strengthening of the region's manpower data base.

The Council has committed itself to regional cooperation in relation to scientific, technical and mathematical subjects in the region's secondary schools.

The Manpower sector of SADCC does not address itself at all to the wider question of education for employment, which is clearly a vital need to improve the linkage of education to job-creation and development. Regional cooperation could greatly benefit the formulation and implementation of appropriate strategies.

Programme and Organisation of the Proposed Seminar

As far as possible, the organisers would like to avoid the presentation of country papers. The emphasis is rather on identifying speakers from the various participating countries, who will be invited to present papers on the themes of the Seminar. The organisers are dividing responsibility for discussion of these themes, for presenting overviews and evaluations, for examining projects and programmes and presenting case studies, among the participating countries. Ministers will be invited to join Panels of Discussants.

Report and Summary Conclusions

A report featuring the papers prepared for the Seminar and containing the Summary Conclusions from the discussions will be jointly edited by the Dag Hammarskjold Foundation and the Foundation for Education with Production and published by the latter in Gaborone, Botswana, with the assistance of the Dag Hammarskjold Foundation.

Annexure 2

LIST OF PARTICIPANTS

ANGOLA

Dr Raul Neto Fernandes
Chancellor
Agostinho Neto University
P. O. Box 815
LUANDA

Telephone: 370581
Telex: 3076 UNIVELA AN
Telegram/Fax: 370417
REITORIA A NETO

Dr A.A. Pereira Garcia
Dean
Faculty of Engineering
P. O. Box 1756
LUANDA

Mr Alvaro Cupessala
Director of Technical Education
P. O. Box 1756
LUANDA

Telephone: 336233

BOTSWANA

Hon. K. P. Morake
Minister of Education
P. Bag 005
GABORONE

Telephone: 355505

Mrs. S. Seisa
Secretary
UNESCO National Committee
P. Bag 005
GABORONE

Telephone: 355605

Mr M.M. Oagile
Directorate of Public Service Management
P. Bag 0011
GABORONE

Telephone: 355522

Mr P.T. Ramatsui
CEO Curriculum Development
P. O. Box 251
GABORONE

Telephone: 373844

LESOTHO

Hon Dr L.B.B.J. Machobane
Minister of Education
Ministry of Education
P. O. Box 47
MASERU

Telephone: 323045

Mr Sabbath Moreke
P. O. Box 266
MASERU

Mr A.S.. Moeketsi
Ministry of Education
P. O. Box 47
MASERU 100

Telephone: 323317

Ms M. Motselebane
Ministry Education
P. O. Box 47
MASERU 100

Telephone: 323045

Ms M. Matabane
Ministry of Planning and Manpower Development
P O Box 630
MASERU

Telephone: 323811

MALAWI

Hon. M.U.K. Mlambala
Minister of Education
P/Bag 328
LILONGWE 3

Telephone: 733922

Mr F.R. Chilingulo
Principal
Malawi College of Distance Education
P/Bag 302
BLANTYRE 3

Telephone: 670088

Mr B.S. Chawani
Curriculum Development
Assistant Chief Inspector
Ministry of Education and Culture
P/Bag 328
LILONGWE 3

Telephone: 733922

Mr S. Nyirenda
Senior Educational Research Officer
MOEC
P/Bag 328
LILONGWE 3

Telephone: 733922

MOZAMBIQUE

Hon. A. Dos Muchangos — Telephone: 743349
Minister of Education
Ministry of Education
MAPUTO

Mr H. Mondlane — Telephone: 744761
Assistant to the Minister
Ministry of Education
MAPUTO

Mr T.A.S. Dos Santos — Telephone 744761
National Director
Ministry of Education
MAPUTO

Mr E Tome — Telephone: 742363
Head of Department
Ministry of Education
MAPUTO

SWAZILAND

Hon. Chief S. Shongwe — Telephone 43308
Minister of Education
Ministry of Education
P O Box 811
MBABANE

Rev. M.B. Mabuza — Telephone 52106/7
Director, Curriculum Development
National Curriculum Centre
P O Box 73
MANZINI

Mr Dlamini Elphas
Senior Planner
Ministry of Education
P O Box 39
MBABANE

Telephone: 42491
Fax: 42496

Mr J.G. Kunene
Acting Chief Inspector, Primary
Ministry of Education
P O Box 39
MBABANE

Telephone 42491

TANZANIA

Mr K.A. Hassan
P O Box 9121
DAR ES SALAAM

Telephone 22373

Mr H.K. Mwenisongole
Ministry of Education
P O Box 9121
DAR ES SALAAM

Telephone: 26948

Mr W. Sabaya
Institute of Curriculum Development
P O Box 35094
DAR ES SALAAM

Telephone: 28189 (Home)
Telex: 41742 TZ

ZAMBIA

Hon. K.S. Musokotwane
Minister of General Education
P O Box 50093
LUSAKA

Telephone 251693

Mr R. Mazonga Telephone 251874
Chief Education Officer
Ministry of Higher Education, Science & Technology
P O Box 50464
LUSAKA

Mr C.D. Mkangaza Telephone 254848
Deputy Director
Curriculum Development Centre
P O Box 50092
LUSAKA

Mr F. Chelu Telephone 211100
Chief Inspector of Schools
Ministry of General Education, Youth & Sport
P O Box 50093
LUSAKA

Mr P.J. Penyani Telephone 212716
Guidance and Counselling Officer
Ministry of Higher Education, Science & Technology
P O Box 50097
LUSAKA

ZIMBABWE

Hon. F.K. Chung Telephone 734051
Acting Minister of Higher Education
Minister of Primary & Secondary Education
Ministry of Primary & Secondary Education
P O Box 8022
Causeway
HARARE

Mr G.W. Sisimayi Tel. 792671
CRADU
Ministry of Higher Education
P O Box UA 275
HARARE

Mr S.C. Mashingaidze Tel. 24084
Curriculum Development Unit
Ministry of Primary & Secondary Education
P O Box MP 133, Mt. Pleasant
HARARE

Mr S. Chinodya
Curriculum Development Unit
Ministry of Primary & Secondary Education
P O Box MP 133, Mt. Pleasant
HARARE

Ms M. Mumbure Tel. 796161/4
Planner
National Planning Agency
Ministry of Finance, Economic Planning
& Development
P/Bag 7705,
Causeway
HARARE

Mr N. Munetzi Tel. 76616
Director of Industrial Training
President's Department
P O Box 567
BULAWAYO

Mr N.N.M. Munetsi Tel. 792671
Ministry of Higher Education
P O Box 387
HARARE

Mr E. Kanyongo Tel. 792035
President's Department
P O Box 2278
HARARE

Ms H. Benoy Tel. 707196
CEO Technical Colleges
Ministry of Higher Education
P O Box UA 275
HARARE

Mr B.S.M. Gatawa Tel. 734051
CEO Curriculum Development Unit
P O Box 8022
Causeway
HARARE

Mr V.R. Nyathi Tel. 703242
ZIMFEP/Ministry of Finance,
Economic Planning & Development
Private Bag 7705
Causeway
HARARE

Mr S.M. Hadebe Tel. 69511
Regional Director Matebeleland North
Ministry of Education
P O Box 555
BULAWAYO

C.E.M. Chikombah Tel. 303211 Ext. 1222
Dean of Education
University of Zimbabwe
P O Box MP 167, Mt. Pleasant
HARARE

Dr O.E. Maravanyika Tel. 303211, Ext. 1259
Lecturer
Department of Curriculum Studies
P O Box MP 167, Mt. Pleasant
HARARE

Mr M.L. Fungate Tel. 795679/0
Zimbabwe Foundation for Education with Production (ZIMFEP)
P O Box 298
HARARE

NAMIBIA (SWAPO)

Mr M. Mbumba Tel. 252250
UN Institute for Namibia
P O Box 33811
LUSAKA, ZAMBIA

SA (ANC)

Mr S. Majombozi Tel. 219656/7
ANC (SA) Education Department
P O Box 31791
LUSAKA, ZAMBIA

Mr O Moloto Tel. 261263
ANC (SA) Manpower Development Department
P O Box 31791
LUSAKA, ZAMBIA

SADCC

Mr E.S.S. Nebwe Tel. 351863-5
Special Advisor to the Executive Secretary Telex 2555 BD
SADCC
Private Bag 0095
GABORONE, BOTSWANA

UNESCO

Mr Bagunywa Tel.e 790921
Area Representative Telex 26472
Sub-Regional Office for Southern Africa
P O Box 4775
HARARE, ZIMBABWE

Mr J.J. Mhlanga Tel. 725430
Zimbabwe National Commission for UNESCO
P O Box UA 275
HARARE, ZIMBABWE

EMPLOYERS ORGANISATIONS

Mr C. Mwalongo Tel. 38031
Tanzania Chamber of Commerce, Telex 41513
Industry and Agriculture
P O Box 1229
DAR ES SALAAM

Mr J.M. Nthongoa
Lesotho Chamber of Commerce and Industries
P O Box 79
MASERU, LESOTHO

Tel. 323482
Telex 4429 LO

Mrs H.A. Katala
National Union of Tanzanian Workers
Luwata Headquarters
P O Box 15359
DAR ES SALAAM, TANZANIA

Tel. 26111, 27301
Telex 41205

NGO's

Ms Selina Cossa
Green Zones of Maputo
Union Geral dos Coop Z.V.
Av. 25 de Septembro
MAPUTO, MOZAMBIQUE

Telex 6-125 GZV
Fax 30101

Mr J.N. Lepheana
Vocational/Technical Training
Institutions, LOIC
P O Box 2542
MASERU, LESOTHO

Tel. 323119

Ms N. Ganedze
Manzini Industrial Training Centre
P O Box 549
MANZINI, SWAZILAND

Tel. 52491/2

Ms J. Rilla B. Hamisi
Presidential Trust Fund for Self-Reliance
P O Box 70000
DAR ES SALAAM, TANZANIA

Tel. 29711, 35927
Telex 41325 PRINTA TZ

Ms P.J. Ozanne | Tel. 322776
Matsieng Development Trust
P O Box 1
MASERU, LESOTHO

Mrs J. Clara Bucar | Tel. 30103
Union Geral dos Coop ZV
Av. 25 de Setembro
MAPUTO, MOZAMBIQUE

Mr Patrick Qorro
P O Box 1500
KARATU, TANZANIA

SPEAKERS AND RESOURCE PERSONS

Dr B. Chidzero
Senior Minister for Finance, Economic
and Planning and Development
P/B 7705,
Causeway
HARARE, ZIMBABWE

Dr Wim Hoppers
SHAPE/Ministry of Higher Education,
Science and Technology
c/o Swedish Embassy
P O Box 30788
LUSAKA, ZAMBIA

Mr A.M.D. Humphrey | Telephone 739833
Confederation of Zimbabwe Industries (CZI) | Telex 2073
109 Rotten Row
HARARE, ZIMBABWE

Dr Kenneth King — Tel. 31-667-1011
Centre of African Studies
Edinburgh University
EDINBURGH, SCOTLAND

Mr Yang Dong Liang — Tel. 658731-2561
Zidan — Telex 22014 SEDC CN
BEIJING, CHINA

Dr M.H. Mills — Tel. 338868
The World Bank
P O Box 30577
NAIROBI, KENYA

Mr Neil Parsons — Tel. 1-853-0331
34 Humber Road
LONDON SE3 7LT, UK

Dr Ernesto Fernandez Rivero — Tel. 61-8811
Ministry of Education
Obispo 160
LA HABANA, CUBA

Mr M. Tsvangirai — Tel. 793093
Zimbabwe Congress of Trade Unions
P O Box 3549
HARARE, ZIMBABWE

ORGANISING COMMITTEE

Mr C.G. Chivanda — Tel. 792671
Ministry of Higher Education
P O Box UA 275
HARARE, ZIMBABWE

Ms H. Benoy Tel. 792671
Ministry of Higher Education
P O Box UA 275
HARARE, ZIMBABWE

Ms D. Masaya
Ministry of Labour, Manpower and Social Affairs
HARARE, ZIMBABWE

Mr V.R. Nyathi Tel. 796191
Ministry of Finance, Economic Planning & Development
P/Bag 7705,
Causeway
HARARE, ZIMBABWE

Mr R. Sisimayi Tel. 24084
Ministry of Primary & Secondary Education
P O Box MP 133, Mt. Pleasant
HARARE, ZIMBABWE

FOUNDATION FOR EDUCATION WITH PRODUCTION

Professor N.A. Kuhanga Tel. 24033
Chairman, FEP
P O Box 9121
DAR ES SALAAM

Mr Patrick van Rensburg Tel/Fax 314311
P O Box 20906 Telex 2753 FEP BD
GABORONE, BOTSWANA

Mr John Conradie
P O Box 20906
GABORONE, BOTSWANA

DAG HAMMARSKJOLD FOUNDATION

Dr S. Hamrell
Executive Director
Dag Hammarskjold Foundation
Ovre Slottsgatan 2
S-752 20 UPPSALA, SWEDEN
Tel. 18-12 88 72
Telex 76234 DH CENTRE

Olle Nordberg
Dag Hammarskjold Foundation

Kerstin Kvist
Dag Hammarskjold Foundation

ADMINISTRATION/SECRETARIAT

Ms R. Chikowore - Ministry of Higher Education, ZIMBABWE
Ms G. Kusotera - Ministry of Primary and Secondary Education, ZIMBABWE
Ms M. Mushaninga - Ministry of Higher Education, ZIMBABWE
Ms B. O'Connor - Famibidzanai Training Centre, Harare ZIMBABWE